THE EVERYTHING® WHEAT-FREE DIET COOKBOOK

Dear Reader,

Research shows that roughly 18 million people suffer from a wheat allergy, sensitivity, or intolerance. It can be quite overwhelming when you are first diagnosed. But once you learn how to avoid foods that contain wheat, you will feel more comfortable at that next social gathering, going out to eat, and even in your own kitchen.

Knowledge is power. Educating yourself on all the foods that contain "hidden" wheat ingredients is the first step. It is crucial for you to read *all* the ingredient labels in your foods. The best way to avoid any discomfort from your wheat intolerance is to prepare your food at home as often as you can. This book will show you how to substitute common foods (and uncommon foods) with those that are wheat-free.

Don't lose hope. Once you learn how many wheat-free options are out there, you will live a happier and healthier life. This book will be your personal guide to delicious, wholesome, wheat-free meals that the whole family will enjoy.

Lauren Kelly

Welcome to the EVERYTHING® Series!

These handy, accessible books give you all you need to tackle a difficult project, gain a new hobby, comprehend a fascinating topic, prepare for an exam, or even brush up on something you learned back in school but have since forgotten.

You can choose to read an Everything® book from cover to cover or just pick out the information you want from our four useful boxes: e-questions, e-facts, e-alerts, and e-ssentials.

We give you everything you need to know on the subject, but throw in a lot of fun stuff along the way, too.

We now have more than 400 Everything® books in print, spanning such wide-ranging categories as weddings, pregnancy, cooking, music instruction, foreign language, crafts, pets, New Age, and so much more. When you're done reading them all, you can finally say you know Everything®!

QUESTION
Answers to common questions

FACT
Important snippets of information

ALERT
Urgent warnings

ESSENTIAL
Quick handy tips

PUBLISHER Karen Cooper

MANAGING EDITOR, EVERYTHING® SERIES Lisa Laing

COPY CHIEF Casey Ebert

ASSOCIATE PRODUCTION EDITOR Mary Beth Dolan

ACQUISITIONS EDITOR Lisa Laing

SENIOR DEVELOPMENT EDITOR Brett Palana-Shanahan

EVERYTHING® SERIES COVER DESIGNER Erin Alexander

Visit the entire Everything® series at www.everything.com

THE EVERYTHING® WHEAT-FREE DIET COOKBOOK

Lauren Kelly, CN

Adamsmedia
Avon, Massachusetts

This book is dedicated not only to those suffering from a wheat allergy or intolerance, but to those simply looking to eliminate wheat from their diets and who are looking for healthy meals that do just that.

Published by Adams Media, a division of F+W Media, Inc.
57 Littlefield Street, Avon, MA 02322. U.S.A.
www.adamsmedia.com

ISBN 10: 1-4405-5680-6
ISBN 13: 978-1-4405-5680-7
eISBN 10: 1-4405-5681-4
eISBN 13: 978-1-4405-5681-4

Printed in the United States of America.

10 9 8 7 6 5 4 3 2 1

Always follow safety and common-sense cooking protocol while using kitchen utensils, operating ovens and stoves, and handling uncooked food. If children are assisting in the preparation of any recipe, they should always be supervised by an adult.

The information in this book should not be used for diagnosing or treating any health problem. Not all diet and exercise plans suit everyone. You should always consult a trained medical professional before starting a diet, taking any form of medication, or embarking on any fitness or weight-training program. The author and publisher disclaim any liability arising directly or indirectly from the use of this book.

This book is available at quantity discounts for bulk purchases.
For information, please call 1-800-289-0963.

Contents

Acknowledgments

Thanks to all my friends and family who have been so supportive during the process of writing this book. I would like to thank my wonderful husband, Steve, and our three small boys for not only graciously taste-testing the recipes, but also for their continued patience and encouragement, allowing me to do what I love. This book could not have been written without all the help from my loving friends, who helped show me that friends are just as important as family. I would also like to thank my mother for introducing me to cooking at a young age. I hope she is smiling down on me with pride.

I would also like to thank my agent, Joëlle Delbourgo, for her guidance during this process, and my editor, Lisa Laing, and all the wonderful people at Adams Media.

Introduction

"WHEAT IS GOOD FOR you. Why a wheat-free cookbook?" That sounds like a fair question, doesn't it? Nutritionists know how important it is to have a well-balanced diet. Over the last decade we have been told how crucial it is to incorporate more whole grains and wheat into our lives as part of a healthy diet. Whole wheat does contain important complex carbohydrates, healthy dietary fiber, vitamins, and minerals, but many people are allergic to or have some type of intolerance to wheat. The main offender for these people is a protein found in wheat called gluten, which can cause great discomfort for the millions of people who suffer from gluten intolerance and other food allergies. A visit to a restaurant, a friend's house, and even your own kitchen can prove hazardous to the uninformed. Each ingredient and food item must be thoroughly inspected, and a well-thought-out approach must be initiated to safeguard against foods containing wheat.

This book will show you that you don't have to make drastic changes to your lifestyle once you know the facts. There are alternative ingredients to wheat flour (corn, rice, almond, and even coconut, to name a few) that will make your meals taste just as delicious without your noticing the difference. And, as an added bonus (although no clinical studies prove this), people who begin a wheat-free diet often lose weight as well.

Studies have shown that wheat is one of several foods that leads to inflammation in the gut. This inflammation has shown to be a contributing factor to certain ailments, such as heart disease, cancer, allergies, asthma, skin rashes, and possibly Alzheimer's disease. Following a wheat-free diet, or simply reducing wheat in one's diet, has been shown to considerably decrease inflammation in the gut, as well as improve overall health. In this book, you will find a wide array of delicious wheat-free meals for any time of the day, and you'll learn about the benefits of using certain ingredients that do not contain wheat.

If you're suffering from wheat-related allergies, would like to reduce inflammation in your body, or simply want to reduce the amount of wheat in your diet, you'll love the variety of soups, poultry, meats, fish, and dessert recipes. *The Everything® Wheat-Free Diet Cookbook* will prove to you that healthy food really can taste delicious.

CHAPTER 1

The Basis of Wheat-Free Cooking

As you begin a wheat-free diet, you might feel discouraged at first and believe you are severely restricted in what you can eat. Adjusting to your wheat-free diet doesn't have to be as overwhelming as you might think. With the public's growing awareness that food allergies are on the rise, ingredients supporting a wheat-free lifestyle are now becoming easier to find. Visit your favorite supermarket or specialty store and you're sure to find many alternatives to wheat. There are also many websites that cater to those with food allergies and that carry specialty ingredients. With a little research and experimentation you'll discover it can actually be fun and easy to cook delicious, healthy, wheat-free meals for the whole family.

Living the Wheat-Free Way

You may feel overwhelmed at first when you discover that you need to follow a wheat-free diet. Many of your concerns are legitimate. Will you need to radically change your lifestyle? What will you be able to eat? Will you have to sacrifice flavor and foods that you love? There is no question you will need to alter your lifestyle to eliminate wheat from your diet. But the change will not be as radical as you might suppose, and you will easily be able to manage your new lifestyle, and eventually, even come to embrace it. And don't worry, there is no need to sacrifice your favorite meals—there are many substitutions for wheat that will make your meals taste delicious.

Wheat is one of the eight most common food allergies, along with peanuts, tree nuts (walnuts, cashews, pecans, almonds, Brazil nuts, macadamia nuts, chestnuts, pine nuts and pistachios), fish, shellfish, eggs, milk, and soy.

People of all ages and from all walks of life are choosing to live the wheat-free way. Various studies have shown that wheat causes inflammation in the body, which leads to several chronic illnesses, so many people give up wheat in order to reduce the inflammation and feel better. Wheat is also a complex carbohydrate, and when people reduce or eliminate carbohydrates from their diet, they often experience weight loss, so some people give up wheat as a way to achieve healthy weight loss. And even more serious, some people have a food allergy or food intolerance to wheat, and they must eliminate it from their diets to maintain proper health and avoid pain and discomfort. So whatever your reason is for wanting to live wheat-free, know that you are not alone.

Celiac Disease Versus Wheat Allergy

Celiac disease and wheat allergies, though similar in some ways, are different disorders with different treatments. Celiac disease is an autoimmune disorder. When a person has celiac disease and eats gluten (a protein found in wheat, barley, and rye), the immune system attacks normal tissue in the intestines. As a result, those who have celiac disease may not have proper absorption of crucial nutrients, including calcium, magnesium, and vitamins B_{12}, D, E, A, and K. This lack of absorption of vital nutrients can lead to vitamin and mineral deficiencies. Celiac disease is a permanent reaction to gluten, and such individuals must avoid any foods containing wheat, barley, or rye.

People with a wheat allergy do not have the same problems with absorption. A person with a wheat allergy is only allergic to the protein found in wheat and must only avoid wheat. One thing to keep in mind is that just because a product is labeled "gluten-free" does not guarantee that it is "wheat-free." According to *www.wheat-free.org*, some manufacturers use wheat that has the gluten removed to make gluten-free foods. Make sure you always read your food labels.

FACT

The main difference between a food allergy and a food intolerance is that food allergies affect the immune system while food intolerances do not. Those who suffer from wheat allergies can experience anything from sneezing, itching, headaches, and nausea to swollen limbs and overall aches and pains. Wheat intolerance is much more common and those who have it usually have a delayed onset of symptoms, as long as two to three days later. These people suffer with various degrees of symptoms, ranging from stomach discomfort to chronic headaches and diarrhea.

Wheat allergies typically develop early in one's life, as a baby or toddler. Generally, children who have a wheat allergy are also allergic to other foods, such as dairy, egg, nuts, or milk. There are also varying degrees in the severity of wheat allergies. Some people may have a slight sensitivity to wheat, which causes some mild discomfort, while others' reactions are more severe. They become extremely ill when consuming wheat or even simply when they come in contact with it. People with a severe wheat allergy must learn how to take every possible precaution in order to prevent serious reactions. The only real remedy for this allergy is to avoid wheat in its entirety. In some cases, children may outgrow a wheat allergy as their immune systems mature. Wheat allergies are not as common in adolescents and adults.

Signs and Symptoms of a Wheat Allergy

A wheat allergy is an unusual reaction in the body to the protein found in wheat. Signs of a wheat allergy differ among individuals, and what may be a symptom for one person may not be for another. The most common indications of a wheat allergy are nasal congestion, asthma, eczema or skin rash, diarrhea, fatigue, chest pains, heart palpitations, bloating, nausea, vomiting, abdominal cramping, throat swelling, joint pain, depression, and a state of "fogginess." The most severe symptom of a wheat allergy is anaphylaxis, a serious, sometimes fatal, allergic reaction. According to the Mayo Clinic (*www.mayoclinic.com*), the signs and symptoms of anaphylaxis are:

- Chest tightness
- Low pulse
- Dizziness
- Extreme breathing difficulties
- Swelling of the throat
- Trouble swallowing
- Nausea
- Vomiting
- Diarrhea
- Skin turning flushed, very pale or even bluish color
- Major decrease in blood pressure

ALERT

In some rare, extreme cases, anaphylaxis is caused by physical activity after the consumption of wheat, called exercise-induced anaphylaxis. If you're allergic to wheat, the best way to prevent this is to avoid eating for several hours before physical activity.

In many cases, wheat allergy sufferers are often misdiagnosed with irritable bowel syndrome (IBS) because the symptoms are very similar. Some wheat allergy symptoms such as gas, bloating, or cramping are signs of early inflammation of the digestive tract. If this inflammation is left untreated, it can develop into long-term illnesses. If you think that you are suffering from one or more of these symptoms and you are not sure whether it is the result of a wheat allergy or intolerance, simply eliminate wheat from your diet for two weeks and see how you feel. If symptoms persist, schedule an appointment with your physician, nutritionist, or health care provider.

In the Event of Contact

For those with severe wheat allergies, there are medical treatments available in the event that they come in contact with wheat. Antihistamines, a type of medication that helps relieve allergy symptoms, should be taken after exposure to wheat. Individuals at risk of more serious reactions, such as anaphylaxis, must carry two doses of emergency medication, epinephrine (synthetic adrenaline), with them at all times. This medication, commonly administered in the form of an EpiPen, allows the victim to breathe better and helps restore blood pressure to normal levels.

Depending on the individual, an allergic reaction can occur within minutes or hours of consuming or inhaling wheat.

What Can You Eat?

Before beginning a wheat-free diet, consult your doctor or health care provider to see if a wheat-free diet is right for you. As overwhelming as it may initially seem, there are many foods that you can still eat on a wheat-free diet. There are also more options available than you may think. You may be surprised by the number of wheat-free choices available in your local grocery or specialty store. You will not be able to use white or wheat flour, but you can certainly use rice, almond, coconut, tapioca, or corn flour. You may not be able to eat ready-made pancakes, but you can easily make your own wheat-free pancakes. Once you have the necessary knowledge to make the correct choices, they will become second nature for you.

FACT

Often, it is the way foods are prepared that poses a problem. For example, once chicken becomes Chicken Parmesan, it is no longer wheat-free. But you could easily use wheat-free bread crumbs and flour and still be able to enjoy this classic dish.

The most important rule for following a wheat-free diet is to read ingredient labels carefully. There are many foods out there that contain some type of wheat ingredient that might surprise you. For example, did you know that soy sauce could contain wheat? Even dairy products like ice cream may have some wheat in them. If you are unsure of which ingredients might contain wheat, call the manufacturer.

When most people think about a wheat-free diet, they assume they will have to give up all foods made with flour. And while you will have to give up traditional flours, there are still plenty of wheat-free starches and flours you can use in your favorite dishes and desserts. According to *www.wheat-free .org*, the following can be tolerated on a wheat-free diet:

- Amaranth flour
- Arrowroot flour
- Barley flour
- Brown rice flour
- Buckwheat flour
- Chia flour
- Chickpea flour (also known as garbanzo bean flour)
- Corn flour and cornmeal
- Flax
- Gluten-free flours (rice, soy, corn, potato, bean)
- Hemp flour
- Hominy (corn)
- Millet flour
- Oat flour

- Potato flour
- Potato starch flour
- Quinoa flour
- Rice flour
- Rye flour
- Sorghum flour
- Soy flour
- Tapioca flour
- Teff flour
- White rice flour

Foods to Avoid

There are many types of flours that may not appear to have wheat in them, but in fact do. Be sure to read the ingredient labels carefully. Simply because it doesn't say wheat in the name, doesn't mean it's wheat-free.

According to The Food Allergy Gourmet (*www.foodallergygourmet.com*), the following types of flour contain wheat and should be avoided:

- Bleached flour
- Bread flour
- Brown flour
- Cake flour meal
- Durum
- Durum flour
- Enriched bleached flour
- Enriched flour
- Graham flour
- Granary flour
- High gluten flour
- High protein flour
- Malted barley flour
- Spelt flour
- Unbleached flour
- Whole meal flour
- Whole wheat flour

In addition to flours and starches, the following foods also commonly contain wheat and should be avoided. (Remember this list is not exhaustive; you must always remember to read the labels on whatever food you buy.)

Some common ingredients that contain wheat that you may not be aware of are: graham, bulghur, wheat germ, modified food starch, spelt, and semolina.

BEVERAGES
- Ale
- Beer
- Fruit drink mixes
- Instant chocolate drink mixes
- Lager
- Malted milk
- Root beer
- Some soft drinks
- Some sports and nutritional powdered drinks

BREAD PRODUCTS
- Bagels
- Bread
- Croutons
- Muffins
- Pastries
- Pies
- Pita bread
- Premade pancake and waffle mixes
- Rolls

BREAKFAST CEREALS
- Cream of Wheat
- Farina
- Some brands of oatmeal

CANDY

- Jordan almonds
- Licorice
- Some caramels
- Some nut candies

CONDIMENTS

- Barley malt
- Ketchup
- Malt vinegar
- Marinades
- Mustard
- Salad dressings
- Soy sauce
- Worcestershire sauce

DESSERTS

- Cakes and frostings
- Chocolates
- Graham crackers
- Ice cream
- Sherbet

GRAINS

- Cereal grains
- Couscous
- Matzo meal
- Orzo
- Seasoned rice mixes
- Spelt
- Tabbouleh
- Triticale (a combination of wheat and rye)

JARRED AND CANNED FOODS

- Alfredo sauce
- Bouillon cubes

- Canned fruits
- Canned meats
- Canned vegetables
- Chicken and beef broth
- Gravies
- Soups
- Tuna fish

MEATS AND SEAFOOD
- Chicken nuggets
- Fish sticks
- Fried or breaded meats
- Hot dogs
- Imitation crab, shrimp, and bacon
- Meatballs
- Processed deli meats
- Sausages

PASTA
- All kinds except those labeled wheat-/gluten-free
- Soba noodles

SNACKS
- Chips
- Cookies (including cookie crumbs and cookie dough)
- Crackers
- Dry-roasted nuts
- Granola bars
- Popcorn
- Pretzels

FOOD ADDITIVES AND INGREDIENTS
- Artificial colors and flavors
- Baking powder
- Caramel coloring and flavoring
- Ground spices and seasonings

- Modified food starch
- Natural flavors
- Natural juices
- Shortening
- Vanilla and other extracts
- Vegetable gum
- Vegetable protein
- Vegetable starch

Even some nonfood items may have wheat in them. If your allergy is severe enough, even simply touching wheat can cause an allergic reaction. Call the manufacturer to find out if there is wheat in products like these that you may use:

- Cosmetics
- Glue
- Lotions and creams
- Medications
- Ointments
- Pet foods
- Play doughs, clays, and putties
- Shampoo
- Sunscreens
- Vitamins

Eating Out

If you are concerned about wheat contained in meals when you are eating out at a restaurant, do not hesitate to call beforehand and ask. Today many restaurants actually prepare and serve gluten- and wheat-free dishes. Know the obvious offenders when reading the menu at your favorite restaurant. Your first inclination must be to exclude any pasta, salad (dressings and croutons may contain wheat), marinades, sauces, and sandwiches. Anything that is deep-fried, breaded, or battered most likely contains wheat.

It's not just food you need to be concerned about on a wheat-free diet. That drink you order with your meal can be just as dangerous. Beer, ale, root beer, malted milk, and even instant chocolate drink mixes can contain wheat. After dinner, you'll also have to be careful of what type of coffee you drink. Many instant coffees have wheat in them. If you are in doubt, be safe and avoid it completely.

Children and the Wheat-Free Lifestyle

It can be very difficult to watch your child suffer from a food allergy. It is even harder when you don't know what the child is suffering from. Symptoms can appear in very young children, even infants, but they can't tell you what's bothering them. If you suspect your child is suffering from a food intolerance or food allergy, consult your pediatrician immediately. Once a positive diagnosis has been confirmed, you will need to modify your child's diet and lifestyle right away. You and your child should not feel alone in this process. You will need the support of friends, family, teachers, and classmates. You might even decide to convert the whole family to a wheat-free diet to make it easier for the child.

ALERT

Be sure to alert your child's school to the fact that your child suffers from a wheat allergy or intolerance. This will help prevent any potential exposures to wheat.

Monitoring your child's diet is much more manageable to do when he or she is at home. Once your child leaves the house, your fears and anxieties will escalate, as there is an increased chance your child could potentially come in contact with an offending food containing wheat. But you can take steps to safeguard your child against these situations. First, contact your child's school. The school nurse will be able to provide you with guidance. Next, the best way to avoid any contact with wheat is to prepare your own child's lunch. Buying lunch at school is not an option. Even though something may appear to be wheat-free, you can never be 100 percent sure it wasn't prepared on a surface that already had wheat on it. Your child can enjoy social gatherings and birthday parties as long as the necessary precautions are taken. If your child is attending a friend's birthday party, pack your own special, wheat-free treats (cupcakes or cookies) so she doesn't feel left out. It is extremely important that your child not feel like she is an outcast because of her allergy. Your child will learn to adapt and eventually embrace this new lifestyle.

ALERT

You must be aware of the nonfood items that contain wheat. For instance, Play-Doh actually contains wheat. Some craft items and glues also contain wheat. Parents need to stay informed about craft supplies that may contain wheat. There are many websites that inform parents about how to make their own wheat-free craft materials such as *www.theglutengal.com*, *www.momsplaceglutenfree.com*, and *www .kidceliac.com*.

Wheat-Free for Life

Over time, and with some creativity and patience, you will be able to enjoy a wheat-free lifestyle. Cooking and baking wheat-free meals can be quite intimidating at first. You may strike out with your first few attempts. Do not be discouraged. Continue to experiment with a wide array of ingredients, and eventually, you will be thrilled with the results.

ESSENTIAL

Make sure you own a food processor or high-speed blender. These appliances come in handy while experimenting with alternative ingredients. Soon you will be creating your own delicious and healthy smoothies, salsas, and sauces. Many of these sauces will be a key staple to a lot of the dishes you prepare for your family.

One very important issue you need to consider in living the wheat-free lifestyle is cross-contamination. Wheat-free foods may come in contact with those containing wheat during the manufacturing process. Oats are a perfect example of this. Some manufacturing companies process oats in the same facility as their wheat products. Today, companies are aware of the potential for cross-contamination and are labeling their products accordingly. You need to be just as disciplined in your own kitchen. You must be vigilant about not using the same cooking utensils that may have been in contact with a food containing wheat. For instance, once you begin your wheat-free lifestyle, you will need to ensure that you clean out your toaster regularly. The crumbs from the wheat bread may come in contact with your new wheat-free bread, resulting in an allergic reaction when consumed. If someone has a severe wheat allergy, it is recommended to have two appliances, one dedicated solely for wheat-free. Also, if your whole family isn't following a wheat-free diet, make sure to use a clean utensil when you spread peanut butter on your wheat-free toast.

Preparing foods in advance will make your life a little easier. On the weekends, prepare some snacks and meals for the upcoming week. If you need to, freeze some for future meals. Prepare your lunch (and your children's lunches) the night before. This way you are carefully packing the next day's lunch and are fully aware of what you (or your child) are eating. Leaving a refrigerated cooler in your car with healthy, wheat-free snacks also alleviates the stress of wondering what you will be able to eat.

You don't need to feel deprived while following a wheat-free diet. You can eat wheat-free meals and desserts that are not only healthy but also delicious. Use your imagination, and remember, it may take you a few times to perfect the dish, but that's the fun part. Have fun while experimenting, read your labels carefully, and stay healthy. You will not only feel better physically, but you will also feel more confident the next time you sit at the dinner table, restaurant, or that next social gathering. Here's to many years of happy, healthy eating!

CHAPTER 2

Appetizers and Salads

Apple, Walnut, Cranberry, and Spinach Salad

The wonderful combination of fruit and nuts makes this salad perfect any time of year.
The dressing can be used for any salad or as a marinade for chicken or vegetables.

INGREDIENTS | SERVES 4

Dressing

½ cup extra-virgin olive oil

½ cup balsamic vinegar

1 clove garlic, crushed

1 teaspoon ground mustard

1 teaspoon honey

1 teaspoon salt

½ teaspoon pepper

Salad

1 (6-ounce) bag organic baby spinach

2 tablespoons chopped walnuts

2 tablespoons dried, unsweetened cranberries

1 fuji apple, cored and chopped

½ medium orange bell pepper, seeded and chopped

2 plum tomatoes, chopped

½ cup kidney beans, thoroughly rinsed and drained

1 tablespoon chia seeds

1. Wisk all the dressing ingredients together in a small bowl. You can also pour into a small, airtight container and shake vigorously.

2. In a large bowl, mix the salad ingredients. Add the dressing and toss before serving.

Tiny Chickpea Crepes

*Chickpea (garbanzo bean) flour gives a slightly nutty flavor
that goes well with many dips and fillings.*

INGREDIENTS | SERVES 12

2 cups chickpea flour

2 cloves garlic, crushed

1 teaspoon Tabasco sauce or other red hot sauce

1 teaspoon salt

1½ cups water

¼ cup olive oil, for frying

1. Mix flour, garlic, hot sauce, salt, and water in a blender, pulsing and scraping the mixture down the sides.

2. Heat the oil in a nonstick pan over medium-high heat. Add 1 tablespoon of the batter for 1½" crepes.

3. Cook until very crisp on the bottom, about 3–4 minutes; do not turn. Remove from pan and place on paper towels or a platter. Now you can add fillings of your choice, cheese or vegetables, and close, or fold each crepe in half.

Classic Caesar Salad

*Caesar salad can be so versatile. Add chicken, shrimp, or even steak
to dress it up as an entrée, or pair it with soup for an easy dinner.*

INGREDIENTS | SERVES 4

1 head romaine lettuce

1 whole egg and 1 egg yolk, beaten

Freshly squeezed juice of ½ lemon

2 cloves garlic, minced

1 teaspoon wheat-free English mustard

1" anchovy paste or 2 canned anchovies, packed in oil, mashed

¾ cup extra-virgin olive oil

1 teaspoon salt

½ teaspoon freshly ground black pepper

5 tablespoons freshly grated Parmesan cheese

24 Fresh Wheat-Free Croutons (see recipe in this chapter)

1. Wash and spin-dry the lettuce; then chop, wrap in a towel, and place in the refrigerator to crisp.

2. In a large bowl, whisk together the egg, egg yolk, lemon juice, garlic, mustard, anchovy paste, and olive oil until very smooth. Add salt and pepper. Add the lettuce and toss.

3. Sprinkle with Parmesan cheese and croutons, and serve.

Sicilian Eggplant Rolls

These make the perfect appetizer or entrée that will definitely impress your guests.

Eggplant Makes a Great Wrap

Eggplant can be sliced thin lengthwise or crosswise and then fried, broiled, or baked. Salting and stacking eggplant slices under a weight will drain off the bitterness that some seem to harbor. Be sure to use a plate with steep sides or a soup bowl under the eggplant—it will release a lot of juice when salted.

1. Cut the eggplant in very thin (⅛") slices with a mandoline or a vegetable peeler. Salt the slices and stack them on a plate; let sit under a weight for 30 minutes to let the brown juices out.

2. Pat the eggplant slices dry with paper towels.

3. Heat the oil in a large skillet or fry pan to 300°F. Dip the eggplant slices in rice flour and fry until almost crisp, about 2 minutes per side.

4. Drain the slices and then place a spoonful of the ricotta cheese and some chopped olives and garlic on the end of each slice. Roll and secure with a toothpick. Place in a greased baking pan.

5. Preheat oven to 300°F. Sprinkle the rolls with Parmesan cheese and bake for 8 minutes. Serve warm.

Wild Rice Salad

This salad is filling and flavorful any time of the year.

INGREDIENTS | SERVES 6

4 cups water
¾ cup wild rice
1 teaspoon salt
½ teaspoon black pepper
1 small red onion, chopped
1 clove garlic, finely chopped
3 stalks celery, finely chopped
1 cup drained and chopped water chestnuts
1 cup jicama, peeled and chopped
1 small gala apple, cored and chopped
1 tablespoon dried cranberries, unsweetened
⅔ cup extra-virgin olive oil
⅓ cup raspberry vinegar
½ cup chopped fresh Italian flat-leaf parsley
6 ounces fresh raspberries

1. Bring water to a boil in a large saucepan or Dutch oven and add the rice. Return to a rolling boil and then reduce heat to simmer and cover tightly. After 30 minutes, add salt and pepper and remove from heat.

2. Add the onion, garlic, celery, water chestnuts, jicama, apple, and cranberries.

3. In a small bowl, whisk the olive oil and vinegar with the parsley. Pour over rice mixture and mix well.

4. Place salad in a large serving dish and serve warm or chilled. Top with raspberries at the last minute.

Cooking Wild Rice

Disregard the directions on the package of wild rice. They tell you to cook for 30–40 minutes, when it takes more like 90 minutes for it to bloom and soften. When cooking, just keep adding liquid if the rice dries out, and keep simmering until it "blooms," or the grains open up.

Fresh Wheat-Free Croutons

These croutons can be made in advance and stored in the refrigerator,
then crisped up at the last moment. They're the perfect addition to any salad.

INGREDIENTS | SERVES 4

½ cup extra-virgin olive oil

2 cloves garlic, minced or put through a garlic press

4 slices wheat-free bread, thickly cut, crusts removed

1½ teaspoons salt

1 teaspoon black pepper

⅛ teaspoon red pepper flakes

1. Preheat the broiler to 350°F.

2. In a small bowl, mix the oil and garlic together. Brush both sides of the bread with the garlic oil. Sprinkle with salt, black pepper, and pepper flakes.

3. Cut each slice of bread into 6 cubes, to make 24 cubes. Spray a cookie sheet with nonstick spray. Place the cubes on the sheet and broil until well browned on both sides, 3–4 minutes each side.

4. Put the cookie sheet on the bottom rack of the oven. Turn off the oven and leave the croutons to dry for 20 minutes.

5. Store in an airtight container until ready to use.

Avocado-White Bean Hummus

Simple yet impressive, this appetizer will wow your guests. It also makes a delicious
and healthy alternative to mayonnaise on your favorite sandwich.

INGREDIENTS | SERVES 10

1 (15-ounce) can cannellini beans, drained and rinsed

1 ripe avocado, pitted and diced

1 large garlic clove, coarsely chopped

¼ cup water, plus more as needed

Juice of 1 lemon

2 tablespoons extra-virgin olive oil

1 teaspoon kosher salt

2 tablespoons coarsely chopped fresh cilantro

Freshly ground black pepper

1. Place the cannellini beans, avocado, garlic, water, lemon juice, olive oil, salt, chopped cilantro and pepper in a food processor fitted with a blade attachment or a high-speed blender.

2. Process until smooth, scraping down the sides of the bowl as needed. If the dip is too thick, pulse in more water, a tablespoon at a time, until the desired consistency is reached. Serve with Baked Corn Tortilla Chips (see recipe in this chapter).

Baked Corn Tortilla Chips

*Who says tortilla chips have to be laden with fat and calories to taste good?
These tasty chips are perfect with all kinds of dips and salsas.*

INGREDIENTS | SERVES 6

24 6-inch round corn tortillas
1 teaspoon kosher salt

Read the Label!

Some corn tortillas are made with wheat
gluten! Thoroughly reading the labels will
help keep you informed because sometimes they don't advertise that they contain
wheat.

1. Preheat the oven to 350°F.

2. Cut tortillas into large triangular slices. Lay slices out in a single layer on a baking sheet and sprinkle with salt.

3. Bake 8–12 minutes, or until chips start to lightly brown. Repeat with remaining tortilla slices. Let cool for 10 minutes before eating.

Classic Red Tomato Salsa

*Once you see how simple it is to make this homemade salsa, you will never want to buy the
store-bought variety again! Serve with Baked Corn Tortilla Chips (see recipe in this chapter).*

INGREDIENTS | SERVES 8

6 large, ripe, juicy red tomatoes
2 cloves garlic
2 jalapeño peppers, cored, seeded, and
chopped
½ cup minced sweet white onion
Juice of 1 lime
1 teaspoon red wine vinegar
1 teaspoon salt
½ cup minced cilantro

Salsa Style

Salsa is a Mexican invention, using the hot
and sweet peppers, tomatoes, herbs, and
spices available. Hot food has a purpose
in a hot climate: it makes you sweat, and
when you sweat, you cool off—a bit. Foods
that are extremely hot do kill taste buds, so
don't punish your mouth.

Place all the ingredients in a food processor and pulse until well blended. Do not purée. Refrigerate 1 hour or overnight before serving.

Light Gorgonzola and Ricotta Torte Appetizer

*This appetizer is light and delicious. You will find that this works best
in a springform pan. Serve warm or at room temperature.*

INGREDIENTS | SERVES 6

16 ounces fresh whole-milk ricotta cheese

4 ounces Gorgonzola cheese, crumbled

1 teaspoon fresh oregano or ¼ teaspoon dried

1 teaspoon fresh lemon juice

1 teaspoon freshly grated lemon zest

1 teaspoon salt

½ teaspoon pepper

3 egg whites, beaten stiff

½ cup walnuts, chopped and toasted

1. Preheat the oven to 350°F.

2. Place the cheeses, oregano, lemon juice, zest, salt, and pepper in a food processor and process until very smooth.

3. Place the mixture in a bowl and fold in the beaten egg whites.

4. Spray the inside of a 10" springform pan with nonstick cooking spray. Add the cheese mixture, and bake for about 30 minutes or until slightly golden.

5. Sprinkle with the walnuts. Cool slightly and serve in wedges.

Devilish Egg-Stuffed Celery

*This is a different take on deviled eggs—you devil the whole egg.
Try garnishing these eggs with either 3 teaspoons salmon caviar, 3 teaspoons capers,
3 teaspoons green peppercorns, chopped fresh parsley, or hot or sweet Hungarian paprika.*

INGREDIENTS | SERVES 12

6 eggs, hard-boiled, cooled in water, cracked, and peeled

2 tablespoons mayonnaise

6 drops Tabasco sauce

½ teaspoon freshly ground white pepper

1 teaspoon celery salt

1 tablespoon Dijon mustard

2 tablespoons chopped onion

1 clove garlic, chopped

1 teaspoon salt

2 tablespoons half-and-half

4 stalks celery, washed and cut into thirds

1. Place all the ingredients except the celery in a food processor and blend until smooth.

2. Spread the resulting mixture into the celery and cover with foil or plastic wrap and chill for 1 hour.

3. Add garnishes of your choice just before serving.

Piquant Artichoke and Spinach Dip

This is the perfect dip for parties and entertaining. Serve with corn or rice crackers or sliced vegetables.

INGREDIENTS | YIELDS 2 CUPS

1 (10-ounce) package frozen chopped spinach, thawed

2 tablespoons extra-virgin olive oil

1 (12-ounce) jar artichoke hearts, drained and chopped

4 ounces cream cheese

8 ounces sour cream

2 cloves garlic, finely chopped

½ bunch scallions, chopped

2 tablespoons fresh lemon juice

¼ teaspoon freshly grated nutmeg

1 tablespoon shredded or grated Parmesan cheese

1. Drain the thawed spinach, squeezing it with paper towels, until the extra liquid is gone.

2. Heat the olive oil in a large skillet over medium heat and add the spinach; cook until just soft, about 5 minutes.

3. Remove pan from heat and add the rest of the ingredients, stirring to mix. Serve warm or cold.

Lemony Garlic Kale-Lentil Salad

This light salad tastes wonderful the first day—and even better as leftovers.
The lemon and kale create a delightful combination.

INGREDIENTS | SERVES 6

1 tablespoon extra-virgin olive oil

3 garlic cloves, chopped

¼ cup chopped onion

2 cups kale, stems removed

½ cup sliced tomatoes

1–2 tablespoons chopped fresh basil

½ teaspoon kosher salt

8 ounces lentils, soaked and cooked

2 tablespoons fresh lemon juice

2 tablespoons shaved Asiago cheese, or any other hard cheese

1. Heat oil in a large skillet over medium-high heat. Add the garlic and onion and sauté for 2 minutes.

2. Add the kale and tomatoes and sauté for 2–3 minutes more, until kale is softened but still crisp. Add basil and salt, and stir until blended.

3. In a large bowl, combine the kale mixture with the cooked lentils. Stir well.

4. Stir in lemon juice and cheese. Serve hot or cold.

Golden Parmesan Crisps

It's important to use a block of fresh Parmesan cheese for this recipe. The bottled stuff won't work as well because it's too fine and too dry. Use the coarse grating blade of a food processor or box grater.

INGREDIENTS | MAKES 12 CRISPS

2 tablespoons unsalted butter (more if necessary)

12 heaping tablespoons coarsely grated fresh Parmesan cheese

1 teaspoon thyme

Freshly ground black or cayenne pepper, to taste

1. Heat the butter in a large fry pan over medium heat until it bubbles.

2. Spoon the cheese by tablespoonfuls onto the butter, pressing down lightly with the back of the spoon to spread, making 12 tablespoon-sized crisps.

3. After about 2 minutes, turn and cook until both sides are lightly golden brown. Add more butter if necessary.

4. Sprinkle with thyme, black pepper or cayenne, or both. Serve at once.

Healthy Shrimp Scampi Appetizer

Shrimp scampi can be healthy and delicious. It's perfect on its own for an appetizer, or you can serve it over wheat-free noodles and steamed spinach for a complete entrée!

INGREDIENTS | SERVES 6

3 tablespoons extra-virgin olive oil

1 pound cleaned, large shrimp, deveined and patted dry

4 cloves garlic, minced

1 cup reduced-sodium chicken broth

¾ teaspoon salt

¾ teaspoon pepper

1 tablespoon unsalted butter

½ cup chopped parsley

½ teaspoon grated lemon zest

Juice of ½ lemon (optional)

1. Heat oil in a 12" heavy skillet over medium-high heat until it simmers, then add the shrimp and sauté them, turning once, until just cooked through, about 2 minutes each side. Transfer shrimp with a slotted spoon to a large bowl.

2. Add the garlic, chicken broth, salt, and pepper to the skillet and bring to a boil. Continue boiling until the liquid is reduced to ½ cup, about 5–7 minutes.

3. Add the butter and stir until melted, then remove skillet from heat and stir in shrimp.

4. Add the mixture to a large bowl and toss with parsley and lemon zest. Squeeze lemon juice on top if desired.

Grilled Pear-Kale Salad with Feta Cheese

These grilled pears are wonderful along with the crisp texture of kale.
Kale has become popular for its health benefits and delicious taste.

INGREDIENTS | SERVES 6

Juice of 1 small lemon

5 tablespoons grapeseed oil, divided

½ teaspoon coarse salt

½ teaspoon ground black pepper

4 pears, halved and cored (Bartlett or Bosc work the best here)

4 cups finely chopped curly kale leaves

¼ red onion, finely chopped

1 tablespoon dried cranberries, unsweetened

¼ cup walnuts

¼ cup feta cheese

Super Kale

Did you know that one serving of kale has 200 percent of your vitamin C daily requirement? Kale has even more vitamin C per serving than an orange! Kale is packed with fiber, vitamins, minerals, and antioxidants.

1. For the dressing, whisk together the lemon juice, 4 tablespoons oil, salt, and pepper in a small bowl. Set aside.

2. Prepare a grill to medium-hot heat (you should be able to hold you hand an inch over the cooking grate for 2–3 seconds). Make sure the cooking grate is well oiled.

3. Brush cut sides of pears with remaining grapeseed oil. Put pears, cut-side down, on the grill. Cover and cook until pear halves are grill-marked and heated through, about 10 minutes. Let them cool and slice into strips.

4. In a large bowl, add the kale, onion, cranberries, and walnuts. Stir to combine. Top with pears, feta cheese, and dressing.

Three Bean Salad

This salad is not too sweet and not too tangy like other bean salads.
It tastes even better when marinated overnight.

INGREDIENTS | SERVES 8

1 (15-ounce) can black beans, thoroughly rinsed and drained

1 (15-ounce) can red kidney beans, thoroughly rinsed and drained

1 (15-ounce) can chickpeas (garbanzo beans), thoroughly rinsed and drained

1 green pepper, finely diced

2 medium red onions, finely diced

⅓ cup cider vinegar

¼ cup extra-virgin olive oil

1 clove garlic, finely diced

1 tablespoon honey

½ teaspoon ground mustard

½ teaspoon salt

½ teaspoon black pepper

Handful of fresh cilantro, chopped

1. In a large bowl, mix the black beans, red kidney beans, and chickpeas. Add the diced pepper and onions and mix well.

2. In a small bowl, combine the vinegar, oil, garlic, honey, mustard, salt, and black pepper. Once thoroughly mixed, pour over bean mixture.

3. Add cilantro and refrigerate for 3–4 hours before serving.

Grilled Portobello Mushrooms with Balsamic Glaze

This vegan salad is so filling and hearty any time of the year.
If you haven't tried to grill portobellos, now is the time!

INGREDIENTS | SERVES 6

4 cups arugula, rinsed and dried
3 large portobello mushrooms
1 cup balsamic vinegar
1 tablespoon turbinado sugar
1 teaspoon wheat-free soy sauce

1. Place the arugula on a large platter. Prepare a grill to medium-hot heat.

2. Clean mushrooms and remove stems and any debris. Grill for 10 minutes, turning once. Place mushroom caps on top of the arugula.

3. In a small saucepan, heat the vinegar, sugar, and soy sauce to a boil. Reduce heat to low and simmer for about 15–20 minutes or until the mixture thickens. Remove from heat and let cool.

4. Once balsamic glaze has cooled a bit, pour evenly over portobellos and arugula. Serve immediately or at room temperature.

Avocado Egg Salad

You will not miss the mayonnaise that traditional egg salads have when you taste the creaminess of the avocado in this recipe. Serve it on a bed of lettuce or wrapped up in a wheat-free tortilla.

INGREDIENTS | SERVES 6

7 hard-boiled eggs, peeled and cooled
1 avocado, peeled, pitted, and cut into 1" pieces
2 tablespoons plain Greek low-fat yogurt
2 tablespoons lemon juice
1 green onion, finely chopped
1 celery stalk, finely chopped
1 teaspoon paprika
½ teaspoon salt
½ teaspoon pepper

1. Separate the whites and the yolks of the eggs. Set aside 3 yolks for another use.

2. Dice the egg whites.

3. In a large bowl, combine the avocado, egg yolks, and yogurt. Mash until the mixture is creamy and smooth.

4. Mix in the lemon juice, onion, celery, paprika, salt, and pepper.

5. Gently add the chopped egg whites and combine. Refrigerate or serve immediately.

Tricolor Tomato-Bean Salad

Take advantage of local summer produce to create this perfect, light salad.

INGREDIENTS | SERVES 6

3 plum tomatoes, seeded and chopped

1 green tomato, seeded and chopped

1 yellow tomato, seeded and chopped

1 small cucumber, peeled and chopped into 1" wedges

1 (15-ounce) can small white beans, thoroughly rinsed and drained

½ red onion, finely chopped

3 tablespoons extra-virgin olive oil

2 tablespoons balsamic vinegar

2 garlic cloves, crushed

1 teaspoon Dijon mustard

Visit Your Local Farmers' Markets

If available, your local farmers' market is the best place to buy the freshest fruit and veggies. Shopping at your local farmers' markets will not only support local farmers, but it will also stimulate your town's economy.

1. Place the tomatoes, cucumber, beans, and onion in medium-sized bowl.

2. In a small bowl, whisk together the oil, vinegar, garlic, and mustard until completely blended.

3. Pour oil and vinegar mixture over chopped vegetables. Stir to thoroughly combine. Refrigerate for at least 1 hour or overnight.

Fresh Tomato and Basil Bruschetta over Portobellos

Don't use canned tomatoes or dried basil for this recipe. The fresh tomato and basil really make a difference. Serve as an appetizer, as a side dish, or in a salad.

INGREDIENTS | SERVES 12

6 plum (Roma) tomatoes, seeded and chopped

2 tablespoons extra-virgin olive oil

½ red onion, chopped finely

4 cloves garlic, minced

2 tablespoons balsamic vinegar

3 tablespoons fresh basil, torn

1 tablespoon Parmesan cheese

½ teaspoon salt

½ teaspoon pepper

6 large portobello mushroom caps, wiped clean, stems removed

Extra-virgin olive oil in Misto sprayer

8 ounces fresh mozzarella, thinly sliced

1. Preheat the oven to 425°F.

2. In a large bowl, combine the tomatoes, olive oil, onion, garlic, vinegar, basil, and Parmesan cheese. Add salt and pepper and mix well.

3. Slice each mushroom cap in half, leaving two half circles, and place on a baking sheet sprayed with nonstick cooking spray. Lightly spray each portobello mushroom cap with Misto sprayer filled with olive oil. Bake for 5 minutes. Remove from oven.

4. Spoon bruschetta mixture on each mushroom half. Top with mozzarella and bake for 2–3 minutes more, until cheese is melted. Serve warm.

Tzatziki Dip

This Greek cucumber-yogurt dip is light and delightful with sliced vegetables. This is a delicious, simple dip for children.

INGREDIENTS | SERVES 12

8 ounces plain Greek low-fat yogurt

2 tablespoons extra-virgin olive oil

1 tablespoon lemon juice

½ teaspoon salt

½ teaspoon ground black pepper

1 tablespoon fresh dill, chopped

2 garlic cloves, minced

2 tablespoons peeled, seeded, and minced English cucumber

1 tablespoon chopped fresh mint

In a medium bowl, mix all the ingredients together until thoroughly combined. Refrigerate for at least 1 hour to let the flavors settle in. Serve cold with sliced raw vegetables.

Tzatziki

Tzatziki—pronounced tsah-ZEE-kee—is a Mediterranean sauce made with yogurt and cucumbers. It is traditionally served as a meze (an appetizer). It can also be used as a spread on gyros (Greek sandwiches) or souvlaki (Greek fast food consisting of meat and vegetables).

Grilled Corn Salad

When you grill corn, it becomes juicy, sweet, and crispy.
This salad is so simple and flavorful, you will want to make it again and again.

INGREDIENTS | SERVES 8

4 ears unshucked corn

2 avocados, peeled, pitted, and cut into 1" squares

½ cup grape or cherry tomatoes, halved

1 green pepper, diced

6 cups arugula, divided

Cilantro-Lime Vinaigrette (see Chapter 10)

2 tablespoons fresh cilantro leaves, torn

1. Pull back the husks of the corn and remove the silk. Pull husks back over corn. Lightly brush grates on grill with olive oil and heat grill to medium.

2. Place corn on the grill and cook for 15–20 minutes, turning occasionally. Remove from the grill and let corn cool.

3. When corn has cooled, shuck corn completely. With a sharp knife, cut down sides of each corn cob to remove kernels, and place grilled corn kernels in a large bowl.

4. Add the avocados, tomatoes, pepper, and 3 cups of arugula to the bowl. Mix well.

5. Add Cilantro-Lime Vinaigrette and stir thoroughly to combine. Refrigerate at least 1 hour to let the flavors soak in.

6. When ready to serve, place remaining 3 cups of arugula on a large platter and top with corn salad. Garnish with cilantro.

CHAPTER 3

Breakfast and Brunch

Crustless Vegetable Quiche Cups

This protein-packed breakfast can be made with whatever vegetables you have on hand.
It's also the perfect way to sneak in your daily dose of vegetables.

INGREDIENTS | SERVES 12

1 tablespoon canola oil

½ cup finely chopped onion

1 cup fresh organic spinach

1 cup fresh grape or cherry tomatoes, halved

1 cup fresh mushrooms, diced

2 whole eggs, beaten

6 egg whites, beaten

1 cup Cheddar cheese

¼ teaspoon thyme

½ teaspoon sweet basil

¼ teaspoon oregano

¼ teaspoon salt

⅛ teaspoon pepper

Powerful Protein

Studies show that people who consume a breakfast that contains protein tend to eat less throughout the day. One quiche cup has over 6 grams of protein!

1. Preheat the oven to 350°F. Lightly spray a 12-cup muffin tin with nonstick cooking spray or line with cupcake liners.

2. Heat oil in a large skillet over medium-high heat. Add the onions and cook, stirring occasionally, until onions are soft, about 2–3 minutes. Stir in spinach, tomatoes, and mushrooms, and continue cooking until veggies have wilted, about 3–4 minutes.

3. In a large bowl, combine the eggs, egg whites, cheese, thyme, basil, oregano, salt, and pepper. Add spinach mixture and stir to blend. Pour into prepared muffin tins.

4. Bake in preheated oven until eggs have set, about 30 minutes. Let cool for 10 minutes before serving.

Coconut Flour Pancakes

Cooking with wheat-free flours can be intimidating, but the sweet taste of coconut flour in these pancakes proves that even wheat-free pancakes can be delicious. You can replace the coconut oil with melted butter and the coconut milk with regular milk if you like.

INGREDIENTS | SERVES 3

2 whole eggs
2 egg whites
4 tablespoons coconut oil, divided
3 tablespoons coconut milk
1½ teaspoons maple syrup
1 teaspoon sea salt
3 tablespoons coconut flour
½ teaspoon wheat-free baking powder
1 teaspoon cinnamon
1 teaspoon allspice
⅓ cup ground flax seed
1 teaspoon wheat-free vanilla extract

1. In a large bowl, using a wire whisk, mix together the eggs and egg whites, 3 tablespoons coconut oil, coconut milk, maple syrup, and salt.

2. Add the coconut flour and baking powder, whisking until thoroughly mixed. Add the cinnamon, allspice, flax seed, and vanilla. Stir to combine thoroughly.

3. Heat remaining tablespoon of coconut oil in a skillet over medium heat.

4. Spoon 2–3 tablespoons of batter onto skillet, making pancakes about 3–4 inches in diameter. Cook for 3–5 minutes, turning once.

The Best Grain-Free Banana Bread Ever

Even those who don't need to be on a wheat-free diet will adore this banana bread. It tastes just as good with or without the walnuts.

INGREDIENTS | SERVES 10

¼ cup butter, softened

⅔ cup turbinado sugar

2 eggs

3 tablespoons plain nonfat Greek yogurt

2 tablespoons water

1 teaspoon wheat-free vanilla extract

2 tablespoons ground flax seed

2 cups brown rice flour or rice flour

1 teaspoon wheat-free baking powder

½ teaspoon wheat-free baking soda

½ teaspoon salt

½ teaspoon cinnamon

1 cup mashed ripe banana (approximately 3 large bananas)

⅓ cup finely chopped walnuts (optional)

Brown Rice Flour

Brown rice flour has more fiber and B vitamins then regular rice flour. It also offers a nutty, slightly sweet taste as opposed to regular rice flour so it may be a better alternative for cookies and baked goods.

1. Preheat the oven to 350°F.

2. In a large bowl, beat the butter and sugar until creamy. Beat in the eggs, one at a time.

3. Stir in yogurt, water, and vanilla and mix well.

4. In a separate bowl combine the flax seed, rice flour, baking powder, baking soda, salt, and cinnamon. Add this mixture to the butter mixture.

5. Stir in the bananas and nuts and mix well.

6. Spoon the mixture into two or three greased mini loaf pans (5½" × 3") or one large loaf pan (5" × 10").

7. Bake 50–55 minutes, or until a wooden pick inserted into the center of the bread comes out clean.

8. Cool in the pans for 2 minutes, then turn out and cool completely.

Raspberry Yogurt Smoothie

Smoothies are a wonderful, healthy, and filling alternative to standard breakfast options. They are so versatile and can be used with so many different ingredients.

INGREDIENTS | SERVES 2

1 cup plain nonfat Greek yogurt

½ cup frozen raspberries

½ cup fat-free milk (almond, soy, or whatever milk you choose)

½ banana

2 tablespoons ground flax seed

Place all of the ingredients in blender and process for 1–2 minutes until thoroughly blended. Serve immediately.

The Benefits of Flax

Flax is a seed that is packed with more antioxidants, fiber, and omega-3 fatty acids than just about anything its size. These omega-3 fatty acids are the ones that fight inflammation in the body and help prevent diseases and chronic illnesses. Ground flax seed can be found in most supermarkets and health food stores.

Chestnut Flour Crepes

Chestnut flour is sweet and nutty, making the most delicious crepes you can imagine. You can stuff them with fruit and whipped cream or with savory fillings.

INGREDIENTS | MAKES 12 CREPES

2 eggs

1 cup milk

½ teaspoon salt

½ cup chestnut flour

½ cup rice flour

2 teaspoons sugar (optional)

1 tablespoon butter (plus more as needed)

Using Nonstick Sauté Pans

Nonstick pans take all of the grief out of making crepes. However, even if your pan is quite new, it's important to use a bit of butter for insurance and extra flavor. Keep the pan well buttered and you have an almost foolproof method for making perfect crepes.

1. In a food processor, add the eggs, milk, and salt, and process until blended.

2. With the motor on low, slowly add the flours, stopping occasionally to scrape down the sides of the container.

3. Add the sugar if you are making sweet crepes with sweet filling; omit if you are going to fill them with savory delights.

4. Heat 1 tablespoon butter in a nonstick sauté pan over medium heat. Pour in batter by the half-cupful into the hot pan. Tilt the pan to spread the batter thinly.

5. Fry the crepes, turning, until browned, about 3–4 minutes on both sides; place on waxed paper and sprinkle with a bit of rice flour to prevent them from sticking.

6. When the crepes are done, you can fill them right away or store them in the refrigerator or freezer for later use.

Vegetable-Egg Scramble with Fontina Cheese

*This light dish will be your favorite way to get your daily requirements of vegetables.
If you don't have broccoli or tomatoes, use whatever vegetables you have in the house.*

INGREDIENTS | SERVES 1

1 tablespoon grapeseed oil
1 clove garlic, chopped
1 cup chopped broccoli
½ cup sliced grape tomatoes
1 whole egg
2 egg whites
2 tablespoons chopped fresh basil
½ teaspoon sea salt
1 teaspoon oregano
1 tablespoon shredded fontina cheese

1. Heat the oil in a medium skillet over medium-high heat. Sauté the garlic for 1 minute, then add the broccoli and tomatoes. Cook for 2–3 minutes until broccoli is tender, but still crunchy.

2. Whisk egg and egg whites in a bowl until frothy.

3. Pour eggs into skillet and continue to mix thoroughly while eggs cook. Add basil, salt, oregano, and cheese and cook for 3–4 minutes until eggs have light brown edges. Remove from heat and serve immediately.

Don't Pass on the Yolks, Folks

Are you using only egg whites? The yolks have a bad reputation, but they really are quite healthy. Yes, the yolks do contain cholesterol and fat, but moderate consumption of yolks will not put you at risk for the diseases they were once thought to have contributed to. The yolks also have a large amount of protein, calcium, and zinc, so don't be afraid to have some whole eggs, too!

Ricotta Torte with Serrano Ham and Parmesan

If you can't find serrano ham, substitute prosciutto.
Do not, however, use low-fat ricotta—it just doesn't taste the same.

INGREDIENTS | SERVES 6

2 shallots, peeled and minced

2 tablespoons butter

3 eggs

1 pound ricotta cheese

½ cup grated Parmesan cheese

¼ cup finely chopped serrano ham or prosciutto

4 tablespoons butter, melted

1 teaspoon dried oregano

1 teaspoon dried basil

⅛ teaspoon nutmeg

½ teaspoon salt

½ teaspoon pepper

1. Preheat the oven to 325°F. In a skillet over medium heat, sauté the shallots in the butter for 2–3 minutes. Place shallots in a pie pan you have prepared with nonstick spray.

2. In a large bowl add the eggs and the rest of the ingredients, and beat constantly until well mixed and frothy. Pour into prepared pie pan and bake for 35 minutes, or until set and golden. Cut into wedges and serve.

Italian Ricotta-Chestnut Fritters

This is a traditional Italian recipe. These fritters are a
wonderful side dish at brunch and are simple to make.

INGREDIENTS | SERVES 4

2 eggs

½ cup sugar

1 teaspoon wheat-free vanilla extract

1 teaspoon wheat-free baking soda

1 cup ricotta cheese

½ cup chestnut flour

½ cup rice flour

Extra-virgin olive oil, for frying

Powdered sugar, to dust fritters

1. In a medium bowl, beat together the eggs and sugar until thick.

2. Slowly add the rest of the ingredients except the olive oil and the powdered sugar. Cover the bowl and let stand for 1 hour.

3. Heat 2 inches of oil over medium-high heat to 375°F. Drop the batter by tablespoonfuls into the oil. Do not overfill the pot. Fry for about 2 minutes, turning as they brown.

4. Drain on brown paper or paper towels and dust with powdered sugar.

Corn Crepes

You can make these crepes in advance and store them in the refrigerator or freezer.

INGREDIENTS | MAKES 12 CREPES

2 eggs

1 cup milk or buttermilk

1 teaspoon salt

1 cup corn flour

2 teaspoons sugar (optional)

2 tablespoons butter, melted

1 tablespoon vegetable oil, plus more if needed

Storing Crepes

To store crepes, simply put a bit of corn flour on sheets of waxed paper and stack the crepes individually. Then put the whole thing in a plastic bag and store in the refrigerator for up to 3 days.

1. Place the eggs, milk, and salt in your food processor and process until smooth.

2. With the motor on low, slowly add the flour, and spoon in the sugar (if you are making sweet crepes). Scrape down the sides of the container often. Add the melted butter.

3. Heat oil in a nonstick pan over medium heat. Pour in ¼ cup batter. Tilt the pan to spread the batter evenly. Cook for 3–4 minutes, turning once. Repeat with remaining batter.

4. Place crepes on sheets of waxed paper that have been dusted with extra corn flour.

5. To store, place in a plastic bag in refrigerator or freezer. You can stuff these with salsa, jack cheese, and sour cream, or you can stuff them with mashed fruit such as blueberries.

Shirred Eggs and Asparagus au Gratin

*This is a very easy brunch or supper dish. Fresh asparagus is definitely better
in this recipe. The trick is arranging the asparagus evenly in the pan.*

INGREDIENTS | SERVES 4

1 pound fresh asparagus, ends trimmed,
or 2 (10-ounce) packages frozen

8 eggs

1 cup crumbled Roquefort cheese

½ teaspoon salt

½ teaspoon pepper

1. Preheat oven to 350°F.

2. Blanch the asparagus in boiling water for 5 minutes.
   Take immediately out of the boiling water and place in
   ice water and drain.

3. Prepare a gratin pan or dish with nonstick spray and
   arrange the asparagus in the bottom in a single layer.
   Break the eggs over the top. Sprinkle with Roquefort,
   salt, and pepper, and bake until eggs are done and
   cheese is hot and runny (about 12 minutes). Serve hot.

Banana Pancakes

For a lighter pancake, separate the eggs and beat the whites stiffly. The bananas can be either sliced onto the cakes or mashed and incorporated into the batter.

INGREDIENTS | MAKES 16 PANCAKES

½ cup milk

2 eggs

1½ tablespoons butter, melted

1 tablespoon wheat-free baking powder

1 banana

1 cup rice flour (or substitute corn, chickpea, or tapioca flour)

Extra butter for frying pancakes

Flour Substitutions

Try substituting rice or potato flour in some recipes, and chickpea flour also makes an excellent savory pancake. You have so many choices—it's fun to exercise them.

1. In the bowl of a food processor, process the milk, eggs, and melted butter together. Slowly add the baking powder, banana, and flour and process until smooth.

2. Heat a griddle pan or large frying pan over medium heat. Drop a teaspoon of butter on it and when the butter sizzles, start pouring on the batter to about 2" diameter.

3. When bubbles come to the top, turn the pancakes and continue to fry until golden brown. Place on a plate in a warm oven to keep the pancakes warm while you make the others.

Egg-and-Cheese-Stuffed Tomatoes

*These are simple but look sophisticated. Their presentation is pretty
and is perfect for a brunch with friends and family.*

INGREDIENTS | SERVES 4

8 medium tomatoes

2 cloves garlic, minced or put through a garlic press

4 tablespoons butter

1 teaspoon salt

1 teaspoon black pepper

1 teaspoon dried oregano

1 teaspoon cumin powder

8 eggs

½ cup grated Monterey jack or Cheddar cheese

8 teaspoons wheat-free corn bread crumbs

Priceless Heirlooms

There are good tomatoes in the supermarket and good tomatoes in cans, but the best tomatoes are homegrown. Recently there has been a trend toward growing ancient varieties of tomato. These "heirlooms," as they are called, have more flavor—sweetness paired with acid—than ordinary tomatoes do. You can buy the seeds and grow them yourself, and some farmers markets have them, too.

1. Cut the tops off the tomatoes, core, and using a melon baller, scoop out seeds and pulp. Place the tomatoes on a baking sheet covered with parchment paper or sprayed with nonstick spray.

2. Preheat the oven to 350°F.

3. In a skillet over medium heat, sauté the garlic in the butter for 2 minutes.

4. In a small bowl, mix together the salt, black pepper, oregano, and cumin. Spread ½ of the mixture on the insides of the tomatoes, saving the rest for topping.

5. Spoon the butter and garlic mixture into the tomatoes. Sprinkle with ½ of the *remaining* spice mixture.

6. Break an egg into each tomato. Sprinkle with the rest of the spice mixture.

7. Loosely spoon the cheese over the eggs, then sprinkle 1 teaspoon corn bread crumbs over each tomato.

8. Bake for 20 minutes. The tomatoes should still be firm, the eggs soft, the cheese melted, and the bread crumbs browned.

Apple-Cinnamon Crepes

The aroma of these delicious crepes will be sure to please children and adults alike. And yes, they taste as delightful as they smell. For a special treat, top them with whipped cream or ice cream.

INGREDIENTS | SERVES 6

2 large tart apples, such as Granny Smith, peeled, cored, and chopped

1 tablespoon butter

1 teaspoon cinnamon

¼ teaspoon ground cloves

2 tablespoons brown sugar, or to taste

4 ounces cream cheese, at room temperature

12 Chestnut Flour Crepes (see recipe in this chapter), made with sugar

1. Preheat oven to 350°F.

2. In a large skillet over medium heat, sauté the apples in butter for 20 minutes. Stir in cinnamon, cloves, and brown sugar.

3. Blend the cream cheese into the hot mixture.

4. Lay out crepes and place a spoonful of filling on each. Roll them and place in a baking dish prepared with nonstick spray.

5. Bake in oven until hot, about 8–10 minutes. Serve warm.

Blueberry or Strawberry Pancakes

These are a healthy and delicious way to get a serving of fruit in your breakfast or brunch. You will get some caramelization from the sugar and fruit—it's delicious. Top with more berries and whipped cream.

INGREDIENTS | MAKES 16 PANCAKES

½ pint blueberries or strawberries

1 teaspoon sugar

1 teaspoon grated orange zest

1½ tablespoons butter

1 batch Banana Pancakes batter (see recipe in this chapter)

1. In a bowl, mix the fruit, sugar, and orange zest. Mash with a potato masher or fork.

2. Heat a griddle over medium heat. Add butter. Pour half-cupfuls of pancake batter on the hot griddle and spoon some berries on top.

3. When bubbles rise to the top of the cakes, flip them over and brown on the other side.

Freezing Fruit in Its Prime

There's nothing like blueberry pie in January, and you don't have to use sugary canned blueberry pie filling. When fresh blueberries are available, just rinse a quart and dry on paper towels. Place the berries on a cookie sheet in the freezer for a half hour and then put them in a plastic bag for future use.

No Grain Bread

This bread is perfect for sandwiches, toast, or even grilled cheese.
The flax seed adds antioxidants and fiber, making this bread nutritious and delicious.

INGREDIENTS | SERVES 12

2½ cups golden flax seed meal

½ cup almond meal

1 tablespoon wheat-free baking powder

¼ teaspoon wheat-free baking soda

1 teaspoon salt

1½ tablespoons sugar

1 teaspoon cinnamon

3 eggs, beaten

½ cup water

3 tablespoons extra-virgin olive oil

1. Preheat oven to 350°F. Place parchment paper in a 5" × 10" loaf pan.

2. In a large bowl, mix flax seed meal, almond meal, baking powder, baking soda, salt, sugar, and cinnamon.

3. Add eggs, water, and oil to dry ingredients and combine well. Let batter set for 2–3 minutes to thicken up, then pour into the prepared pan.

4. Bake for about 20 minutes, until the top is brown and the loaf springs back when you touch the top.

5. Cool and cut into slices. Store leftovers in the refrigerator to preserve freshness for up to 5 days.

Dark Chocolate–Coconut Scones

These wheat-free scones are perfect with a cup of coffee or tea.
You can use carob chips to make them dairy free as well.

INGREDIENTS | SERVES 8

1½ cups wheat-free, all-purpose flour
¼ cup coconut flour
½ teaspoon xanthan gum
¼ cup turbinado sugar
2 teaspoons wheat-free baking powder
⅛ teaspoon salt
¾ cup finely shredded coconut, unsweetened
½ cup coconut oil
2 large eggs
⅓ cup coconut milk
1 teaspoon wheat-free vanilla extract
¼ cup dark chocolate chunks or chips
Coconut or additional turbinado sugar for sprinkling (optional)

1. Preheat the oven to 400°F. Line a baking sheet with parchment paper or use a silicone mat.

2. In a large bowl, mix together the flours, xanthan gum, sugar, baking powder, salt, and coconut. Work in the coconut oil until the mixture is crumbly.

3. In a separate bowl, whisk together the eggs, milk, and vanilla until frothy. Add to the dry ingredients, stirring until well blended. The dough will be sticky. Fold in the chocolate chunks.

4. Drop the dough onto the parchment paper or silicone mat and form into a circle in the center of baking sheet. Cut circle into 8 triangles.

5. Sprinkle the scones with coconut or turbinado sugar if desired. Bake for 15–20 minutes, or until golden brown. Remove from the oven and let cool for 5 minutes before serving.

Egg and Avocado Breakfast Burrito

Breakfast burritos are easy enough to make even on your busiest mornings.

INGREDIENTS | SERVES 4

3 whole eggs
3 egg whites
¼ cup shredded Cheddar cheese
⅓ cup milk
1 tablespoon grapeseed oil
¼ yellow onion, finely chopped
½ green pepper, diced
2 avocados, peeled, pitted and mashed
¼ teaspoon salt
½ teaspoon pepper
4 corn or rice flour tortillas, warmed
⅔ cup crumbled goat cheese
¼ cup wheat-free salsa

1. In a medium bowl, beat together the eggs, egg whites, cheese, and milk until frothy.

2. Heat the oil in a medium skillet over medium-high heat. Sauté the onion and green pepper until onion is translucent, about 2–3 minutes.

3. Pour the egg mixture into skillet and cook, stirring, until eggs are scrambled.

4. Season the mashed avocados with salt and pepper.

5. Place tortillas one at a time in a separate skillet and cook until warm, about 2–3 minutes.

6. Spread equal amounts of avocado on one side of tortillas and layer with equal amounts of goat cheese and scrambled eggs. Roll up into burritos and serve immediately with salsa on the side.

Chocolate–Peanut Butter Smoothie

This smoothie is so delicious, you won't even believe that it is healthy!

INGREDIENTS | SERVES 2

2 tablespoons unsweetened cocoa powder

2 tablespoons natural creamy peanut butter

½ banana, frozen

½ cup almond milk (or milk of your choice)

½ cup plain Greek low-fat yogurt

½ teaspoon wheat-free vanilla extract

4–5 ice cubes

Combine all ingredients in a blender and blend until thick and creamy. Serve immediately.

Blueberry-Oatmeal Smoothie

Wheat-free rolled oats add a wonderful texture to your average smoothie.

INGREDIENTS | SERVES 2

½ cup wheat-free rolled oats

1 cup soy milk or milk of choice

1 banana, frozen

¾ cup fresh or frozen organic blueberries

1 teaspoon honey (optional)

4–5 ice cubes (if using fresh blueberries)

Place the oats in a blender and blend for 1–2 minutes until they are ground into a fine powder. Add the rest of the ingredients, blend and enjoy!

Freeze-Ahead Fruit

Frozen fruit is perfect for smoothies and you can always keep it in your freezer. Feel free to mix it up and use whatever fruit you have on hand.

Chocolate Chip–Zucchini Bread

You will never know that there are vegetables in this yummy bread or that it's wheat-free. It's a perfect way to sneak vegetables into those picky children!

INGREDIENTS | SERVES 8

2 eggs
½ cup turbinado sugar
½ cup grapeseed oil
½ cup unsweetened applesauce
1 tablespoon wheat-free vanilla extract
1 cup brown rice flour
½ cup almond flour
½ cup cornstarch
1 teaspoon xanthan gum
½ teaspoon wheat-free baking soda
¼ teaspoon wheat-free baking powder
½ teaspoon salt
1 tablespoon cinnamon
¼ teaspoon ground cloves
¼ teaspoon nutmeg
1½ cups fresh zucchini, shredded
½ cup chocolate chips

1. Preheat oven to 350°F. Grease a 9" × 5" loaf pan with cooking spray.

2. In a large mixing bowl, beat together the eggs, sugar, oil, and applesauce. Add the vanilla and mix well.

3. In a separate bowl, combine the flours, cornstarch, xanthan gum, baking soda, baking powder, salt, cinnamon, cloves, and nutmeg.

4. Add the dry ingredients to wet ingredients and mix well.

5. Add zucchini and chocolate chips and stir to combine.

6. Pour into the greased loaf pan and bake for 60–70 minutes. Place a toothpick in center of bread and if it comes out clean, it's done.

CHAPTER 4

Casseroles and Entrées

Healthy Mexican Casserole

This one-dish meal is so easy and delicious your family will ask you to make it again and again.
Serve the casserole with Baked Corn Tortilla Chips (see Chapter 2).

INGREDIENTS | SERVES 8

1 tablespoon extra-virgin olive oil
1 pound lean ground turkey
½ teaspoon cumin
¼ teaspoon chili powder
¼ teaspoon red pepper flakes
⅛ teaspoon coriander
2 tablespoons water
1 (15-ounce) can black beans, rinsed thoroughly and drained
1 (15-ounce) can pinto beans, rinsed thoroughly and drained
4–5 plum tomatoes, chopped and seeds removed
1 teaspoon chopped chili peppers
½ cup frozen corn
¼ cup Mexican blend shredded cheese

1. Preheat the oven to 350°F.

2. Heat the oil in a skillet over medium-high heat. Cook turkey in hot oil for 5–8 minutes, until the meat is browned.

3. Stir in cumin, chili powder, red pepper flakes, coriander, and water.

4. Add black and pinto beans, tomatoes, chili peppers, and corn. Stir well.

5. Place the meat mixture in a 9" × 13" casserole dish and add cheese on top.

6. Bake for 20 minutes until cheese is melted.

Ditch the Packet

The packets of taco seasoning that you can find in the grocery store are loaded with sodium and preservatives. One little packet can has as much as 1,500 mg of sodium! It is easy and more economical to make your own taco seasoning blend using these simple ingredients.

Las Chalupas with Crepe-atillas

You can make these delightful crepes in advance, then either refrigerate or freeze them. You can also use ground turkey or chicken in this recipe.

INGREDIENTS | SERVES 4

2 eggs

1½ cups milk

1½ teaspoons salt, divided

1¼ teaspoons pepper, divided

1 cup corn flour (masa harina)

¼ tablespoon grapeseed oil for frying

1 pound lean ground beef

1 small onion, chopped

2 pickled jalapeños, chopped, and 2 ounces of their juice

1 teaspoon garlic powder

1 cup salsa

1 tablespoon chili powder

2 cups shredded Monterey jack or Cheddar cheese

2 cups shredded iceberg or romaine lettuce

1 cup chopped tomato

½ cup chopped black or green olives

1 cup Guacamole (see Chapter 13)

1 cup sour cream

1. Place the eggs, milk, ½ teaspoon salt, ¼ teaspoon pepper, and flour in a blender. Process until smooth, stopping once to scrape down the sides of the container. Let batter rest for 30 minutes or more. After resting, the batter should be very loose. If it is too thick, add extra milk, 1 tablespoon at a time.

2. In a medium nonstick skillet, heat the oil over medium heat. Pour about ¼ cup batter into the pan and tilt the pan so that the crepe is 6" in diameter. Fry until lightly golden on both sides, about 2–3 minutes each side.

3. Set crepe aside on waxed paper that you have sprinkled with flour. Repeat until you have 8 crepes.

4. In another skillet, sauté the beef and onion until beef is no longer pink and onion is translucent, about 10 minutes. Stir in jalapeños, garlic powder, salsa, chili powder, and the remaining salt and pepper. Cook until heated through.

5. Place the crepes on plates and top with ground beef mixture. Set out bowls of cheese, lettuce, tomato, olives, guacamole, and sour cream for toppings. Let your guests add their favorite toppings to create their own chalupas.

Scalloped Potatoes with Leeks and Prosciutto

This is the ideal comfort food. It's filling and tasty and is an excellent brunch or supper dish.

INGREDIENTS | SERVES 6

1½ cups grated Parmesan cheese

1 cup coarsely grated fontina cheese

½ cup corn flour

½ teaspoon salt

½ teaspoon freshly ground pepper

6 large Idaho or Yukon Gold potatoes, peeled and sliced thinly

4 leeks, thinly sliced crosswise, white parts only

1 pound prosciutto, diced

3 cups milk

4 tablespoons butter (for greasing baking dish and dotting on potatoes)

1. Preheat oven to 350°F. Grease a 9" × 13" baking dish or prepare it with nonstick spray.

2. Mix together the cheeses, corn flour, salt, and pepper.

3. Place a layer of potatoes in the baking dish, then one of leeks, and dab with bits of prosciutto. Sprinkle with the mixture of cheeses, corn flour, and spices. Repeat until you get to the top of the baking dish. Add the milk, sprinkle with cheese mixture, and dot with butter.

4. Bake for about 90 minutes. The top should be brown and crispy, the inside soft and creamy.

Veal Loaf with Red Peppers and Gorgonzola

The water bath (or bain-marie) technique used here will make this tender meat loaf almost custard-like.

INGREDIENTS | SERVES 4–6

1½ pounds ground veal

1 small onion, quartered

2 cloves garlic

2 eggs

1 cup wheat-free bread crumbs

1 tablespoon oregano

1 teaspoon marjoram

½ teaspoon salt

½ teaspoon pepper

½ cup wheat-free chili sauce

2 roasted red peppers, packed in olive oil

3 ounces Gorgonzola cheese, crumbled

2 tablespoons grated Parmesan cheese

1. Preheat the oven to 325°F.

2. Add the veal, onion, garlic, eggs, bread crumbs, oregano, marjoram, salt, pepper, and chili sauce to a food processor and process until smooth.

3. Prepare a standard 9" × 5" bread pan with nonstick spray. Pour half of the mixture into the bread pan. Spread a layer of roasted red peppers on top and crumbled cheese over that. Add the rest of the veal mixture. Sprinkle with Parmesan cheese.

4. Place the bread pan inside a large roasting pan, and add enough boiling water to come halfway up the sides of the bread pan. Place pans in oven and bake for 1 hour.

Basil

Basil is a versatile herb—raw or cooked, dry or fresh, it adds immeasurably to many main dishes, sauces, salads, and soups. In old Italian lore, it was considered bad luck to chop basil with a knife—one was told to tear it carefully. The edges from tearing are not so clean and sharp, so perhaps they let more aroma and flavor out of the leaves. Basil also comes in a number of different varieties with different flavors. The standard Italian basil is fine for everything. At the end of the summer, pick all of the basil in bunches, tie them, and let them dry. They will last all winter.

Zucchini with Tomato and Bacon

This recipe is best when made with medium-sized zucchini, about 10"–12" each, and can also easily be made vegetarian by omitting the bacon.

INGREDIENTS | SERVES 6

6 medium zucchini

1 small onion, minced

2 cloves garlic, minced

1 serrano pepper, cored, seeded, and minced

2 tablespoons butter or extra-virgin olive oil

1 cup cooked rice

1 cup crushed tomatoes

2 tablespoons freshly squeezed lemon juice

2 eggs, slightly beaten

1 tablespoon dried oregano leaves or 2 tablespoons fresh oregano

½ teaspoon salt

½ teaspoon pepper

6 strips bacon

1. Preheat the oven to 350°F. Spray a 9" × 13" baking dish with nonstick spray or oil.

2. Cut the top quarter off the zucchini, lengthwise. Hollow out the zucchini with the small side of a melon baller or with a half-teaspoon measuring spoon; reserve the pulp.

3. In a skillet over medium heat, sauté the onion, garlic, pepper, and zucchini pulp in the butter until soft, about 3–4 minutes. Add all the remaining ingredients except the bacon.

4. Divide the filling among the zucchini boats. Lay a bacon strip on top of each stuffed zucchini. Place in the prepared baking dish. Bake until the "boats" are hot and the bacon is brown and crisp, about 10–12 minutes. Serve hot or at room temperature.

Stuffed Vegetables

There are many vegetables you can successfully stuff with lots of different, delicious ingredients. Chopped meat, shrimp, fish, and crabmeat all make wonderful stuffing. A baked clam–stuffed mushroom is also a real treat. Ricotta cheese, used to stuff pastas such as ravioli and lasagna, also makes an excellent stuffing.

Thick and Creamy Corn and Black Bean Casserole

This makes a satisfying meal that can be made vegetarian, or you could add some ham for extra flavor. Feel free to substitute half-and-half for the whipping cream to lighten it up.

INGREDIENTS | SERVES 4–5

2 tablespoons unsalted butter

½ sweet onion, chopped finely

½ cup minced celery

½ cup minced celeriac (celery root)

¼ cup sweet red pepper, roasted and chopped

2 tablespoons corn flour, potato flour, or cornstarch

½ cup rich chicken broth

1 (15-ounce) can black beans, thoroughly rinsed and drained

1 (10-ounce) package frozen corn kernels

2 eggs, well beaten

1½ cups whipping cream

1 teaspoon salt

1 teaspoon sweet paprika

1 teaspoon ground black pepper

1 teaspoon ground coriander

½ teaspoon ground allspice

1 cup wheat-free bread crumbs

1 cup grated Cheddar cheese

Better Than Canned

Stay away from canned creamed corn and stick with fresh or frozen, making your own cream sauce. It's easy and wheat-free, and tastes so much better than the ones made with soups or mixes.

1. Preheat the oven to 350°F.

2. Melt the butter in a large ovenproof casserole. Add the onion, celery, celeriac, and red pepper and sauté over low heat until soft, about 10 minutes.

3. Mix in the corn flour or starch and stir, cooking gently for 3 minutes.

4. Add the chicken broth, black beans, and corn. Bring to a boil, and then lower the heat to a simmer and cook until the black beans are slightly softened, about 20 minutes. Take off the heat.

5. In a small bowl, mix together the eggs and cream. Blend the mixture quickly into the vegetables. Mix in the salt and spices.

6. Place in a well-buttered casserole or keep in the same ovenproof pan that you've been using for cooking. Sprinkle the top with bread crumbs and cheese.

7. Bake until golden brown and bubbling, about 15 minutes. Serve hot.

Chicken Divan

Chicken lovers will be asking for second helpings when they try this mouthwatering dish.

INGREDIENTS | SERVES 6

3 pounds chicken breasts, boneless and skinless, cut into strips

1 cup corn flour

1 tablespoon sea or kosher salt

Ground black pepper, to taste

½ cup extra-virgin olive oil, or more as needed

1 pound broccoli florets, cut into bite-sized pieces, cooked, and drained

1½ cups Incredible Hollandaise Sauce (see recipe in this chapter)

2 tablespoons Parmesan cheese

Sprinkle of paprika (optional)

1. Preheat oven to 350°F.

2. Roll the chicken in the flour, then sprinkle with salt and pepper.

3. Heat the olive oil in a sauté pan over medium heat. Sauté the chicken for 5 minutes on each side until golden brown, adding more oil if the pan gets dry.

4. Butter a 2-quart casserole or prepare it with nonstick spray. Place the broccoli in the bottom and spoon some Hollandaise over the top. Arrange the chicken over the broccoli and pour on the rest of the sauce. Sprinkle with Parmesan cheese and paprika. Bake for 30 minutes.

Incredible Hollandaise Sauce

This sauce is so adaptable and can be used on fish, lobster, or hot vegetables, especially asparagus, artichokes, and broccoli.

INGREDIENTS | MAKES 1¼ CUPS

2 sticks (1 cup) unsalted butter

1 whole egg, plus 1 or 2 egg yolks, depending on the richness desired

1 tablespoon freshly squeezed lemon juice

⅛ teaspoon cayenne pepper

Salt, to taste

Hollandaise Sauce

The name implies that this sauce was created in Holland, a land of high butter use. However, it is one of the five master sauces in French cuisine. It is believed to have been created by French chefs to mimic a Dutch sauce. But in any area where there is plentiful butter, hollandaise sauce, with its rich, smooth texture, will reign. And although people tend to think of it in terms of eggs Benedict, it's good on most green vegetables.

1. Melt the butter in a small, heavy saucepan over very low heat.

2. Place the eggs, egg yolks, lemon juice, and cayenne in a blender or food processor. Blend well.

3. With the motor running on low, add the hot butter, a little at a time, to the egg mixture.

4. Return the mixture to the pan you used to melt the butter. Whisking, thicken the sauce over low heat, adding salt to your taste, about 5–7 minutes. As soon as it's thick, pour the sauce into a bowl, a sauce boat, or over the food. (Reheating the sauce to thicken it is the delicate part. You must not let it get too hot or it will scramble the eggs, or even curdle them. If either disaster happens, add a tablespoon of boiling water and whisk vigorously.)

Chestnut Cannelloni with Sage, Mushrooms, and Wine Sauce

The number of cannelloni you make depends not on the recipe but on how large and thick you make them. Plan on two stuffed tubes per person.

INGREDIENTS | SERVES 6

2 eggs

1½ teaspoons salt, divided

1 teaspoon freshly ground white pepper, divided

1 cup milk

1 cup Italian chestnut flour

¼ cup vegetable oil for frying

1 cup ricotta cheese

2 eggs

¼ teaspoon nutmeg

½ cup smoked ham, thinly sliced and shredded

½ cup chopped fresh Italian flat-leaf parsley

¼ cup fresh basil leaves, torn into small pieces

1 cup freshly grated Parmesan cheese, divided

2 shallots, minced

2 cups mushrooms, sliced

½ cup extra-virgin olive oil

1 tablespoon cornstarch

1 cup dry white wine

½ cup chicken broth

10 fresh sage leaves, chopped

Variation on a Theme

This is wonderfully delicious and easy to make in advance, storing the pasta for future use. A fine variation is to add some spinach to the ricotta stuffing. You can also substitute prosciutto for regular ham.

1. Preheat oven to 350°F. Prepare a baking dish with butter.

2. Put the eggs, 1 teaspoon salt, ½ teaspoon pepper, milk, and flour into the blender or food processor and process until smooth.

3. Heat oil in a nonstick pan over medium heat. Pour ⅓ cup batter into the hot pan, moving the pan around in circles to evenly spread the batter.

4. Fry for 2–3 minutes per side; don't over- or undercook or the pasta will tear. Stack on sheets of waxed paper and store in a plastic bag in the refrigerator until ready to use (if making it in advance).

5. In a large bowl, mix the ricotta cheese, eggs, nutmeg, ham, parsley, basil and ½ cup Parmesan cheese. Lay out 1 sheet of pasta and spread 1 tablespoon of ricotta mixture across one edge. Carefully roll the pasta into a tube and place in baking dish. Repeat with remaining pasta and filling. Set aside.

6. In a skillet over medium heat, sauté the shallots and mushrooms in the olive oil for 2–3 minutes. Add the starch and stir until thickened, about 5 minutes. Blend in the wine, broth, sage, and remaining salt and pepper. Pour over the cannelloni and sprinkle with remaining Parmesan cheese. Bake for 30 minutes.

Red Rice and Sausage

This is so easy—and perfect for when you are low on time.
Kids love it and grown-ups do too.

INGREDIENTS | SERVES 4–6

1 pound sweet or hot Italian sausage, cut into 1" pieces

1 medium onion, chopped fine

2 cloves garlic, chopped

1 cup red rice, uncooked

2¾ cups chicken broth

1 teaspoon dried rosemary or 1 tablespoon fresh rosemary

½ cup grated Parmesan cheese

¼ cup chopped fresh parsley

What Is Red Rice?

Yes, there is more out there than white or brown rice! Red rice is often found in Europe, Southeast Asia, and India. Red rice has a similar nutritional profile as brown rice, as they are both high in fiber. When red rice is cooked, the natural red color of the bran leeches out and turns the rest of the rice a reddish-pink color.

1. Brown the sausage pieces, onion, and garlic in oven-safe skillet over medium-high heat for 5–8 minutes. If the sausage is very lean, add a bit of olive oil to prevent the food from sticking.

2. Stir in the rice and toss with the sausage and vegetables. Add the broth and rosemary and cover. Cook on very low heat or place in a 325°F oven for 45–60 minutes.

3. Just before serving, sprinkle the top with Parmesan cheese and brown under the broiler. Add the chopped parsley and serve.

Tuscan Bean, Tomato, and Parmesan Casserole

This is fantastic comfort food. If you are looking for a satisfying, warming, and delicious meal, this is it!

INGREDIENTS | SERVES 4–6

4 slices bacon

¼ cup extra-virgin olive oil

4 cloves garlic, chopped coarsely

1 medium onion, peeled and chopped coarsely

½ fresh fennel bulb, coarsely chopped

1 tablespoon rice flour

2 (15-ounce) cans white beans, drained and rinsed

16 ounces tomatoes, chopped (canned is fine)

1 medium zucchini, chopped

1 tablespoon chopped fresh basil

1 teaspoon dried oregano

1 teaspoon dried rosemary

½ cup fresh Italian parsley, rinsed and chopped

1 teaspoon dried red pepper flakes, or to taste

1 teaspoon salt, or to taste

½ cup freshly grated Parmesan cheese

2 tablespoons unsalted butter, cut into small pieces

1. Preheat oven to 350°F.

2. Fry the bacon in a skillet until almost crisp. Place on paper towels to drain. Remove all but 1 teaspoon of bacon fat from pan. Chop bacon and set aside.

3. Add the oil, garlic, onion, and fennel to the skillet. Sauté over low heat for 10 minutes, or until softened but not browned.

4. Blend the flour into the mixture and cook for 3 minutes, mixing well.

5. Add the beans, tomatoes, and zucchini. Mix well and pour into a casserole dish.

6. Add the herbs, red pepper flakes, and salt, and stir. Mix in the reserved chopped bacon.

7. Sprinkle Parmesan cheese and butter over the top and bake for 25 minutes, or until the cheese is lightly browned.

Eat More Beans

There are more varieties of legumes than it's possible to list here. They are delicious and loaded with protein, vitamins, minerals, and fiber. If a culture, or a household, needs to stretch its food supply, beans are the answer. They come in red and pink, green and orange, black and white, speckled or solid. Some have black eyes and others look like cranberries. Beans—legumes—are available in many sizes and shapes, from tiny peas to big kidneys.

Turkey and Fruit

Vary the flavors in this dish by adding fresh sage or fresh parsley.
The fruit lends a delightful sweetness that is a wonderful complement to the turkey.

INGREDIENTS | SERVES 4

2 tablespoons butter

½ cup chopped sweet onion

2 stalks celery, chopped

2 tart apples, peeled, cored, and chopped

2 ripe pears, peeled, cored, and chopped

½ cup dried cranberries

¼ cup golden raisins

1 teaspoon dried thyme leaves

2 teaspoons dried rosemary spikes, crumbled

1¼ pounds sliced fresh turkey breast or thigh

½ teaspoon salt

½ teaspoon pepper

½ cup apple cider

½ cup chicken broth

1½ cups wheat-free corn bread crumbs

1. Preheat oven to 350°F. Prepare a baking dish with nonstick spray.

2. Melt the butter in a skillet over medium-high heat and add the onion and celery. Lower the heat to low and sauté until soft, about 10 minutes.

3. Add the fruit and seasonings. Cook until just tender, about 5 more minutes.

4. Sprinkle the turkey with salt and pepper and place it in a baking dish. Spread the fruit mixture over the turkey.

5. Add the cider and broth. Sprinkle the top with corn bread crumbs. Bake for 45 minutes.

Serve with Rice

More varieties of rice are now on the market. It used to be just Uncle Ben's and Carolina. Today, you can buy arborio rice from Italy and basmati rice, the staple of the Indian and Chinese diets. You can also buy purple rice, brown rice, and sticky rice. Arborio and basmati rice are short grained and stubby. They make a lot more "cream" than other varieties do. Try them all and you will find favorites. Basmati and arborio varieties are wonderful in risotto, baked rice, and rice pudding.

Beef Stroganoff

This is an elegant, historic recipe, named after the Russian general who is said to have invented it. You can serve it with potato pancakes on the side, or with wild rice.

INGREDIENTS | SERVES 6

2 tablespoons extra-virgin olive oil

1 medium white onion, chopped

8 ounces tiny button mushrooms, brushed clean, stems removed

2 garlic cloves, minced

2 tablespoons tapioca flour, plus ¼ cup for coating the meat

1 teaspoon dried mustard

Salt and pepper, to taste

1½ cups beef broth, warmed

1 cup dry red wine

1 teaspoon wheat-free Worcestershire sauce

2 pounds filet mignon, cut into bite-sized cubes

2 tablespoons unsalted butter

2 tablespoons snipped fresh dill weed

1 cup sour cream or crème fraîche

Why Not to Wash Mushrooms

Mushrooms are grown in a safe and sanitary medium that has been treated with thermophilic bacteria. This kills any germs by naturally heating the growing medium to a very high temperature. Also, washing mushrooms makes them mushy because they absorb the water. Please don't peel them, either—just brush them off.

1. In a large sauté pan, heat the oil over medium heat and add the onion, mushrooms, and garlic. Cook for 5 minutes to soften.

2. Add the flour, mustard, and salt and pepper to the pan, and stir to blend.

3. Mix in the warmed beef broth, cook, and stir to thicken. Stir in the wine and Worcestershire sauce and bring to a boil. Turn off the heat.

4. On a large piece of waxed paper, roll the beef in flour.

5. Heat the unsalted butter in a separate pan. Sear the beef in the butter for 1 minute to quickly brown and seal in the juices.

6. Spoon the beef into the mushroom sauce, add the dill weed, and stir to blend. Simmer for 10–15 minutes; the beef should be medium rare.

7. Just before serving, add the sour cream. Spoon over a bed of wild rice or serve with potato pancakes on the side.

Tuna-Noodle Casserole

This creamy, kid-friendly dish is simple to make and can be a wonderful lunch or dinner.

INGREDIENTS | SERVES 6

8 ounces brown rice noodles

1 tablespoon butter

½ medium onion, finely chopped

2 large carrots, finely chopped

1 red bell pepper, sliced

1 garlic clove, minced

1½ cups milk

1 cup chicken broth

½ teaspoon marjoram

3 tablespoons cornstarch

½ teaspoon salt

1 teaspoon pepper

2 (6-ounce) cans white albacore tuna, drained and flaked

1 cup shredded sharp Cheddar cheese

2 tablespoons Asiago cheese

1. Preheat the oven to 375°F. Spray a 9" × 13" baking dish with cooking spray.

2. Bring a large pot of lightly salted water to a boil. Add noodles, cook for 6–8 minutes, until al dente, and drain.

3. Melt the butter in a skillet over medium-low heat. Stir in the onion, carrots, red pepper, and garlic, and cook for 5 minutes, until tender.

4. Increase the heat to medium-high, and continue to cook and stir for 5 minutes, or until most of the liquid has evaporated.

5. In a medium-sized saucepan, mix the milk, broth, marjoram and cornstarch and stir until thoroughly mixed. Cook over medium heat for 5 minutes, until the sauce is smooth and slightly thickened. Season with salt and pepper.

6. Stir in the tuna, carrot mixture, cooked noodles, and Cheddar cheese. Transfer to the prepared baking dish.

7. Bake for 25 minutes, or until bubbly and lightly browned. Top with Asiago cheese.

Baked Mushroom and Fontina Risotto

You can add so many other ingredients—cubes of cooked chicken or turkey, chopped pears or apples, and your favorite herbs.

INGREDIENTS | SERVES 6–8

3 tablespoon butter, divided

3 tablespoons extra-virgin olive oil

1 small onion, minced

2 garlic cloves, minced

½ teaspoon salt

½ teaspoon pepper

½ teaspoon ground oregano

6 large leaves fresh sage, ripped or cut up, or 2 teaspoons dried sage, crumbled

1 cup long grain rice

2½ cups chicken broth

½ cup white vermouth

8 ounces mixed mushrooms (shiitake, porcini, morels, chanterelles)

⅓ cup grated fontina cheese

A Misunderstood Italian Staple

Most cooks think that risotto is simply rice that has been boiled with broth and herbs. But it's so much more—the technique for making risotto is simple but demanding. The secret is the rice and how it's slow cooked, adding a bit of liquid until it's absorbed and then a bit more. It's been said that the rice will tell you when to add liquid—it hisses and sizzles, asking for the broth!

1. Preheat the oven to 350°F.

2. Heat 1 tablespoon butter and the olive oil in an ovenproof casserole. Sauté the onion and garlic over low heat until softened, about 2–3 minutes.

3. Add the salt, pepper, oregano, sage, and rice. Stir to coat the rice. Add the broth and vermouth. Cover the dish and place in the oven.

4. After the rice has cooked for 20 minutes, heat the remaining butter in a skillet and sauté the mushrooms for 3–4 minutes.

5. Stir the mushroom/butter mixture into the rice. Re-cover the casserole and continue to cook for 15 minutes.

6. Just before serving, stir in the fontina cheese.

Egg and Turkey Sausage Casserole

*This healthy and simple dish is perfect to make the night before for brunch or breakfast.
Feel free to experiment with different types of vegetables and cheeses too.*

INGREDIENTS | SERVES 6

1 tablespoon extra-virgin olive oil

1 (16-ounce) package lean turkey breakfast sausage

2 cups baby spinach, rinsed and dried

¼ cup shredded Cheddar cheese

6 whole eggs

6 egg whites

½ cup skim milk

1. Preheat the oven to 350°F. Spray a 9" × 13" casserole dish with cooking spray to prevent sticking.

2. In a large skillet, heat oil over medium-high heat. Cook breakfast sausage for about 5–7 minutes, or until no longer pink inside. Place on a plate covered with paper towels to drain. Let cool, then cut into 1" slices.

3. Place the spinach on the bottom of casserole dish. Top with sausage slices and sprinkle shredded cheese on top.

4. In a large bowl, whisk eggs and egg whites with milk. Continue to beat until frothy.

5. Pour egg and milk mixture over casserole and bake for 35 minutes until completely set.

Enchilada Casserole

This is definitely a crowd-pleaser.
You can adjust the spices according to your guests' tastes.

INGREDIENTS | SERVES 6

2 tablespoons extra-virgin olive oil

½ medium onion, chopped

1 garlic clove, minced

2 pounds lean ground beef

1 tablespoon chili powder

1 tablespoon cumin

⅛ teaspoon cayenne pepper

1 tablespoon chopped fresh cilantro

1 (15-ounce) can black or pinto beans, thoroughly rinsed and drained

1 cup diced tomatoes or 1 (14-ounce) can diced tomatoes

½ cup green pepper, diced

1 large carrot, shredded

1 can diced green chili peppers

1 cup frozen corn

¼ teaspoon salt

8–12 corn tortillas, amount depends on how many you want to use

2 cups sharp Cheddar or Monterrey jack cheese, shredded

2 scallions, finely chopped

1 avocado, peeled, pitted, and sliced

1 cup sour cream

½ cup sliced black olives

1 cup salsa

1. Preheat the oven to 425°F.

2. Heat oil in a very large, deep skillet or Dutch oven and cook onion and garlic for 3–4 minutes until they soften.

3. Add the ground beef, chili powder, cumin, cayenne pepper, and cilantro and cook for 5–8 minutes, until beef turns brown.

4. Add the beans, tomatoes, green pepper, carrot, chili peppers, and corn. Season with salt and cook additional 1–2 minutes until thoroughly combined.

5. Spray a 9" × 13" casserole dish with nonstick cooking spray. Layer the corn tortillas, then meat mixture, then cheese. Repeat again until all ingredients are used.

6. Bake for 15 minutes until the cheese is melted. Top with scallion, avocado, sour cream, olives, and salsa.

Eggplant Parmesan

This popular Italian dish is transformed into an easy, healthy casserole.

INGREDIENTS | SERVES 10

2 medium eggplants, peeled and thinly sliced

1 teaspoon sea salt

3 large eggs, plus 2 egg whites, lightly beaten

2 cups wheat-free bread crumbs

¾ cup ground flax seed

1 teaspoon oregano

4 garlic cloves, minced

½ cup Parmesan cheese, divided

6 cups Easy Pizza Sauce (see Chapter 9) or spaghetti sauce

2 cups mozzarella cheese, shredded

1 tablespoon fresh basil

Why Do You Need to "Sweat" Out Eggplant?

Eggplants are very bitter. Once you remove moisture from it, the eggplant will become less bitter. The salt helps remove the moisture from the eggplant. Just be sure to rinse it thoroughly so it isn't too salty.

1. Preheat oven to 350°F.

2. Slice eggplant and place in 9" × 13" casserole dish. Add salt to eggplant and let sit for 1 hour to let eggplant "sweat" out extra moisture. After the hour, put eggplant in colander and rinse excess salt off. Pat dry with paper towels.

3. Place beaten eggs in shallow bowl.

4. In another shallow bowl, add the bread crumbs, flax seed, oregano, garlic, and ¼ cup Parmesan cheese. Stir well to combine.

5. Spray a baking sheet with nonstick cooking spray. Dip eggplant in egg, then bread crumb mixture and place onto baking sheet. Bake for 10 minutes on each side.

6. Spread ½–¾ cup pizza sauce on the bottom of the casserole dish. Place a layer of eggplant on top of sauce layer. Sprinkle with Parmesan and ½ cup–¾ cup mozzarella cheese. Repeat another layer of sauce, eggplant, and cheese until ingredients run out.

7. Top with fresh basil. Bake for 20 minutes or until golden brown and cheese is melted.

CHAPTER 5

Poultry

Parmesan–Chia Seed Crusted Chicken

Chia seeds pack a nutritional punch in this chicken dish. You won't even miss the bread crumbs in this fantastic entrée. Serve this chicken topped with Warm Tomato Bean Salad (see recipe in this chapter).

INGREDIENTS | SERVES 4

1 cup wheat-free, all-purpose flour
1 tablespoon finely shredded Parmesan cheese
1 garlic clove, finely chopped
1 teaspoon dried basil
3 tablespoons ground chia seeds
1 egg
3 egg whites
4 boneless, skinless organic chicken breasts

1. Preheat the oven to 350°F.

2. Place the flour, cheese, garlic, basil, and chia seeds in a shallow bowl. Stir until well blended.

3. In another shallow bowl, whisk the eggs and egg whites until well blended.

4. Dip each chicken breast in egg mixture first, then dredge in flour/chia seed mixture until completely covered. Place in a 9" × 13" casserole dish.

5. Bake for 30–35 minutes, turning over halfway through the cooking time, until chicken is no longer pink.

Warm Tomato Bean Salad

This salad can be served as a light side dish or as a delightful first course.

INGREDIENTS | SERVES 4

1 tablespoon grapeseed oil
3 cloves garlic, chopped
1 (15-ounce) can white cannellini beans, rinsed and drained
5 plum tomatoes, chopped
1 cup baby spinach

1. Heat the grapeseed oil in a skillet over medium-high heat, and sauté the garlic for 1–2 minutes, until soft.

2. Pour the beans and chopped tomatoes into the skillet. Reduce heat to medium-low and simmer for 5–10 minutes, until the tomatoes are soft.

3. Remove from heat and stir in spinach until wilted.

4. Serve over chicken or as a side dish.

What Is Grapeseed Oil?

Grapeseed oil is extracted from the seeds of grapes. It has a very high smoke point, which makes it optimal for sautéing and frying foods. It has a clean, light taste that blends nicely with foods. Grapeseed oil also works well in baked goods. It is packed with vitamins and healthy omega fatty acids.

Indian-Style Chicken with Lentils

In countries with huge populations, it's both wise and popular to stretch meat, fish, and seafood with all kinds of legumes.

INGREDIENTS | SERVES 4–6

1 cup lentils

3 cups water

½ teaspoon salt, divided

1 teaspoon pepper

2 cloves garlic, minced

1 medium onion, finely minced

2 tablespoons lemon juice

1 teaspoon cumin

¼ teaspoon red pepper flakes

½ cup chopped fresh parsley

1 pound boneless, skinless chicken breasts, cut into bite-sized pieces

1 cup plain Greek low-fat yogurt

1 tablespoon curry powder

1 teaspoon Tabasco sauce

1. Preheat broiler. Line a baking sheet with aluminum foil.

2. Place the lentils and water in a saucepan. Bring to a boil, reduce heat, and simmer.

3. Just before the lentils are cooked (when barely tender, after about 25 minutes), add ¼ teaspoon salt, pepper, garlic, onion, lemon juice, cumin, red pepper flakes, and parsley.

4. Toss the chicken with the yogurt, curry powder, remaining salt, and Tabasco sauce. Place chicken on foil-lined baking sheet and broil for 5 minutes per side.

5. Mix the chicken into the lentils and serve with rice.

Tasty Turkey Parmesan

Adding your favorite herbs and seasonings can modify this dish,
which is a wonderful variation of the classic chicken Parmesan.

INGREDIENTS | SERVES 4

1¼ pounds boneless, skinless turkey breast

1 cup wheat-free cornbread crumbs

1 clove garlic, chopped

½ teaspoon dried oregano

½ teaspoon dried basil

1 cup Parmesan cheese, divided

1 egg

1 cup corn flour

¼ cup extra-virgin olive oil

2 cups tomato sauce

½ pound whole-milk mozzarella, shredded or thinly sliced

What's in the Stuffing?

The key to buying wheat-free food is reading every label carefully. Store-bought corn bread stuffing may have wheat flour mixed in with the corn flour and cornmeal. Corn muffins, also a favorite in making homemade stuffing, can have a mixture of wheat flour and cornmeal. In the long run, the safest way to provide wheat-free stuffing is to make the corn bread yourself.

1. Preheat the oven to 350°F.

2. Flatten the turkey breast with a meat pounder. Cut into 4 serving pieces.

3. In a shallow bowl, mix the corn bread crumbs, garlic, oregano, and basil with ½ cup Parmesan cheese.

4. In another shallow bowl, beat the egg.

5. Pour the corn flour onto a plate. Dip the turkey in the flour, then in the egg, and finally in the crumb mixture.

6. Heat oil in a large skillet over medium-high heat. Fry turkey in oil until golden brown, about 4–5 minutes; drain on paper towels.

7. Spray a 9" × 13" baking dish with nonstick spray. Pour a little tomato sauce into the baking dish. Add the turkey pieces. Sprinkle with remaining ½ cup Parmesan cheese. Cover with tomato sauce. Spread the mozzarella over the top.

8. Bake in oven until hot and bubbling, about 20 minutes. Serve hot.

Mexican Chicken and Rice

This dish is not too spicy, but it is well seasoned.
To save time, cook the rice while the chicken is simmering.

INGREDIENTS | SERVES 4–6

½ cup corn flour

¼ teaspoon salt

½ teaspoon pepper

1 (3½-pound) chicken, cut in serving-sized pieces, rinsed and dried on paper towels

½ cup corn oil

4 cloves garlic, thickly sliced

1 large red onion, chopped coarsely

4 tomatillos, peeled and chopped

1 hot pepper, such as serrano or poblano, cored, seeded, and chopped

1 sweet red pepper, cored, seeded, and chopped

½ cup frozen corn

10 mushrooms, chopped

1½ cups chopped fresh or canned tomatoes

1 cup dry red wine

1 lemon, thinly sliced, seeded

½ teaspoon cinnamon

1 cup short grain rice, uncooked

2 cups chicken broth

½ cup chopped flat-leaf parsley or cilantro

1. Mix the corn flour, salt, and pepper on a sheet of waxed paper. Dredge the chicken in it.

2. Heat the oil in a large frying pan or Dutch oven over medium-high heat. Brown the chicken for 5–7 minutes. Remove the chicken from the pan and drain on paper towels.

3. Add the garlic, onion, tomatillos, hot pepper, sweet pepper, corn, and mushrooms. Sauté until soft, about 10 minutes.

4. Add the tomatoes, wine, lemon, and cinnamon. Mix well.

5. Return the chicken to the pan and add rice and broth. Bring to a boil. Then reduce heat to low, cover, and simmer for 45 minutes.

6. Just before serving, add the parsley or cilantro. Serve immediately.

Texas Influence

Mexican cooking is well seasoned, with layers of flavors coming from herbs, aromatic vegetables, and, yes, some spices. It's the Texas influence and the American passion for burning up the taste buds that has given Mexican cooking a reputation for being overly spiced.

Roasted Turkey

For the sweetest, juiciest bird, try to find a turkey that is 9–12 pounds.
Make extra gravy by adding a can of wheat-free chicken broth to the basting liquid.

INGREDIENTS | SERVES 15

1 (10-pound) turkey

¼ pound butter, softened

1 teaspoon dried thyme

½ cup fresh Italian flat-leaf parsley, rinsed and minced

1 garlic clove, chopped

½ teaspoon salt

1 teaspoon pepper

1 batch Sausage, Apple, and Sage Stuffing (see recipe in this chapter)

4 strips bacon

½ cup dry white wine

2 bay leaves

2 teaspoons cornstarch

Roasting Turkeys

Always start the turkey breast-side down so the juices run into, rather than out of, the breast. The bacon prevents the breast from sticking to the roasting pan and adds a nice flavor to the juices. If, like most families, yours likes extra stuffing, make 3–4 cups extra and roast it in a casserole while you are roasting the turkey.

1. Rinse the turkey in cold water and pat dry. Set aside the giblets, wing tips, and neck. Preheat the oven to 325°F.

2. In a medium bowl, mix the butter, thyme, parsley, garlic, salt, and pepper together thoroughly.

3. Gently loosen the skin of the turkey and rub butter mixture underneath the skin. Be careful not to tear the skin.

4. Stuff the turkey with the stuffing and tie the legs together. Close the neck cavity with a skewer.

5. Place the bacon on the bottom of a large roasting pan and place the turkey breast-side down on the bacon and place in the oven.

6. In a saucepan, place the giblets, wing tips, and neck with the wine, and add water to cover. Add the bay leaves. Bring to a boil over high heat, then reduce heat to medium-low. Simmer for 2 hours while the turkey is cooking. Add extra water as needed to keep the giblets, wing tips and neck from drying out.

7. After 30 minutes, turn the turkey over and arrange the bacon over the breast and legs. Roast for 3 hours, basting every 20 minutes with the prepared giblet stock and the pan juices. Roast until the thickest part of the turkey registers 155°F on a meat thermometer. Let the turkey rest for 15 minutes before carving.

8. Make gravy by mixing cornstarch with ¼ cup water in a small bowl and blending with pan juices.

Sausage, Apple, and Sage Stuffing

*Make your own wheat-free corn bread for stuffing a day or two before,
cube, and place in the refrigerator in a plastic bag until ready to use.*

INGREDIENTS | SERVES 6–8

4 tablespoons butter

2 cloves garlic, minced

1 medium onion, finely chopped

4 stalks celery with tops, finely chopped

1 pound bulk breakfast sausage

10 cups cubed wheat-free corn bread

1 cup unsalted butter, melted with ½ cup water

2 teaspoons dried thyme

10 fresh sage leaves, minced, or 2 tablespoons dried

1 clove garlic, chopped

2 large tart apples, peeled, cored, and chopped

¼ teaspoon salt

½ teaspoon pepper

1. In a large frying pan, heat 4 tablespoons butter over medium-high heat. Add the garlic, onion, and celery, and sauté for 8–10 minutes, until soft.

2. Add the sausage and break it up with a wooden spoon. Cook until sausage is no longer pink and vegetables are tender, about 15 minutes. Place mixture in a large bowl.

3. Add the rest of the ingredients to the bowl. With your hands inside large plastic bags, use your hands to mix the ingredients well.

4. Stuffing can be cooked inside a turkey as it roasts, or in a casserole dish at 325°F for 30–40 minutes.

Sesame-Crusted Chicken Breasts

Serve this with rice and steamed vegetables. Leftovers can be chopped, mixed with a spicy sauce, and used to fill Corn Crepes or Chestnut Flour Crepes (see Chapter 3) as a delicious snack.

INGREDIENTS | SERVES 4

2 large boneless, skinless chicken breasts, halved

¼ cup pineapple juice

¼ cup orange juice

1 tablespoon lime juice

½ cup wheat-free soy sauce

1" piece gingerroot, peeled and minced

2 cloves garlic, or to taste, minced

1 teaspoon chili oil, or to taste

½ cup sesame seeds

1 tablespoon ground chia seeds

1 egg, beaten

1 tablespoon vegetable oil

1. Rinse the chicken breasts and pat dry with paper towels.

2. In a nonreactive bowl or glass pan large enough to hold the chicken, whisk together the juices, soy sauce, ginger, garlic, and chili oil.

3. Add the chicken to the sauce and turn to coat. Cover and refrigerate for 4 hours.

4. In a shallow bowl, mix the sesame seeds with ground chia seeds.

5. Drain the chicken. Dip the chicken in the beaten egg and then in sesame seed mixture.

6. Heat oil in a large skillet over medium-high heat. Sauté breasts for 6 minutes per side. Serve hot.

Chili and Other Hot Sauces

Chinese, Indians, and other groups in Asia, Southeast Asia, and Asia Minor make their own versions of chili for cooking. Chili oil is extremely hot. Chili paste comes in green and red and is popular in Thailand. The Chinese make a chili-and-garlic paste that is called Sichuan chili. Tabasco sauce, freshly chopped chilies (red and/or green), cayenne pepper, and red pepper flakes can be substituted.

Classic Southern Fried Chicken

Fried chicken is perfectly delicious for entertaining or for a quiet meal at home with the family.

INGREDIENTS | SERVES 4

1 (6-pound) chicken, cut into 8 pieces (drumsticks, thighs, breasts, and wings)
1 cup buttermilk
1½ cups corn flour
1 clove garlic, chopped
1 teaspoon salt
1 teaspoon black pepper
1 teaspoon wheat-free baking powder
1 egg, beaten
½ cup wheat-free, buckwheat beer
1½ cups cornmeal
½ cup vegetable oil

Frying with Corn Flour

When you use corn flour or cornmeal for frying, you can mix it with either rice flour or potato flour for good results. For a light, tempura-like crust, try cornstarch mixed with water and egg as a coating. Wheat-free cooking does require a whole new chemistry.

1. Rinse the chicken pieces and dry on paper towels, then place in a resealable plastic bag with the buttermilk and marinate for 2–3 hours.

2. In a large paper bag, mix together the corn flour, garlic, salt, pepper, and baking powder. Add the chicken pieces to the corn flour mixture one at a time, then close the bag and shake until the chicken is well coated.

3. In a medium bowl, whisk the egg and beer together. Spread the cornmeal on a large piece of waxed paper. Dip the chicken in the beaten egg/beer mixture. Then roll in the cornmeal, pressing it down into the mixture.

4. Bring 1" of oil to 365°F in a fryer, or ½" of oil in a frying pan. Fry the chicken for 20–25 minutes, turning every 4–5 minutes. Watch the chicken carefully to make sure that it doesn't burn. Drain on paper towels.

Chicken Cacciatore

This classic, tasty dish can be served over rice or spaghetti squash.

INGREDIENTS | SERVES 4–6

1 (3½-pound) chicken, cut into 8 pieces

1 cup potato or corn flour

¼ teaspoon salt

½ teaspoon pepper

¼ cup fresh basil, torn, or 2 tablespoons dried basil

1 teaspoon oregano, crumbled

¼ cup extra-virgin olive oil

1 teaspoon butter

1 medium onion, diced

2–3 cloves garlic, minced

2 tablespoons fresh rosemary

2 cups mushrooms, brushed off and chopped

1 (16-ounce) jar wheat-free marinara sauce or 16 ounces canned tomatoes

4 ounces dry red table wine

½ cup Parmesan cheese

1 bunch fresh parsley, chopped

1. Rinse the chicken and pat dry with paper towels. In a large bowl combine the flour, salt, pepper, basil, and oregano. Dredge the chicken in the mixture.

2. In a large frying pan over medium-high heat, heat the oil and butter together until butter melts.

3. Brown chicken in butter and oil, for 5 minutes per side.

4. Add the onion, garlic, rosemary, and mushrooms. Sauté for 5 minutes.

5. Add the marinara sauce (or tomatoes) and red wine. Cover and simmer over very low heat for 1 hour.

6. Remove cover, place chicken on a platter, and continue to simmer sauce until reduced by half, about 15 minutes.

7. Spoon sauce over the chicken and sprinkle with cheese and fresh parsley.

Easy Turkey Meat Loaf

This is classic comfort food. Serve with roasted or mashed potatoes and roasted vegetables. You can also use ground chicken or beef for this recipe. For an extra touch, drape 2 slices of bacon over the top of the meat loaf before cooking.

INGREDIENTS | SERVES 6–8

1½ pounds ground turkey
½ cup chili sauce
½ cup milk
3 eggs
1 cup wheat-free cornbread crumbs
Salt and pepper, to taste
2 garlic cloves, minced
1 small onion, minced
1 teaspoon dried rosemary, crumbled
2 teaspoons Lea & Perrins steak sauce
½ teaspoon nutmeg

1. Preheat oven to 350°F.

2. Place all the ingredients into the large bowl of a food processor, and process together.

3. Treat a 9" × 5" bread pan with nonstick spray. Pour in the meat loaf mixture.

4. Place a roasting pan in the middle of the oven. Add 1" of hot water to the roasting pan. Place the bread pan containing the meat loaf in the water. Bake for 80 minutes.

A Hot Water Bath

Baking your meat loaf in a hot water bath enables it to stay juicy. Processing the ingredients makes a much smoother meat loaf than the coarse stuff that you have to chew for a long time. The water bath is called a *bain-marie*, and it keeps baked foods soft, creamy, and moist.

Elegant Duck and Fruit-Filled Corn Crepes

This would be a delicious dinner or lunch served over baby spinach or fresh salad greens.
The sweetness of the duck works with the fruit—a marriage made in heaven.

INGREDIENTS | SERVES 4

½ cup chicken broth

1 tablespoon cornstarch

⅔ pound boneless, skinless duck breasts

½ cup corn flour

3 tablespoons unsalted butter, divided

½ teaspoon salt

2 teaspoons freshly ground black pepper

½ cup dried cranberries soaked in ⅔ cup apple juice or wine

¼ cup dried cherries soaked in ½ cup orange juice

¼ cup chopped celery tops

24 pearl onions

1 tablespoon rosemary leaves, dried and crumbled

½ teaspoon dried thyme

½ cup apple brandy (such as Calvados)

8 large Corn Crepes (see Chapter 3)

1. In a small bowl, mix the chicken broth and the cornstarch and set aside.

2. Dredge the duck breasts in the corn flour.

3. Heat 2 tablespoons butter over medium heat. Sauté the duck breasts for 3–4 minutes, turning once.

4. Add the salt and pepper and the chicken broth/cornstarch mixture to the pan, stirring to make a sauce.

5. Add the soaked fruit, celery tops, onions, rosemary, thyme, and apple brandy. Cover and cook for 20 minutes over low heat.

6. Preheat the oven to 350°F.

7. Cool and remove the duck from the pan. Cut it into small pieces and shred. Return the duck to the sauce. Divide the duck and sauce mixture between the 8 crepes. Roll the crepes and place them, seam-side down, in a greased baking dish.

8. In a small saucepan, melt the remaining butter and drizzle over the crepes. Heat in the oven for 10–15 minutes.

Thai Chicken with Peanut Dipping Sauce

The chicken or other meat for satay should be grilled over hot coals.
You can use tender beef instead of chicken. The marinade is perfect with any meat.

INGREDIENTS | SERVES 4

Dipping Sauce

½ cup unsweetened coconut milk

1 cup dry-roasted peanuts

1 tablespoon lemon or lime juice

1 tablespoon dark brown sugar

1 tablespoon wheat-free dark soy sauce

1 teaspoon fresh ginger, minced

½ teaspoon chili oil

2 tablespoons peanut oil

2 tablespoons finely chopped sweet onion

2 cloves garlic, minced

Chicken

1½ pounds boneless, skinless chicken breast

½ cup wheat-free soy sauce

1 tablespoon coconut milk

2 teaspoons Thai red chili paste, or to taste

2 tablespoons minced fresh gingerroot

1 tablespoon sesame oil

2 tablespoons dry sherry

1. Make the dipping sauce: In a food processor, combine the coconut milk, peanuts, lemon or lime juice, brown sugar, soy sauce, ginger, and chili oil. Process until very smooth.

2. Heat the peanut oil in a large saucepan. Add the onion and garlic, and cook over medium heat until just soft, about 3 minutes. Pour the peanut mixture into the pan and mix well. Heat on low for 2–3 minutes but do not boil. Set aside.

3. Set 12 (10") skewers to soak in water to cover for at least 40 minutes.

4. Rinse the chicken, pat it dry, and cut it into bite-sized pieces.

5. Mix the rest of the chicken ingredients together and add to the chicken in an airtight container. Cover and marinate for 2 hours.

6. String the chicken on the skewers and grill over glowing coals for 4–5 minutes per side. Serve with dipping sauce.

Wooden Skewers Must Be Soaked!

Wooden skewers must be soaked, or they will burn when on the grill or under the broiler. Place them in a pan of water for an hour. You can also get very fancy skewers with decorative handles or metal at the ends. Simple metal skewers are also available. When using metal skewers, be sure to oil them or use nonstick spray to keep the food from sticking.

Roasted Cornish Game Hens with Ginger-Orange Glaze

This is simple and tastes fantastic. It tastes just as delightful as leftovers the next day.

INGREDIENTS | SERVES 4

2 Cornish game hens, split open
2 tablespoons extra-virgin olive oil
½ teaspoon salt
¾ teaspoon pepper
1 tablespoon orange marmalade
2 tablespoons peanut oil
1 tablespoon wheat-free soy sauce
2 tablespoons orange juice
½ medium white onion, finely chopped
1 tablespoon minced fresh gingerroot

Fresh Gingerroot

You can use fresh gingerroot in all kinds of dishes, from dinners to desserts. Dried ground ginger, ginger snaps, and candied ginger are often used in cooking. Unpeeled fresh ginger freezes beautifully and can be added to sauces, salad dressings, and desserts such as puddings. When you want to use it, cut off an inch or two and peel it, then grate it, mince it, or chop it finely.

1. Preheat the oven to 375°F.

2. Rinse the hens, pat dry with paper towels, brush with olive oil, and sprinkle with salt and pepper.

3. In a small saucepan over low heat, stir the rest of the ingredients together to make glaze; set aside.

4. Roast the hens in a baking dish or pan, cut-side up, for 15 minutes. Turn hens and brush with glaze. Continue to roast for another 20 minutes, brushing hens with glaze every 5 minutes. Serve with roasted vegetables, rice, or mashed potatoes.

Chicken in Apple Cider and Brandy

You can prepare this dish in advance. Reheat when you're ready to serve,
adding the cream at the last minute.

INGREDIENTS | SERVES 4–6

2 small chickens, cut into quarters
4 tablespoons butter
1 cup chopped onion
1 tablespoon cornstarch
¼ cup apple brandy or applejack
1¼ cups apple cider
Salt and pepper, to taste
½ cup heavy cream or half-and–half
1 teaspoon dried rosemary

1. Rinse and pat the chicken dry.

2. Heat the butter in a large skillet over medium heat. Add the chicken pieces and brown for 5 minutes per side.

3. Add the onion and cook until softened, about 2–3 minutes. Stir in the cornstarch.

4. Add the brandy and flame it by setting it on fire with a long match. (Be careful not to burn yourself.) After the flames die out, add the cider, salt, and pepper. Cover and simmer for 25 minutes.

5. Just before serving, place the chicken on a platter. Add the cream to the sauce in the pan, and heat for 2 minutes. Spoon sauce over chicken, sprinkle with rosemary and serve.

Ginger, Soy, and Kale Chicken

This recipe has a wonderful combination of ginger and soy.
Marinate it the night before to let the chicken thoroughly absorb the flavors.

INGREDIENTS | SERVES 2

4 tablespoons low-sodium wheat-free soy sauce

1 tablespoon toasted sesame oil

1 tablespoon honey

½ teaspoon fresh grated gingerroot

2 garlic cloves, crushed

2 boneless, skinless organic chicken breasts, cut into 1" cubes

1 tablespoon extra-virgin olive oil

2 cups kale

Are You Familiar with Kale?

Kale is a powerhouse of nutrition as well as being a member of the cabbage family. Kale is packed with fiber, calcium, vitamin B$_6$, vitamin A, vitamin K, and vitamin C. Kale can be eaten raw or cooked and can replace your other leafy greens in all varieties of recipes.

1. In a small bowl, whisk together the soy sauce, sesame oil, honey, gingerroot, and garlic.

2. Place chicken in a zip-top plastic bag and pour half of the soy mixture into bag. Make sure the bag is closed and shake it up so all the chicken is covered. Let marinate for at least a half hour or overnight.

3. Remove chicken from the marinade. Heat olive oil in a skillet over medium-high heat. Sauté the chicken for 5–8 minutes, until fully cooked and no longer pink.

4. Add the kale and cook until it is still bright green but only a little soft, about 2 minutes. Add remaining soy mixture and mix well.

Hot and Spicy Turkey Meatballs

*Meatball recipes usually include bread crumbs as a filler and sometimes
for an outside coating. This recipe uses ground potato chips.
The eggs will hold the meatballs together, and who doesn't love potato chips?*

INGREDIENTS | MAKES 10–12 MEATBALLS

1 pound ground turkey

2 eggs

2 cloves garlic, minced

1 teaspoon dried oregano

1 teaspoon dried basil

½ teaspoon cinnamon

½ teaspoon fennel seeds

½ cup finely grated Parmesan cheese

2 cups crushed low-salt potato chips, divided

½ teaspoon salt

½ teaspoon pepper

4 tablespoons canola oil

1. In a large bowl, mix the turkey, eggs, garlic, oregano, basil, cinnamon, fennel seeds, cheese, 1 cup potato chip crumbs, salt, and pepper.

2. Place a large sheet of waxed paper on the counter. Sprinkle remaining cup of chip crumbs on it.

3. Form 1" meatballs from the turkey mixture. Roll meatballs in crumbs to coat.

4. Heat oil in a large skillet over medium-high heat. Fry meatballs until well browned, about 5 minutes. Drain on paper towels and then either refrigerate, freeze, or serve with the marinara sauce of your choice.

Kick Up Those Meatballs

You can add flavor to your meatballs by grinding up some sweet or hot Italian sausage and mixing it with the ground turkey or beef. A truly great Italian sausage has aromatics like garlic and herbs, and spices such as anise seeds.

Spicy Olive Chicken

The key to this flavorful dish is simmering while covered for a while.
Don't forget to pour the extra sauce on top of the chicken and over your side dish as well.

INGREDIENTS | SERVES 4

1 (3-pound) chicken, cut into 8 pieces

1 teaspoon salt, divided

1 teaspoon pepper, divided

4 tablespoons unsalted butter

2 garlic cloves, chopped

⅔ cup chopped sweet onion

½ cup chicken broth

½ cup dry white wine

24 green olives, pitted

1 teaspoon prepared Dijon mustard

¼ teaspoon hot sauce

Fresh parsley, chopped

1 tablespoon capers

Capers

Capers are flavorful berries. Picked green, they can be packed in salt or brine. Try to find the smallest—they seem to have more flavor than the big ones do. Capers are great on their own or incorporated into sauces. They are also good in salads and as a garnish on many dishes that would otherwise be dull.

1. Sprinkle the chicken pieces with ½ teaspoon salt and ½ teaspoon pepper. Heat butter in a skillet over medium-high heat. Brown chicken pieces for about 5 minutes per side. Remove from pan and set aside.

2. In the same pan, sauté the garlic and onion for 5–10 minutes, until onions are soft. Add the broth, wine, and olives. Using a fork, whisk in the mustard.

3. Return chicken to the pan. Cover and simmer until the chicken is done, about 45 minutes. Add hot sauce and remaining salt and pepper.

4. Pour sauce and olives over mashed potatoes, rice, or rice noodles. Garnish with chopped parsley and capers.

Balsamic Chicken with Sun-Dried Tomatoes and Roasted Red Peppers

This tangy chicken dish can be served over rice or quinoa for a perfect, balanced meal.

INGREDIENTS | SERVES 6

3 boneless, skinless chicken breasts, rinsed and sliced in half

½ teaspoon salt

½ teaspoon pepper

1 tablespoon vegetable oil

1 small onion, chopped

2 garlic cloves, chopped

¼ cup balsamic vinegar

½ teaspoon brown sugar

¼ cup low-sodium chicken broth

1 teaspoon dried rosemary

1 teaspoon dried basil

1 teaspoon dried oregano

1 (6-ounce) bag sun-dried tomatoes, sliced in quarters

1 (12-ounce) jar roasted red peppers, drained and sliced

1. Season the chicken breasts with salt and pepper.

2. Heat the oil in a skillet over medium heat. Add the onion and garlic and sauté for 2–3 minutes, until tender. Add chicken and brown about 5 minutes per side.

3. In a small bowl, combine the balsamic vinegar, brown sugar, chicken broth, rosemary, basil, and oregano.

4. Add the tomatoes and red pepper to the chicken. Pour the balsamic mixture over the chicken and vegetables. Turn heat to high and let the liquid come to a boil. Reduce heat to medium-low and simmer for about 15 minutes, or until the chicken is no longer pink inside.

What Kind of Balsamic Vinegar Do You Use?

All balsamic vinegars are *not* the same. Just like fine wine, balsamic vinegar tastes better when aged. The longer it ages, the thicker and sweeter it becomes. Although the aged balsamic vinegars may be more expensive, you have to remember that a little goes a long way.

Chicken Piccata

This zesty, traditional Italian dish is packed with flavor and has become extremely popular in restaurants. Serve it with rice or wheat-free pasta.

INGREDIENTS | SERVES 8

1 cup low-sodium chicken broth

½ cup dry white wine or vermouth

2 tablespoons lemon juice

4 skinless, boneless chicken breasts, sliced in half

½ teaspoon salt

½ teaspoon ground black pepper

1 tablespoon butter

½ medium onion, chopped

4 garlic cloves, minced

1 (13.75-ounce) can artichoke hearts, rinsed and drained

4 tablespoons capers

2 tablespoons freshly minced flat-leaf parsley

½ lemon, thinly sliced

1. In a small bowl, whisk together the broth, wine, and lemon juice. Set it aside.

2. Place a halved chicken breast between two pieces of plastic wrap. Using the flat side of a mallet, pound each breast until about ¼" thick.

3. Remove the top of the plastic wrap and sprinkle one side of the chicken with half of the salt and pepper.

4. Heat butter in a large skillet over medium heat. Place chicken in the skillet with the salt and pepper side down. Add remaining salt and pepper to the other side.

5. Cook chicken about 4 minutes per side, until no longer pink in the middle. Remove chicken from the skillet and place on a plate. Keep warm.

6. Add broth mixture, onion, and garlic to the same skillet, cover and reduce heat to low. Let simmer for 5–10 minutes until liquid reduces to about half.

7. Add browned chicken, artichoke hearts and capers. Let simmer on low heat, uncovered, for a few minutes so sauce thickens. Top with parsley and lemon slices.

Orange Chicken Lettuce Wraps

Crisp lettuce makes a perfect, crunchy wrap for this mildly orange teriyaki chicken.

INGREDIENTS | SERVES 6

2 tablespoons canola oil, divided
½ green onion, chopped
1 tablespoon gingerroot, minced
1 pound boneless, skinless chicken breasts, rinsed and cut into 1" cubes
1 tablespoon wheat-free soy sauce
½ teaspoon red pepper flakes
1 clove garlic, chopped 2 tablespoons wheat-free teriyaki sauce
2 tablespoons rice vinegar
½ cup orange juice
1 tablespoon honey
1 cup shredded carrots
½ cup chopped water chestnuts
12 large lettuce leaves, iceberg or Bibb

1. Heat 1 tablespoon oil in large skillet over medium heat. Add the onion and gingerroot, and sauté a few minutes, until onion becomes translucent, about 2–3 minutes.

2. Add the chicken and stir-fry until no longer pink, about 8–10 minutes. Remove from skillet.

3. In a large bowl, whisk the remaining oil, soy sauce, red pepper flakes, garlic, teriyaki sauce, vinegar, orange juice, and honey.

4. Add the cooked chicken, carrots, and water chestnuts and mix until thoroughly combined.

5. Serve chicken mixture alongside lettuce leaves to make individual wraps.

CHAPTER 6

Meat

Tenderloin of Pork with Spinach and Water Chestnuts

For convenience, use fresh baby spinach, prewashed and packed in a bag.
This dish can be served with any variety of rice or roasted potatoes.

INGREDIENTS | SERVES 4

2 pork tenderloins, about ¾ pound each

¼ cup potato flour

1 clove garlic, minced

¼ teaspoon nutmeg

¼ teaspoon ground cloves

Salt and pepper, to taste

¼ cup extra-virgin olive oil

2 tablespoons lemon juice

1 teaspoon wheat-free Worcestershire sauce

1 (8-ounce) bag fresh baby spinach or 1 (10-ounce) box frozen chopped spinach, thawed

½ cup sliced water chestnuts

1. Trim the pork and cut into serving pieces. On a sheet of waxed paper, mix together the flour, garlic, and seasonings. Dredge the pork in the mixture.

2. In a large skillet, heat olive oil over medium heat and sauté the pork for about 6 minutes per side; it should be medium.

3. Add the lemon juice, Worcestershire sauce, spinach, and water chestnuts. Stir to wilt the spinach. Sprinkle with more olive oil, if the pan is dry.

Buying Pork

You can get "heirloom" or "heritage" pork on the Web. Or you can get pork tenderloin in almost any supermarket. The tenderloin is about the best and juciest cut available.

Garlic Balsamic Crusted Pork Tenderloin

*This is wonderful for entertaining. Mashed potatoes and
roasted vegetables pair perfectly with this tenderloin.*

INGREDIENTS | SERVES 4

3 cloves garlic, minced

2 tablespoons balsamic vinegar

½ teaspoon ground mustard

1 teaspoon salt

¼ teaspoon pepper

2 tablespoons extra-virgin olive oil, divided

1–1¼ pounds pork tenderloin

2 tablespoons fresh parsley, for garnish

1. In a small bowl, mix together the garlic, balsamic vinegar, mustard, salt, pepper and 1 tablespoon olive oil. Rub the paste all over pork. Marinate for at least 2–3 hours or overnight if you'd like.

2. Preheat the oven to 400°F. Heat remaining oil in large skillet over medium-high heat. Working in batches if necessary, add pork and brown tenderloin all over, about 4–5 minutes.

3. Transfer pan to preheated oven. Roast the pork, turning occasionally, until the internal temperature reaches 160°F, about 20–30 minutes.

4. Transfer the pork to a cutting board and let rest 10 minutes before slicing. Top with fresh parsley if desired.

Baby Rack of Lamb with Herbed Crust

*The herbs and cornmeal give a delicious flavor in this dish
and are a wonderful substitution for bread crumbs.*

INGREDIENTS | SERVES 4–6

2 racks of lamb (1½–2 pounds each),
most of the fat removed

2 teaspoons salt

Freshly ground black pepper, to taste

1 cup cornmeal

2 tablespoons dried rosemary or 4
tablespoons finely chopped fresh

3 tablespoons minced fresh parsley

2 tablespoons minced chives

2 tablespoons minced garlic

½ green onion, finely minced

½ cup extra-virgin olive oil

6 sprigs fresh mint and lemon wedges,
for garnish

1. Preheat the broiler to 450°F.

2. Rub the lamb with salt and pepper. Place on a broiler pan, bone-side up. Broil for 5 minutes.

3. Turn and continue to broil for another 5 minutes.

4. While the lamb is broiling, mix the rest of the ingredients, except the garnishes, together in a medium bowl. Press the herb mixture into the meat by making small incisions on top and pressing mixture into it and change the setting from broil to bake. Bake the lamb at 450°F for another 10–12 minutes.

5. Cut into chops and garnish with fresh mint and lemon wedges.

Mincing Chives

Of course, you can use a knife to mince chives; however, a pair of sharp kitchen scissors works faster and better than a knife. The scissors work well with any number of other ingredients too, such as scallions, bacon, and so on. As with any cutting tool, the sharper, the better—and safer. Dull tools are dangerous—they can slip off a tomato, for example—and inefficient.

Stuffed Filet Mignon with Red Wine Sauce

Stuffing a whole filet mignon with mushrooms and garlic will turn it into a luscious feast. Using chestnut flour will add a nutty and delightful flavor.

INGREDIENTS | SERVES 10–12

4 tablespoons unsalted butter

4 cups exotic mushrooms such as creminis, morels, shiitake, or oysters, brushed off, stems removed, chopped finely

6 shallots, minced

4 cloves garlic, minced

1 tablespoon wheat-free Worcestershire sauce

¼ cup chestnut flour, mixed with salt and pepper to taste

½ cup dry red wine

4 sage leaves, torn in small pieces

½ teaspoon dried rosemary

½ teaspoon dried thyme

1 (6-pound) filet mignon, fat trimmed

½ cup chestnut flour

1 tablespoon coarse salt

1 teaspoon black pepper

1 cup beef broth

2 tablespoons extra-virgin olive oil

1. In a large skillet over medium heat, melt the butter. Add the mushrooms, shallots, and garlic, and sauté until the vegetables are soft and the mushrooms are wilted, about 3–4 minutes.

2. Add the Worcestershire sauce. Add ¼ cup flour seasoned with salt and pepper and blend. Stir in ½ cup red wine and the sage, rosemary, and thyme. Reduce the mixture to about 1½ cups, about 5–7 minutes.

3. Preheat oven to 350°F.

4. Make a tunnel down the middle of the filet mignon— use a fat knitting needle or the handle of a blunt knife. Stuff the mushroom mixture into the tube. If there are extra mushrooms, save them for the sauce.

5. Coat the outside of the filet with ½ cup chestnut flour, salt, and pepper. Place the beef broth in the bottom of a roasting pan with the filet. Sprinkle with olive oil and roast in oven for 20 minutes per pound.

Drippings Make the Perfect Sauce

Use the drippings for a sauce, served on the side. If the pan juices get too reduced, add some boiling water or more beef broth.

Roast Leg of Veal with Mustard Crust

You will probably have to special order the veal from your butcher—
try to get one that does not exceed 7 pounds. It is the perfect dish for a special occasion.

INGREDIENTS | SERVES 10–12

½ pound unsalted butter, at room temperature

½ cup Dijon-style mustard

1 cup rice or potato flour

1 teaspoon garlic powder

1 teaspoon dried basil

2 teaspoons dried oregano

1 (7-pound) veal leg roast, well trimmed

Salt and pepper, to taste

1 cup dry (white) vermouth

Lemon slices

The Versatility of Veal

When you prepare veal chops, scallops, stew, or a roast, you can vary the accompanying vegetables, herbs, and spices. Veal should be very young; old veal is beef. The paler the color, the more mild and tender the meat will be. Cuts from the leg make the scallops.

1. Preheat the oven to 400°F.

2. In a large bowl, add the butter, mustard, flour, garlic powder, basil, and oregano. Mix together to make a paste. Rub the veal with salt and pepper. Cover the veal with the paste.

3. Place the veal in the oven in a 9" × 13" baking pan, and add the vermouth around the veal. Roast for 15 minutes or until the crust hardens.

4. Arrange the lemon slices on top of the veal. Baste every 15 minutes. Roast for 15 minutes per pound, until it reaches internal temperature of 145°F. Carve and serve with pan juices. (Heavy cream can be added to the pan juices to make more sauce.)

Gascony Style Pot Roast

This is a traditional holiday dish, often made on Christmas Eve to serve on Christmas Day. Serve with mashed potatoes and winter vegetables.

INGREDIENTS | SERVES 6

1 (4-pound) top or bottom round beef roast
4 cloves garlic, slivered
1 teaspoon salt
1 teaspoon freshly ground black pepper
Pinch cinnamon
Pinch nutmeg
1 slice bacon, cut into pieces
4 shallots, peeled and halved
2 medium red onions, quartered
2 large carrots, sliced
¼ cup cognac
2 cups red wine
1 cup rich beef broth
1 teaspoon thyme
4 whole cloves
¼ cup cornstarch mixed with ⅓ cup cold water, until smooth

1. Preheat the oven to 250°F.

2. Make several cuts in the meat and put slivers of garlic in each. Rub the roast with salt, pepper, and pinches of cinnamon and nutmeg.

3. Heat the bacon on the bottom of a Dutch oven. Remove the bacon before it gets crisp, and brown the roast for 3–4 minutes on each side.

4. Surround the roast with shallots, onions, and carrots. Add the cognac, wine, beef broth, thyme, and cloves.

5. Place in the oven for 5–6 hours. When the meat is done to your liking, place the roast on a warm platter.

6. Add the cornstarch-and-water mixture to the pan juices and bring to a boil. Remove from heat. Slice the roast. Serve the sauce over the pot roast with the vegetables surrounding the meat.

A Hearty, Delectable Pot Roast

Slow cookers are excellent for cooking a pot roast. Either a top or bottom round is great. Chuck tends to be stringy. Trim the roast well but do leave a bit of fat on it. You can also marinate a pot roast overnight in red wine and herbs. That will give you a deliciously tender piece of meat.

Greek Pork-Stuffed Eggplants

You can do most of this recipe in advance, refrigerate, and then put it in the oven for 10 minutes. This is wonderful over a bed of greens.

INGREDIENTS | SERVES 4 FOR LUNCH, OR 8 AS AN APPETIZER

8 small eggplants, about 4–5" in length
½ cup extra-virgin olive oil
½ cup minced onion
4 cloves garlic, minced
½ pound lean ground pork
Salt and pepper, to taste
½ cup fresh tomato, finely chopped
¼ teaspoon ground coriander
Juice of ½ lemon
Yogurt and finely chopped tomato, for garnish

1. Preheat oven to 400°F.

2. In a large skillet over medium-high heat, fry the whole eggplants in olive oil for 5 minutes. Remove from pan and when cool enough to handle, make a slit from top to bottom but do not cut through.

3. In the same pan over medium heat, fry the onion, garlic, pork, salt, pepper, tomato, and coriander. Add the lemon juice.

4. Keep stirring to blend and break up the pork. Set aside to cool for 15 minutes.

5. Place the eggplants on a baking sheet that has been covered with aluminum foil. Spread the eggplants open, scoop the seeds out, and fill with pork stuffing.

6. Bake for 10 minutes. Serve with a dollop of yogurt on each eggplant and garnish yogurt with chopped tomato.

Stuffed Pork Chops

Ask the butcher for thick rib chops, and to slit a pocket in each.
By doing this, it will allow stuffing the pork chops to be less complicated.

INGREDIENTS | SERVES 4

1 tart apple, peeled, cored, and chopped

½ cup chopped onion

1 tablespoon dried rosemary, crumbled, or 2 tablespoons chopped fresh

¼ cup finely chopped Italian flat-leaf parsley

1 tablespoon dried basil

¾ cup extra-virgin olive oil, divided

½ cup wheat-free corn bread crumbs

Salt and pepper, to taste

4 thick-cut pork rib chops

4 garlic cloves, chopped

2 medium onions, chopped

½ cup chicken broth

½ cup dry white wine

Zest and juice of ½ lemon

2 ripe pears, peeled, cored, and quartered

2 teaspoons cornstarch mixed with ¼ cup cold water (to thicken the gravy)

1. Sauté the apple, onion, and herbs in ½ cup olive oil over medium heat for 5 minutes.

2. Once the apples are softened, add the corn bread crumbs, salt, and pepper. Remove from heat. When cool enough to handle, stuff into the chops and secure with toothpicks.

3. Add remaining ¼ cup olive oil to the pan and brown the chops over medium-high heat for 4–5 minutes each side. Add the rest of the ingredients, except for the cornstarch-and-water mixture, and cover. Simmer for 40 minutes over very low heat.

4. Remove the chops and place on a warm platter. Add the cornstarch-and-water mixture to the gravy in the pan if you want it to be thicker. Add salt and pepper to taste. Serve gravy either alongside the chops or poured over the chops.

Spicy Beef-Stuffed Mushrooms

The mushrooms should be 2½" across. This is a great side dish or appetizer.

INGREDIENTS | SERVES 4

½ pound chopped sirloin

½ cup minced onion

2 cloves garlic, minced

1" piece gingerroot, peeled and minced

1 teaspoon ground oregano

2 tablespoons cooking oil

1 tablespoon wheat-free Worcestershire sauce

Salt and freshly ground black pepper, to taste

1 egg, slightly beaten

12–16 large mushroom caps, stems removed, brushed off

1. Sauté the meat, onion, garlic, gingerroot, and oregano in the oil, mixing constantly to break up lumps. When the meat turns pink (but not gray or brown), remove from the heat and add the Worcestershire sauce; taste and add salt and pepper. When almost cool, blend in the egg.

2. Preheat the oven to 350°F. Divide the stuffing among the mushrooms in a baking pan. Pour enough water to come ¼" up the sides in the pan.

3. Bake the mushrooms for 25 minutes. You can sprinkle them with chopped fresh herbs of your choice when done.

Herb-Stuffed Veal Chops

This recipe calls for thick-cut chops. You can use double rib chops with a pocket for the aromatic herbs and vegetables. These can be grilled or sautéed.

INGREDIENTS | SERVES 4

½ cup minced shallots

½ medium onion, finely chopped

2 tablespoons chopped fresh rosemary

2 teaspoons dried basil or 1 tablespoon chopped fresh basil

½ teaspoon ground coriander

2 tablespoons unsalted butter

1 teaspoon salt

Pepper, to taste

4 veal rib chops, 1½–2" thick, a pocket cut from the outside edge toward the bone in each

¼ cup extra-virgin olive oil

1. In a skillet over medium heat, sauté the shallots, onion, and herbs in butter for 2–3 minutes. Add salt and pepper. Let sit for 5 minutes.

2. Stuff the chops with the mixture. Rub chops with olive oil, salt, and pepper.

3. Using an outdoor grill or broiler, sear the chops over high heat, 1–2 minutes per side.

4. Lower heat to medium and cook the chops for 4–5 minutes per side for medium chops or rare chops, depending on the thickness.

Spicy Marinated Beef and Baby Spinach

After you have marinated the beef, the dish takes but a few minutes to cook.
This dish will surely delight your guests.

INGREDIENTS | SERVES 4

2 cloves garlic, minced

2 tablespoons plus 2 teaspoons sugar, divided

½ teaspoon salt, or to taste

1 teaspoon red pepper flakes, or to taste

2 tablespoons canola oil

1½ pounds filet mignon, trimmed and cut into ½" slices

¼ cup dry white wine

¼ cup white wine vinegar

2 tablespoons fish sauce

2 tablespoons canola or peanut oil

½ green onion, finely diced

4 cups fresh baby spinach, rinsed, spun dry, stems removed

1 tablespoon butter

Wheat-free soy sauce, chopped scallions, lemon or lime slices, for garnish

Fish Sauce

Fish sauce, available at Asian markets, is an important ingredient in Southeast Asian, Chinese, and Indonesian cuisines. It is extremely aromatic and it is important to remember that a little goes a long way in most recipes.

1. In a large bowl or glass baking dish, mix together the garlic, 2 tablespoons sugar, salt, pepper flakes, and canola oil. Add the slices of filet mignon, turning to coat. Cover and refrigerate for 2 hours.

2. In a small bowl, mix together the wine, vinegar, 2 teaspoons sugar, and fish sauce; set aside.

3. When ready to cook, heat a nonstick pan over very high heat and add canola or peanut oil and green onion, cook for 2 minutes.

4. Remove the meat from the marinade and add it to the pan. Quickly sauté the filets until browned on both sides, about 2 minutes per side. Arrange the meat over a bed of spinach.

5. Add the wine mixture and butter to the pan and deglaze, reducing quickly, about 1–2 minutes. Pour over the spinach and meat. Serve with soy sauce and chopped scallions on the side and slices of lemon or lime.

Sausage and Asparagus Risotto

This flavorful one-pot meal will leave you asking for a second helping. You can use turkey or chicken sausage as well.

INGREDIENTS | SERVES 6

4 tablespoons extra-virgin olive oil

1 green onion, chopped

2 cloves garlic, minced

1 pound mild Italian sausage links, casings removed

2 cups shiitake mushrooms, wiped clean and stems removed

2 cups arborio rice

½ cup dry white wine or vermouth

5¼ cups low-sodium chicken broth, warmed

1 pound asparagus stalks, stems removed and cut into 2" pieces

1 teaspoon ground oregano

1 teaspoon ground basil

⅓ cup freshly grated Parmesan cheese

1. In a large skillet over medium heat, cook the oil, onion, and garlic for 2–3 minutes.

2. Add the sausage links and cook while breaking them apart with a spoon. Once the sausages are browned, about 5–7 minutes, add mushrooms and stir for 1–2 minutes to combine.

3. Add rice and wine, and continue to stir and cook until liquid is completely absorbed, about 15–20 minutes.

4. Add chicken broth, 1 cup at time, while making sure all the liquid is absorbed before adding another cup.

5. After adding all the broth, add chopped asparagus and herbs, and continue to stir. When risotto is firm, yet creamy, it is finished. Top with grated Parmesan.

Ginger-Teriyaki Flank Steak

This Asian-inspired dish pairs perfectly with steamed vegetables and rice.
This marinade can be used on a variety of meats such as chicken, pork, and other cuts of beef.

INGREDIENTS | SERVES 4

½ cup water
1 tablespoon sesame oil
½ teaspoon grated gingerroot
2 garlic cloves, minced
¼ cup wheat-free soy sauce
1 tablespoon honey
1 tablespoon cornstarch
1½ pounds beef flank steak

What Does It Mean to Slice Against the Grain?

Lines in the flank steak run from right to left down the length of the steak. By cutting across these lines, the knife will cut through the fibers, which makes it easier to chew. Slicing the steak on a 45-degree angle creates an elegant presentation.

1. In a small bowl, mix water, sesame oil, gingerroot, garlic, soy sauce, honey, and cornstarch. Stir thoroughly to ensure the cornstarch has been mixed in well.

2. Place the steak in zip-top bag and pour the marinade on top. Make sure the bag is sealed and shake until well blended. Place in refrigerator and let sit for at least 4 hours or, even better, overnight.

3. When ready to cook the steaks, remove them from the bag and discard the leftover marinade.

4. Place steaks on preheated grill or on a grill pan and cook on each side for about 6–8 minutes, until you have reached your desired degree of doneness. The internal temperature should read at least 145°F.

Spicy Steak Fajitas

*Skirt steak rubbed with spicy seasoning and chopped peppers
and served with warmed corn tortillas makes for the perfect family meal.*

INGREDIENTS | SERVES 8

1 tablespoon cornstarch

2 teaspoons chili powder

1 teaspoon salt

1 teaspoon paprika

½ teaspoon red pepper flakes

1 teaspoon wheat-free Worcestershire sauce

1 teaspoon fresh lime juice

1 teaspoon turbinado sugar

¼ teaspoon cumin

3 pounds skirt steak

4 garlic cloves, minced

½ onion, chopped

1 green bell pepper, sliced

1 red or yellow bell pepper, sliced

½ bunch fresh cilantro

Corn tortillas

10 ounces shredded Monterey jack cheese

1. In a small bowl, mix the cornstarch, chili powder, salt, paprika, red pepper flakes, Worcestershire sauce, lime juice, sugar, and cumin.

2. Rub the steaks with the garlic and the prepared seasoning mixture and then cut it into strips.

3. Heat oil in a large skillet over medium heat. Cook the onion, peppers, and cilantro for 3–4 minutes. Add steak strips and cook, stirring frequently, until cooked through, about 7 minutes.

4. Remove from heat and spoon the meat into a corn tortilla. Top with cheese and roll them up.

Healthy Goulash

This one-dish meal is filled with flavor. This is not Hungarian goulash,
which is more of a beef stew with potatoes.

INGREDIENTS | SERVES 8

2 pounds lean ground beef

2 large yellow onions, chopped

3 cloves garlic, chopped

3 cups water

2 (15-ounce) cans low-sodium tomato sauce

2 (14.5-ounce) cans diced tomatoes

1 tablespoon wheat-free soy sauce

1 tablespoon wheat-free Worcestershire sauce

2 tablespoons dried Italian herb seasoning (or 1 teaspoon each basil, oregano, rosemary, and thyme)

3 bay leaves

½ teaspoon dry mustard

1 teaspoon paprika

¼ teaspoon salt

2 cups uncooked brown rice noodles (preferably elbows)

¼ cup shredded white sharp Cheddar cheese

1. In a large Dutch oven, cook and stir the ground beef over medium-high heat, breaking the meat up as it cooks, until the meat is no longer pink and has started to brown, about 10 minutes.

2. Skim off excess fat, and stir in the onions and garlic. Cook and stir the meat mixture until the onions are translucent, about 10 more minutes.

3. Stir in water, tomato sauce, diced tomatoes, soy sauce, Worcestershire sauce, Italian seasoning, bay leaves, dry mustard, paprika, and salt. Bring the mixture to a boil over medium heat. Reduce the heat to low, cover, and simmer 20 minutes, stirring occasionally.

4. Stir in the macaroni, cover, and simmer over low heat until the noodles are tender, about 25 minutes, stirring occasionally.

5. Remove from heat, discard bay leaves, and top with shredded cheese. Mix well and serve.

Garlic-Rubbed Prime Rib

This exquisite dish is perfect for a holiday or special occasion.
Prime rib is usually served rare or medium rare.

INGREDIENTS | SERVES 8–10

10 cloves garlic, minced
2 tablespoons extra-virgin olive oil
1½ teaspoons salt
2 teaspoons ground black pepper
1 tablespoon balsamic vinegar
1 teaspoon dried thyme
1 teaspoon dried rosemary
1 (10-pound) prime rib roast

Internal Temperatures Are Crucial for Preparing the Perfect Prime Rib

For a rare roast, remove from the oven at ~100°F and let it sit until it reaches ~120°F. For medium-rare prime rib, take out of the oven at ~120°F and let it sit until it reaches a final temperature of ~130°F. For a medium roast, remove from the oven at ~130°F until it reaches ~140°F.

1. In a small bowl, mix together the garlic, oil, salt, pepper, balsamic vinegar, thyme, and rosemary.

2. Place the roast in a roasting pan with the fatty side up. Cut slits in the fatty layers. Rub the garlic mixture throughout the fatty side and all over the entire roast. Insert meat thermometer in the thickest part of the roast. Cover roast with aluminum foil and let sit out at room temperature for 2 hours.

3. Preheat oven to 450°F. Once preheated, place the roast in the oven and bake the roast for 12 minutes.

4. Lower the temperature to 400°F and cook for 8 minutes.

5. After 8 minutes, lower the temperature to 325°F, and cook for 90 minutes, or until the desired internal temperature is reached (see sidebar).

6. Remove from oven, cover with aluminum foil and let roast sit out for 20 minutes, or until it reaches the desired internal temperature (see sidebar). The roast will continue to cook even when it's removed from the oven.

Slow Cooker Pulled Pork

You will love how your house smells when this is slow cooking.
Feel free to use chicken if you don't eat pork. Serve with Raw Broccoli Slaw with Fruit,
Veggies, and Walnuts (see Chapter 8) or Balsamic Roasted Vegetables (see Chapter 13).

INGREDIENTS | SERVES 6

2 medium yellow onions, chopped

5 garlic cloves, minced

1 cup beef broth

1 tablespoon brown sugar

1 tablespoon chili powder

2 teaspoons kosher salt

1 teaspoon cumin

½ teaspoon cinnamon

½ teaspoon dried oregano

1 (5-pound) pork shoulder, boneless or bone-in

1 cup wheat-free barbecue sauce

1 teaspoon wheat-free soy sauce

1. Place the onions, garlic, and broth in a slow cooker.

2. In a small bowl, combine the sugar, chili powder, salt, cumin, cinnamon, and oregano and mix well.

3. Pat the pork with a paper towel and rub the prepared mixture all over it. Place pork on top of broth in slow cooker.

4. In the same small bowl, mix the barbecue sauce and the soy sauce. Stir to combine. Pour on top of pork making sure the mixture is spread evenly on top. Cover and cook on low for 8 hours.

5. Remove pork from slow cooker and allow to cool slightly. If using bone-in pork, discard bone. Place pork in 9" × 13" casserole dish.

6. Shred the pork using a fork. Add additional barbecue sauce and slow cooker mixture if you'd like. Serve warm in wheat-free buns or tortillas.

Fruit and Corn-Crusted Pork Tenderloin

The colorful filling makes this a very pretty presentation. It also is delicious—and perfect for entertaining.

INGREDIENTS | SERVES 4–6

6 dried apricots, chopped
½ cup dried cranberries
¼ cup white raisins (sultanas)
1 cup warm water
Juice of ½ lemon
2 pork tenderloins, about ¾ pound each
2 tablespoons wheat-free Worcestershire sauce
1 cup cornmeal
1 teaspoon salt
Freshly ground black pepper to taste
½ cup extra-virgin olive oil

1. Put the dried fruit in a bowl with the warm water and lemon juice. Let stand until most of the water is absorbed, about 3–4 hours.

2. Preheat the oven to 350°F.

3. Make a tunnel through each tenderloin using a fat knitting needle or the handle of a blunt knife. Stuff the fruit into the tunnels.

4. Sprinkle both roasts with Worcestershire sauce.

5. In a small bowl, make a paste with the cornmeal, salt, pepper, and olive oil. Spread it on the pork.

6. Roast for 30 minutes. The crust should be golden brown and the pork pink.

CHAPTER 7

Seafood

Coconut-Lime Shrimp

*This dish can be served as an appetizer or as a main dish
on top of rice, quinoa, or a plate of wheat-free noodles.*

INGREDIENTS | SERVES 4

1 egg
½ cup all-purpose gluten-free flour
⅔ cup coconut milk
Juice from 2 limes
Zest from 1 lime
1½ teaspoons wheat-free baking powder
¼ cup plus 2 tablespoons coconut flour
1¼ cups finely shredded coconut
24 shrimp, deveined with tails on
½ cup grapeseed oil
Fresh lime wedges, for squeezing

1. In medium bowl, combine the egg, all-purpose flour, coconut milk, lime juice, lime zest, and baking powder.

2. Place coconut flour and shredded coconut in 2 separate bowls.

3. Hold shrimp by tail, and dredge in flour, shaking off excess flour. Dip in egg/milk mixture; allow excess to drip off. Roll shrimp in coconut, and place on a baking sheet lined with waxed paper. Refrigerate for 30 minutes.

4. Heat oil in grill pan or skillet.

5. Sauté the shrimp in batches: cook, turning once, for 2–3 minutes, or until golden brown.

6. Using tongs, remove shrimp to paper towels to drain. Serve warm with fresh lime wedges.

Red Snapper in White Wine Sauce

This sauce can be used with any fish or meat, mashed potatoes, or rice. Feel free to adjust the amount the herbs or add some sliced mushrooms, olives, capers, or green peppercorns.

INGREDIENTS | SERVES 2

2 (8-ounce) red snapper fillets
1 teaspoon salt
1 teaspoon ground black pepper
½ cup minced sweet onion
1 garlic clove, minced
2 tablespoons unsalted butter
1 tablespoon extra-virgin olive oil
3 tablespoons cornstarch
1 cup chicken broth, warmed
½ cup dry white wine or white vermouth
½ teaspoon prepared Dijon mustard
¼ cup chopped parsley
1 teaspoon shredded fresh basil
½ teaspoon dried tarragon or rosemary
1 tablespoon extra-virgin olive oil

1. Season the filets with salt and pepper on both sides.

2. In a skillet over medium heat, sauté the onion and garlic for 4 minutes in the butter and oil. Whisk in the cornstarch and cook for 3–4 minutes.

3. Whisk in the warm chicken broth, stirring until smooth. Then add the wine or vermouth. Swirl in the mustard and herbs. Simmer over low heat for 10 minutes, stirring occasionally.

4. While sauce is simmering, place olive oil in a skillet over medium heat. Add fish and cook approximately 3–4 minutes on each side. Pour the sauce over the top and serve hot.

Crispy Beer-Battered Fried Shrimp

You can do everything in advance but fry the shrimp. Beer batter is delicious, just be sure to use buckwheat beer. Don't be afraid of the name, buckwheat beer is actually wheat-free.

INGREDIENTS | SERVES 4

½ cup corn flour
¼ teaspoon salt
1 tablespoon butter, melted
1 whole egg
½ cup flat buckwheat beer
Old Bay Seasoning, to taste
1 teaspoon paprika
1¼ pounds shrimp, peeled and deveined
¼ cup golden rum
2 tablespoons wheat-free soy sauce
Light oil such as canola, for frying
1 egg white, beaten stiff

1. Make the batter in advance by mixing together the first seven ingredients (flour through paprika). Let stand for 1 hour.

2. Marinate the cleaned shrimp in rum and soy sauce for 20 minutes, covered, in the refrigerator.

3. Bring the oil for frying to 375°F. Add the egg white to the batter.

4. Dip the shrimp in the batter a few times to coat. In small batches, gently lower each shrimp into the oil. Fry for about 4 minutes, or until well browned. Drain on paper towels and serve.

Savory Shark and Bacon

Shark is a melt-in-your-mouth kind of fish—and it really deserves to be cooked more often. It is sweet and tender.

INGREDIENTS | SERVES 4

2 tablespoons chili sauce
1 tablespoon concentrated orange juice
1 tablespoon wheat-free Worcestershire sauce
Juice of ½ lemon
1 teaspoon Tabasco sauce, or to taste
1¼ pounds boneless shark steak, cut into serving pieces
Salt and pepper, to taste
4 strips bacon

1. Preheat the broiler to 450°F.

2. Mix the chili sauce, orange juice concentrate, Worcestershire sauce, lemon juice, and Tabasco sauce in a small bowl.

3. Rinse and pat the shark steaks dry. Sprinkle with salt and pepper. Paint them with the sauce mixture.

4. Place them on a broiler pan that you have treated with nonstick spray. Arrange the bacon on top of the shark and broil for 3 minutes. Turn the bacon and broil for 2 more minutes. Turn off the broiler and close the door to let the shark cook through, about 6 minutes.

Orange-Ginger Salmon

This is so simple and only has a few ingredients.
This wonderful marinade can be used on various meats and fish.

INGREDIENTS | SERVES 6

¾ cup orange juice

1 tablespoon honey

1 teaspoon wheat-free soy sauce

2 teaspoons balsamic vinegar

1 teaspoon finely chopped fresh gingerroot

2 pounds salmon fillet

Salt and ground black pepper, to taste

All Salmon Is Not the Same

There are several varieties of salmon, with wild Alaskan salmon being the healthiest. Wild Alaskan salmon has a diet that is considered safe and healthy for the environment. Atlantic farmed salmon may consume antibiotics and even food coloring. Always choose "wild salmon" over "farmed salmon."

1. Preheat the oven to 400°F.

2. Place orange juice, honey, and soy sauce in a small saucepan over medium-low heat. Cook and stir 10–15 minutes, until reduced by about half and thickened. Remove from heat, and allow to cool.

3. Stir balsamic vinegar and gingerroot into orange juice mixture.

4. Line a baking pan with parchment paper. Place salmon fillets with the skin side down. Season with salt and pepper and pour half of the orange juice mixture on top of the salmon fillets.

5. Bake salmon for about 10–15 minutes until it easily flakes with a fork.

6. Cover the cooked salmon with the remaining orange juice mixture. Serve immediately.

Seafood à la King

You can make the sauce the day before and add the seafood at the last minute.
Serve with rice or stuff into crepes. This dish is fantastic for entertaining.

INGREDIENTS | SERVES 4

½ cup shallots, minced

1 tablespoon white onion, finely minced

1 garlic clove, minced

¼ cup unsalted butter

20 small white mushrooms, cut in half

20 pearl onions, fresh or frozen, cut in half

2 tablespoons cornstarch

¼ cup cold water

1 tablespoon tomato paste

2 tablespoons brandy

1½ cups cream

Salt and pepper, to taste

½ pound shrimp, cleaned and deveined

½ pound bay scallops

2 tablespoons red salmon caviar, for garnish

1. Sauté the shallots, minced onion, and garlic in the butter over moderate heat for 5 minutes. Add the mushrooms and pearl onions. Stir, cooking for 2–3 more minutes.

2. Mix the cornstarch with cold water and add to the pan, stirring to blend.

3. Blend in the tomato paste and brandy.

4. Warm the cream slightly, then stir it into the sauce in the pan. (You can prepare this dish in advance up to this point. Store in the refrigerator until ready to serve.)

5. Reheat the sauce but do not boil. Add salt and pepper to taste, then add the seafood. When the shrimp turns pink, the dish is done, about 3–4 minutes. Garnish with caviar and serve.

Long Live the King!

This dish was created at the Brighton Beach Hotel on Long Island, New York, by Chef George Greenwald for his boss, E. Clarke King II. It became very popular when Campbell's came out with canned cream of mushroom soup, used as a base.

Crab Cakes

*These crab cakes can be served as an entrée over a bed of greens
or they can be made into smaller cakes for an appetizer.*

INGREDIENTS | SERVES 4

1 tablespoon extra-virgin olive oil

2 green onions, finely chopped

12 ounces jumbo lump crabmeat

2 garlic cloves, chopped

2 eggs

1 tablespoon mayonnaise

1½ cups wheat-free bread crumbs, divided

½ teaspoon ground cayenne pepper

½ teaspoon ground basil

½ teaspoon ground oregano

Salt and ground pepper, to taste

½ cup extra-virgin olive oil, for frying

What to Do If You Don't Have Wheat-Free Bread Crumbs?

Wheat-free bread crumbs have become more readily available in supermarkets and specialty stores, but if they are expensive, or you can't find them, why not make your own? Take day-old wheat-free bread, remove the crusts and tear into small pieces. Place the bread in your food processor or blender and you have bread crumbs!

1. Heat 1 tablespoon olive oil in a skillet over medium-high heat. Sauté green onions for 1–2 minutes, until tender. Remove from heat.

2. In a large bowl, combine the crabmeat, garlic, egg, mayonnaise, ½ cup bread crumbs, cayenne pepper, basil, oregano, salt and pepper. Form into small patties, about ½" thick.

3. In a separate bowl, place remaining 1 cup of bread crumbs. Dredge patties in the bread crumbs thoroughly.

4. Heat ½ cup oil in a skillet over medium-high heat. Place crab cakes in oil and cook until golden brown, making sure to cook evenly on both sides. Once cooked, place on paper towels to drain. Serve with Garlic Aioli Sauce (see recipe in this chapter).

Sole Florentine

Sole is an adaptable fish; mild and sweet, it goes with many different flavors. Frozen spinach works fine for this. Just make sure you completely squeeze the water out.

INGREDIENTS | SERVES 4

3 tablespoons unsalted butter

1 shallot, minced

1 garlic clove, minced

3 tablespoons cornstarch

2 (10-ounce) packages frozen chopped spinach, thawed, moisture squeezed out

⅔ cup heavy cream

¼ teaspoon nutmeg

4 sole fillets, rinsed and dried on paper towels

1 egg, well beaten

½ cup rice or potato flour

Salt and pepper, to taste

⅔ cup extra-virgin olive oil

¼ cup Parmesan cheese

1. In a skillet over medium heat, melt the butter and sauté the shallot and garlic until softened, about 5 minutes. Blend in the cornstarch, cooking until smooth.

2. Add the spinach, cream, and nutmeg. Cook and stir until thickened, about 3–4 minutes. Pour into a baking dish treated with nonstick spray and set aside.

3. Dip the pieces of sole in the beaten egg. Then, on a sheet of waxed paper, mix the flour, salt, and pepper. Dredge the sole in the flour mixture.

4. In a separate skillet, heat the olive oil over medium heat. Add the sole and sauté until lightly browned, about 2–3 minutes each side.

5. Arrange the sole over the spinach in the baking dish. Sprinkle with the cheese. Run under the broiler until very brown and hot, about 3 minutes.

Garlic Aioli Sauce

This condiment is perfect as a dipping sauce or for spreading on a sandwich.
Greek yogurt not only adds protein and lightens it up, but also adds a little tang.

INGREDIENTS | SERVES 4–6

½ cup mayonnaise

2 tablespoons plain Greek yogurt

3 cloves garlic, chopped

2 tablespoons freshly squeezed lemon juice

½ teaspoon salt

½ teaspoon ground pepper

¼ teaspoon dried cumin

Place all the ingredients in a small bowl and mix until thoroughly blended. Refrigerate for at least 1 hour so the flavors blend.

Lobster with Sherry Sauce

This adaptation is a unique way to serve lobster. Garnish with fresh lemon wedges.

INGREDIENTS | SERVES 4–6

4 chicken lobsters, 1–1¼ pounds each

1 teaspoon Asian five-spice powder

1 clove garlic, minced

1 teaspoon parsley

¼ cup sesame seed oil

¼ cup sherry

Juice of ½ lemon

2 tablespoons minced gingerroot

1. Boil the lobsters for 20 minutes, then split them and crack the claws.

2. Preheat the broiler to 500°F.

3. In a saucepan, mix the rest of the ingredients together to make the sauce. Bring to a boil and spoon over the lobsters.

4. Broil for 3 minutes. Serve.

Marseille Whipped Cod and Potatoes

You can use either salt cod or fresh cod in this dish. You can also substitute half-and-half for the milk or cream if you would like to lighten it up.

INGREDIENTS | SERVES 4

2 cups salt cod or 1¼ pounds fresh cod

3 large or 4 medium potatoes, about 2 pounds

2 tablespoons extra-virgin olive oil

½ cup rich milk or light cream, use more or less depending on the consistency of the potatoes

Salt and pepper, to taste

1 teaspoon dried basil

½ cup chopped chives and parsley

1. Soak the cod overnight in cold water to cover. Change water once or twice.

2. Boil the potatoes in their skins until a knife slides into the flesh easily. The timing varies by the size of the potato.

3. Using a long-handled fork, spear the boiled potatoes and peel them. Put the potatoes through a ricer and into a bowl. Whisk in the olive oil and the milk or cream, then add salt, pepper, and basil and keep warm.

4. Steam the cod, salted or fresh, about 15 minutes, until very tender. Make sure there are no bones.

5. Place the cod in a food processor and process until smooth.

6. Fold the cod into the potatoes and mix in the chives and parsley. Blend with a fork until fluffy. Serve hot.

Southern Fried Oysters

These are so crunchy on the outside and succulent on the inside, you will probably have to make an extra batch. Best when served with a squeeze of fresh lemon juice.

INGREDIENTS | SERVES 4

1 quart shucked oysters
½ cup corn flour
1 cup cornmeal
1 teaspoon wheat-free baking powder
¼ teaspoon nutmeg
½ teaspoon dried parsley
½ teaspoon salt, or to taste
Freshly ground black pepper, to taste
2 beaten eggs
Oil for deep-frying

1. Place the oysters in a colander to drain.

2. In a large bowl, thoroughly mix the flour, cornmeal, baking powder, nutmeg, parsley, salt, and pepper.

3. Dip the oysters in the beaten egg and then in the flour-and-cornmeal mixture.

4. Bring the oil in a pot to 375°F and fry for about 3–4 minutes or until browned.

5. Remove with a slotted spoon. Drain on paper towels.

Seafood Loves to Be Saucy

Even the tastiest of mollusks and crustaceans love to be dipped or bathed in sauces. And there are a variety of options and substitutions. Any citrus can be substituted for just about any other—for example, limes for lemons, grapefruit for orange, and you can blend them together for intriguing outcomes using your own original flair for flavors. Throw in some ginger, curry powder, or mustard, and you'll add another layer of flavor.

Spicy Dipping Sauce for Shrimp and Oysters

A lovely dipping sauce that has dozens of uses. Make in advance and store in the refrigerator.

INGREDIENTS | MAKES 1½ CUPS

1 cup chili sauce

1 teaspoon orange bitters

2 teaspoons lemon juice

1 teaspoon grated horseradish, or to taste

1 teaspoon minced fresh gingerroot

1 teaspoon brown sugar, or to taste

1 teaspoon cider vinegar

½ teaspoon garlic powder

½ teaspoon ground cayenne pepper

Salt and pepper, to taste

Place all ingredients in the blender and process until well blended. Serve.

Citrus Dipping Sauce for Shrimp and Oysters

One of the best things about this sauce is its versatility.
You can use it with fried scallops, cold seafood, or chicken.

INGREDIENTS | MAKES 1½ CUPS

½ cup marmalade

¼ cup wheat-free soy sauce

¾ cup fresh orange juice

1 teaspoon Dijon mustard

1 teaspoon honey

Juice of ½ lime

Juice of ½ lemon

1" piece gingerroot, peeled and minced

Salt and pepper, to taste

Place all ingredients in a saucepan and boil until well blended. Cool and store in the refrigerator.

Golden Sautéed Diver Scallops

This recipe calls for caramelizing the scallops. It tastes wonderful.
You'll find lots of excuses to serve these.

INGREDIENTS | SERVES 4

½ cup corn flour

½ teaspoon ground parsley

2 tablespoons white sugar

1 teaspoon salt

½ teaspoon white pepper

1½ pounds large diver scallops, each about 2" across

2 tablespoons unsalted butter

2 tablespoons extra-virgin olive oil

1. On a sheet of waxed paper, mix the flour, parsley, sugar, salt, and pepper. Roll the scallops in the flour mixture.

2. In a large skillet, heat the butter and oil over medium-high heat. Add the scallops and watch them. They will brown quickly. Cook for 2–3 minutes per side. Serve with any of your favorite sauces.

Baked Risotto with Seafood

This is perfect for a dinner party where you want to impress your guests but don't want to spend all day making the risotto.

INGREDIENTS | SERVES 6–8

3 tablespoons extra-virgin olive oil

1 tablespoon butter

1 small onion, minced

1 garlic clove, minced

Salt and pepper, to taste

1 tablespoon fresh rosemary, crushed, or 2 teaspoons dried, broken up

1 teaspoon saffron threads

1 cup long grain rice

2½ cups chicken broth

2 tablespoons Marsala or sherry wine

1 pound raw shrimp, peeled, deveined, and rinsed; or 1 pound bay scallops, rinsed; or 1 pound crabmeat

1. Preheat oven to 350°F.

2. In a cast-iron or ovenproof skillet over medium heat, heat the oil and butter. Add the onion and garlic, and sauté until softened for 2–3 minutes.

3. Add salt, pepper, rosemary, saffron, and rice, and mix to cover the rice with the oil. Add the broth, cover tightly, and place in the oven.

4. After the rice has cooked for 10 minutes, add the Marsala or sherry wine. Return to the oven and cook for another 10 minutes.

5. Add the shrimp or other seafood and continue to bake for 7 minutes more. Uncover and serve.

Risotto Doesn't Have to Be Boring

You can use shrimp, scallops, crabmeat, lobster, or crayfish in place of mushrooms or other vegetables. The trick is to put any raw shellfish in at the end of the cooking so it will not be overdone. By the same token, you can substitute 2 cups sliced mushrooms that have been sautéed separately in butter for the seafood.

Corn and Lobster Newburg

*Have your fishmonger cook and remove the meat from three small
(1¼ pounds each) lobsters, or buy frozen lobster meat. Serve with rice and salad.*

INGREDIENTS | SERVES 6

2 tablespoons unsalted butter

2 shallots, minced

1 garlic clove, minced

4 egg yolks

2 cups cream

1 cup fresh corn, cut off the cob, or frozen corn, blanched and drained

1½ pounds, or 4 cups, lobster meat

2 tablespoons dry sherry

2 tablespoons chopped parsley, for garnish

Extra Egg Whites or Yolks

The recipe for Lobster Newburg calls for 4 egg yolks. This gives you the opportunity to make a marvelous dessert meringue with the whites. Or if you have a recipe that calls for whites and not yolks, you can make mayonnaise or custard with the yolks. There is a use for everything but the shells.

1. In a skillet over medium heat, melt the butter and sauté the shallots and garlic for 5–6 minutes, until soft.

2. In a small bowl, beat the egg yolks.

3. Put the cream into a large pan over medium heat; scald the cream but do not boil. Remove from the heat.

4. Mix 2 tablespoons of hot cream into the beaten egg yolks and whisk vigorously.

5. Pour the egg mixture into the hot cream and return to the heat. Continue to whisk until thick. Add the corn and lobster. Heat, stirring, until very hot but not boiling. Add the sherry. Serve garnished with parsley.

Cod Broiled on a Bed of Paper-Thin Potatoes

Cod is one of the world's most beloved and versatile fish. It can be baked, broiled, steamed, poached, salted, or cooked with milk in a stew. This dish is simple yet delicious.

INGREDIENTS | SERVES 4

2 pounds Idaho or Yukon Gold potatoes, peeled and sliced paper-thin

¼ cup extra-virgin olive oil

2 tablespoons butter, melted

Salt and pepper, to taste

4 cod fillets or steaks, about 5 ounces each

1 tablespoon butter

Chopped parsley and lemon wedges, for garnish

1. Preheat the oven to 400°F.

2. In a baking pan that has been treated with nonstick spray, toss the thinly sliced potatoes with oil and melted butter, salt, and pepper.

3. Bake the potatoes for 40 minutes or until the top is brown and crisp and the inside soft.

4. When the potatoes are done, lay the fish on top, sprinkle with salt and pepper, dot with butter, and turn the oven to broil.

5. Broil until the fish is done—8–10 minutes, depending on the thickness of the fish. If the potatoes start to burn, move the pan to a lower shelf in the oven.

6. Sprinkle with chopped parsley and serve with lemon wedges.

Parmesan Crusted Tilapia

*These crispy tilapia fillets would be perfect served with rice and a green salad.
Feel free to sprinkle extra grated Parmesan cheese on top too.*

INGREDIENTS | SERVES 2

2 tablespoons extra-virgin olive oil, divided

¼ cup wheat-free bread crumbs or cornmeal

¼ cup grated Parmesan cheese

1 teaspoon dried basil

½ teaspoon dried oregano

½ teaspoon onion powder

½ teaspoon red pepper flakes

½ teaspoon dried rosemary

2 garlic cloves, minced

½ teaspoon salt

¼ teaspoon ground black pepper

1 tablespoon freshly squeezed lemon juice

3–4 tilapia fillets, depending on their size, washed and dried

1. Preheat oven to 425°F.

2. Combine 1 tablespoon olive oil, bread crumbs, Parmesan cheese, seasonings, garlic, salt, and pepper in a medium-sized bowl. Stir to combine.

3. On a medium-sized plate, pour lemon juice.

4. Dip each fillet in lemon juice and then in the bread crumb mixture evenly on both sides. Place in baking dish that is well oiled. Sprinkle with remaining 1 tablespoon olive oil and additional Parmesan cheese, if you desire. Cover with aluminum foil so fish remains moist.

5. Bake for 20 minutes, or until the edges are browning. Take baking dish out of the oven and put the broiler on. Broil on medium for about 2 minutes so fillets get crispy.

Crispy Calamari

This lovely dish can be served as an appetizer with Spicy Marinara Sauce (see Chapter 11), or it can make a wonderful addition to any salad. This recipe is very simple and delicious.

INGREDIENTS | SERVES 10

1–2 cups peanut oil for frying (you may need more or less)

12 squid, cleaned and cut into small rings

¼ cup cornmeal

¼ cornstarch

1 teaspoon sea salt

¼ teaspoon ground black pepper

2 cloves garlic, minced

½ tablespoon parsley, dried

1 teaspoon oregano

¼ cup wheat-free bread crumbs

1 lemon, sliced into wedges for garnish

1. Preheat oil in a very large, deep-frying pan or wok. Oil must be very hot so let sit for a few minutes over medium heat.

2. While oil is heating, rinse squid with water and dry with paper towel. The calamari should be damp enough so the flour/bread crumbs will stick but not too damp or the mixture will clump.

3. In a medium-sized bowl, combine the cornmeal, cornstarch, salt, pepper, garlic, and seasonings. Dip the calamari rings into the batter, then coat with bread crumbs.

4. Deep-fry in small batches for 1–2 minutes, or until very light brown. Even if you think it may not be brown enough, stop cooking after 1–2 minutes or the calamari will be overcooked. Lay cooked calamari on paper towels to absorb any liquid. Serve with Spicy Marinara Sauce (see Chapter 11) or serve over a bed of greens in a salad.

Classic Creole Jambalaya

This traditional one-dish meal is easy and scrumptious.

INGREDIENTS | SERVES 4

2 tablespoons butter

8 ounces andouille sausage, cut into ¼"
rounds

1 tablespoon paprika

1 tablespoon cumin

¼ teaspoon cayenne pepper

1 teaspoon oregano, dried

2 cloves garlic, minced

1 cup diced tomatoes

1 green pepper, seeded and diced

1 celery stalk, diced

3 green onions, sliced

1 large carrot, shredded

1 bay leaf

½ teaspoon salt

1 cup brown rice, uncooked

2 cups low-sodium chicken broth

1 pound large shrimp, peeled and
deveined

Chopped fresh parsley (optional)

1. Place the butter and sausage in a large pot or Dutch oven. Stir well and cook for 5–8 minutes, until sausage is fully cooked.

2. Stir in the paprika, cumin, cayenne pepper, oregano, and garlic. Cook for another minute until well combined.

3. Add the tomatoes, pepper, celery, onions, carrot, bay leaf, and salt.

4. Stir in the rice and broth, mix well, and bring to a boil. Cover and reduce heat to low. Let simmer about 50 minutes until rice is fully cooked and tender.

5. Add the shrimp and let cook about 5 minutes. Remove bay leaf before serving. Garnish with extra chopped onion and fresh parsley if desired.

Jambalaya a Different Way

There are so many variations of jambalaya these days. You could add chicken, ham, or even duck. Traditional Creole jambalaya typically uses tomatoes and chicken broth, whereas Cajun jambalaya typically uses no tomatoes, just broth.

Fish Tacos with Tropical Fruit Salsa

These folded tacos can be stuffed with a number of different toppings.
Although tacos originated in Mexico, fish tacos are said to have derived from Baja California.

INGREDIENTS | MAKES 12 TACOS

½ teaspoon chili powder

1 teaspoon oregano, dried

2 cloves garlic, minced

1 teaspoon cumin

1 teaspoon cilantro, minced

½ teaspoon red pepper flakes

1 pound boneless cod fillets, fresh, or frozen and thawed

Juice of 1 lime

Salt and pepper, to taste

12 corn tortillas, warmed

Tropical Fruit Salsa (see Chapter 9)

Shredded lettuce, sliced avocado, sour cream, extra cilantro, for garnish

1. Preheat oven to 375°F.

2. In a small bowl, mix chili powder, oregano, garlic, cumin, cilantro, and red pepper flakes.

3. Place cod fillets on a large sheet of aluminum foil and squeeze lime juice over top of them. With a spoon, sprinkle prepared seasonings on each side of the fillets. Season with salt and pepper. Fold the foil around the fish, and seal top to create a pouch. Place pouch on a baking tray.

4. Bake in the oven for 20 minutes or until fish easily flakes with a fork. Divide fish among the corn tortillas and top with Tropical Fruit Salsa and desired garnishes.

CHAPTER 8

Vegetarian Entrées

Asparagus, Mushrooms, Edamame, and Sun-Dried Tomatoes in Balsamic Glaze

This vegan entrée can be served either warm or cold. Fresh asparagus and mushrooms will work best in this recipe.

INGREDIENTS | SERVES 6

1 pound asparagus, ends trimmed and cut into 1" pieces

1 package sliced mushrooms, wiped clean and stems cut off

1 cup organic shelled and cooked edamame

½ cup sun-dried tomatoes (not in oil), sliced in half

2 tablespoons extra-virgin olive oil

1 tablespoon balsamic vinegar

3 cloves garlic, crushed

½ teaspoon salt

⅛ teaspoon pepper

Fresh parsley, for garnish

1. Preheat the oven to 350°F.

2. Place the asparagus, mushrooms, edamame, and sun-dried tomatoes in a large zip-top bag.

3. In small bowl, mix the olive oil, vinegar, garlic, salt, and pepper together with wire whisk.

4. Pour marinade over vegetables in the bag. Close the bag and shake until evenly coated.

5. Place veggie mixture on baking sheet, top with chopped parsley. Roast for 45–60 minutes, checking periodically to turn veggies and to make sure they do not overbrown.

What Are Edamame?

Edamame are actually immature, green soybeans. They are so versatile and super easy to add to all types of dishes. They are a favorite for vegans and vegetarians since they are a complete protein. Edamame are also packed with fiber, B vitamins, omega-3 fats, iron, calcium, and zinc.

Fiesta Lime-Lentil Salad

This is the perfect meatless dish that even carnivores will love.

INGREDIENTS | SERVES 8

1 (16-ounce) bag dried lentils
4 cups water
½ teaspoon sea salt
2 tablespoons freshly chopped cilantro
1 tablespoon grapeseed oil
½ cup broccoli, chopped
¼ cup carrots, sliced
½ cup green cabbage, chopped
¼ cup radish, chopped
½ green pepper, chopped
1 celery stalk, chopped
2 cloves garlic, minced
¼ teaspoon ground chili pepper
½ teaspoon dried oregano
1 teaspoon dried basil
1 teaspoon dried cumin
½ teaspoon dried paprika
½ teaspoon ground cayenne pepper
Juice of 1 lime

Steamed Lentils Save Time

Do you want to save time and preparation? Purchase steamed lentils, which are available in the refrigerated section of most grocery stores. Simply take the steamed lentils out of their container and add to sautéed vegetables (step #6) and follow the rest of the instructions.

1. Rinse the lentils under running water and pick through them to remove any bits of soil or rocks.

2. Add the lentils and water to a saucepan (with a lid) and bring to a boil. Turn heat down to low and cover to let the lentils simmer, but leave the lid ajar a bit so that they don't boil over. Check on them occasionally to make sure the water has not boiled down below the level of the lentils; add more water as needed. When the lentils are tender and can easily be mashed with a fork, they are done. It usually takes about 30–45 minutes for them to cook.

3. Add salt and cilantro in about the last 15 minutes of cooking time—when the lentils are starting to get soft. (Cooking often neutralizes the taste of the salt, so if you add it at the start you end up having to add more salt to get the same flavor.)

4. When they are finished cooking, take the saucepan off the heat and cover tightly with the lid. Leave to sit for 5–10 minutes. The lentils will absorb more of the water, making them juicier and more tender.

5. In a skillet over medium heat, add the oil and chopped veggies and sauté for 5 minutes.

6. Add lentils and seasonings and stir. Let sit on medium-low heat for 5–8 minutes until the veggies soften.

7. Remove from heat, add fresh lime juice, and stir until well blended.

Warm Chickpea Salad with Spinach

Chickpeas (or garbanzo beans) are loaded with protein and fiber. If you use canned beans, make sure you rinse them thoroughly before using. Serve this with a side green salad for a balanced meal.

INGREDIENTS | SERVES 4

1 tablespoon extra-virgin olive oil

4 cloves garlic, minced

½ onion, diced

2 cups fresh baby spinach

1 (12-ounce) can chickpeas, rinsed and drained thoroughly

½ teaspoon cumin

½ teaspoon salt

⅛ teaspoon curry

Juice from ½ freshly squeezed lemon

¼ cup vegetable broth

1. Heat the olive oil in a skillet over medium-low heat. Cook the garlic and onion in the oil until translucent, about 5 minutes.

2. Stir in the spinach, chickpeas, cumin, salt, and curry. Continue to stir for a few minutes. Add lemon juice and broth, and stir. Allow to cook until thoroughly heated.

The Benefits of Beans

Beans are low in fat and help regulate blood sugar levels. They are also high in dietary fiber, which studies have shown can help lower cholesterol, reduce blood pressure, and support proper digestive health.

Indian Vegetable Cakes

This is a great way to get kids to eat their veggies!
A nonstick pan helps prevent sticking. Sour cream makes a very good garnish.

INGREDIENTS | SERVES 4–6

1 tablespoon extra-virgin olive oil

1 (10-ounce) package frozen chopped spinach, thawed and squeezed of excess moisture

5 ounces frozen baby peas, thawed

½ bunch scallions, chopped

1 teaspoon curry powder

½ teaspoon turmeric

½ teaspoon ground black pepper

Salt and hot pepper sauce, to taste

¼ cup cornmeal

5 extra-large eggs, well beaten

½ cup Parmesan cheese

1. Heat olive oil in a nonstick pan over a medium heat.

2. In a large bowl, mix together all the ingredients except the Parmesan cheese. Form into patties.

3. Drop patties, 3 or 4 at a time, into the pan and fry until delicately browned, 3–4 minutes per side. Turn and sprinkle with cheese before serving.

Terrific Turmeric

Do you know about the health benefits of turmeric? Curcumin, a main ingredient in turmeric, has been shown to reduce inflammation. Some studies indicate that it may help ease the pain and symptoms of arthritis and rheumatoid arthritis. Other research shows that turmeric may protect against diseases, such as certain cancers, Alzheimer's disease, high cholesterol, and heart disease, to name a few. Try adding turmeric to your favorite dishes for some health benefits.

Spinach, Tomatoes, and Gnocchi in Classic Pesto Sauce

This meal is so simple to prepare that you will amazed how delicious it tastes.

INGREDIENTS | SERVES 8

1 (12-ounce) package wheat-free gnocchi

1 (6-ounce) bag organic baby spinach

1 pint organic grape tomatoes, halved

1 teaspoon extra-virgin olive oil

1 garlic clove, chopped

Classic Pesto Sauce (see recipe in this chapter)

Parmesan cheese, for garnish (optional)

Gnocchi

Gnocchi is an Italian-style potato dumpling and can be substituted for pasta in many popular dishes. Be advised, just because you hear "potato" dumplings don't assume they are wheat-free. Read your ingredient lists carefully because many of them are made with wheat flour. There are many brands that offer wheat-free gnocchi in specialty grocery stores and many local supermarkets.

1. Cook the gnocchi according to the package directions.

2. Place the spinach and grape tomatoes in skillet with oil and garlic, and sauté until soft, about 2–3 minutes. Add in the gnocchi and stir until well blended.

3. Place everything in large bowl. Pour pesto on top. Stir to combine. Top with Parmesan if desired.

Classic Pesto Sauce

This wonderful sauce takes only a few minutes to prepare.
Feel free to double this recipe, as it stores well in the freezer.

INGREDIENTS | SERVES 8

½ cup extra-virgin olive oil

3 garlic cloves

1½ ounces pine nuts

2 ounces Parmesan cheese

2 ounces fresh basil leaves, torn

Salt and pepper, to taste (optional)

1. Add all the ingredients to a food processor or high-speed blender in the order listed.

2. Blend for 1 minute or until blended smooth. Depending on your blender or processor you may need to also stir the pesto by hand to make sure all the ingredients are combined.

Pesto Possibilities

When it comes to pesto, try thinking outside of the box. You can substitute pine nuts with walnuts, cashews, pistachios, almonds, or even pumpkin seeds. To add different flavors and textures you can also add different vegetables and cheeses. The possibilities are endless!

Pesto, Arugula, and Yellow Tomato Pizza with Cauliflower Pizza Crust

Pizza doesn't have to consist of just cheese and sauce.
It's fun to be creative with different vegetables and sauces.

INGREDIENTS | SERVES 4

2 cups Easy Pizza Sauce (see Chapter 9)

1 Cauliflower Pizza Crust (see recipe in this chapter)

½ cup Classic Pesto Sauce (see recipe in this chapter)

3 cups fresh arugula

1 tablespoon extra-virgin olive oil

1 clove garlic, minced

1 cup part skim mozzarella cheese, shredded or fresh

1 pint yellow cherry tomatoes, sliced in half

¼ cup freshly torn basil leaves

1. Preheat oven to 350°F.

2. Spread the pizza sauce evenly over the top of the cauliflower crust.

3. Spread the pesto evenly on top of the pizza sauce.

4. Sauté the arugula in a small pan with 1 tablespoon olive oil and garlic until wilted, about 1–2 minutes. Once done, pour evenly over pizza.

5. Sprinkle with the cheese, and add sliced tomatoes and fresh basil on top.

6. Bake for about 10–15 minutes, until the edges are browned.

7. Place under the broiler, on high heat, until cheese is melted, approximately 1–2 minutes.

Cauliflower Pizza Crust

Being on a wheat-free diet doesn't mean you can't have pizza!
This makes a 1" thick crust, but it can be doubled for a larger pizza.

INGREDIENTS | SERVES 4

1 cup raw cauliflower, grated (or chopped in food processor)
1 egg
½ cup Parmesan cheese
1 teaspoon oregano
2 teaspoons parsley
Handful of fresh basil
1 garlic clove, finely diced

Cauliflower Pizza Crust Tips

Approximately 2¼ cups of cauliflower, chopped into 1" pieces, would grate into 1 cup of grated cauliflower. Be careful not to spread the crust too thin, or it will fall apart and its edges will burn. Alternatively, spreading the crust too thick will leave the middle uncooked.

1. Preheat oven to 425°F. Spray a cookie sheet with nonstick spray or use parchment paper.

2. In a medium bowl, combine the cauliflower, egg, Parmesan cheese and all the seasonings. Press evenly on baking pan or pizza stone. Bake for 15–20 minutes, until the edges start to brown. You may turn over once if desired.

3. Remove the pan from the oven. Add sauce and desired toppings.

4. Place under the broiler, on high heat, until cheese is melted.

Raw Broccoli Slaw with Fruit, Veggies, and Walnuts

Why not try a broccoli slaw without mayonnaise?
This is perfect for outdoor picnics and cookouts.

INGREDIENTS | SERVES 6

1 (12-ounce) bag broccoli slaw

1 cup diced organic Fuji apple, peeled

1 organic kiwi, peeled and sliced

1 organic red bell pepper, seeded and chopped

2 tablespoons dried cranberries (unsweetened)

2 tablespoons sliced walnuts

Chia-Balsamic Vinaigrette (see recipe in this chapter)

1. Place broccoli slaw in large bowl. Add chopped apple, kiwi, and pepper. Mix it all together.

2. Top with cranberries and walnuts. Mix again. Add vinaigrette just before serving.

Chia-Balsamic Vinaigrette

You can make more of this dressing and keep it in your refrigerator.
It goes well with veggies, meats, and any kind of salad.

INGREDIENTS | SERVES 6–8

1 tablespoon Dijon mustard

5 tablespoons balsamic vinegar

1 tablespoon extra-virgin olive oil, or oil of your choice

1 tablespoon chia seeds, ground

Salt and freshly ground black pepper, to taste

1 large garlic clove, finely chopped

1–2 tablespoons fresh basil leaves

1. In a clean, empty jar or Tupperware container with a lid, add the mustard, balsamic vinegar, oil, chia seeds, salt, and pepper.

2. Add the chopped garlic along with the fresh basil leaves.

3. Cover the jar and shake well to blend. Store up to 5 days in airtight container.

Corn and Spinach Pockets Stuffed with Cheese and Artichokes

Simply because a dish is vegetarian does not mean it has to be tasteless. This recipe is a perfect example.

INGREDIENTS | SERVES 8

1 (10-ounce) box frozen artichoke hearts, thawed

1 (10-ounce) box frozen spinach, thawed, moisture squeezed out

1 cup ricotta cheese

4 ounces cream cheese

¼ cup minced chives

1 clove garlic, chopped

¼ teaspoon freshly ground nutmeg

Salt and pepper to taste

1 egg

8 large (8–9" in diameter) Corn Crepes (see Chapter 3)

Beaten egg, for sealing pockets

1. Preheat oven to 350°F. Add the defrosted artichokes to a food processor with the spinach, process, and slowly add the cheeses, chives, garlic, seasonings, and egg.

2. Lay out the crepes on a nonstick baking sheet or one covered with a sheet of aluminum foil.

3. Divide the filling among the crepes, spooning the mixture onto one half and leaving the other half plain.

4. Wet the rims of the crepes with beaten egg. Fold over and press lightly to seal, and then bake for 20 minutes or until well browned and filling is bubbling out.

Selecting and Preparing Artichokes

If you use fresh artichokes, look for ones that are tightly closed. Take a pair of kitchen scissors and clip off the sharp points. You can use a knife to cut off the tops. They are hearty when stuffed with many kinds of delicious foods. If you eat fish, salmon mixed with rice makes an excellent stuffing.

Tofu and Vegetables with Macadamia Nuts and Asian Citrus Sauce

The tastes and textures come together beautifully in this Asian-inspired dish. Serve over rice.

INGREDIENTS | SERVES 4

1 tablespoon sesame seed oil

3 tablespoons peanut or other vegetable oil

1 bunch scallions, chopped

1 clove garlic, minced

1" piece gingerroot, peeled and minced

⅔ pound sugar snap peas, ends trimmed

2 cups mung bean sprouts

2 cups shredded Chinese cabbage

½ teaspoon brown sugar

½ orange, juice and rind, pulsed in the food processor

1 teaspoon Asian five-spice powder

1 teaspoon Chinese mustard or Japanese wasabi, or to taste

¼ cup sake or dry white wine

¼ cup light wheat-free soy sauce

1 pound satin tofu, cubed

1. Heat the oils in a wok. Add the scallions, garlic, and gingerroot. Lightly mix in the rest of the vegetables and toss in the oil for 3–4 minutes. Place the cooked vegetables in a large, warm serving bowl.

2. In a small bowl, mix together the brown sugar, orange juice and rind, five-spice powder, mustard or wasabi, sake or wine, and soy sauce.

3. Stir into the wok until blended. Add the tofu cubes and vegetables, and mix to coat. Serve hot.

A Source of Protein for Vegetarians

Tofu, long used in Asia because meat and milk were both scarce and expensive, has become an important part of the vegetarian diet. It can be flavored to taste like many kinds of meat. Or it can be sweetened and prepared with fruit for desserts. It's delicious in soups and with vegetables.

Stuffed Portobello Mushrooms

This vegetarian dish can be prepared as an entrée with a bed of greens,
or you can use smaller portobello mushrooms to make these into an appetizer.

INGREDIENTS | SERVES 2

2 large portobello mushrooms, stems and gills removed, wiped down with insides scooped out and set aside

3 cups water

1 teaspoon vegetable bouillon

1 cup brown rice, uncooked

1 medium red onion, finely chopped

¼ cup sun-dried tomatoes

3 cloves garlic, minced

¼ cup fresh basil, torn

1 cup baby spinach

½ cup Parmesan cheese, grated

1. Preheat the oven to 250°F.

2. Place the portobello mushrooms onto a baking sheet lined with aluminum foil.

3. Bring 3 cups of water and bouillon together to a boil.

4. Add rice, onion, tomatoes, garlic, basil, and spinach to the boiling water. Stirring occasionally, continue to boil until all the water is absorbed and the rice is fully cooked, about 15–20 minutes. Remove from heat and add the scooped-out insides of mushrooms. Stir to combine.

5. Pour rice mixture into each of the mushroom caps and top with Parmesan cheese.

6. Place mushrooms in the oven for about 20–30 minutes, or until cheese is melted.

Crispy Potato Pancakes

This can be served traditionally with applesauce for an entrée, alongside eggs for breakfast or brunch, or even as an appetizer with an aioli dipping sauce.

INGREDIENTS | MAKES ABOUT 10 PANCAKES

4 large Idaho potatoes, peeled and coarsely grated

2 medium mild onions, chopped fine

1 tablespoon parsley, finely chopped

½ cup scallions, chopped (including the green part)

2 eggs, well beaten

½ cup potato flour

Salt and pepper, to taste

2 cups cooking oil (such as canola)

Sour cream, applesauce, fruit preserves, salsa, or chutney, for garnish

1. Mix the grated potatoes, onions, parsley, scallions, and eggs in a bowl. Sprinkle with potato flour, salt, and pepper. Form into cakes.

2. Heat the oil in a skillet to 350°F and spoon in the potato cakes, pressing down to make a patty.

3. Fry until golden, about 5 minutes per side. Drain on a paper towel, keep warm, and serve with garnish of choice.

The Origins of Potato Pancakes

During the long winters in northern and eastern Europe, when fresh fruits and vegetables were not available, winter storage of carrots, potatoes, beets, Brussels sprouts, apples, and dried fruits was crucial to prevent scurvy, or ascorbic acid deficiency. As Mother Nature would have it, these vegetables are packed with vitamins and minerals. Potato pancakes with sour cream, applesauce, or fruit syrups became a staple in harsh climates.

Classic Polenta with Herbs and Parmesan

Use 7 cups of water if you want soft polenta the consistency of mashed potatoes; use 6½ cups if you prefer it firm enough to cut into squares to broil, grill, or fry.

INGREDIENTS | SERVES 4–6

6½ or 7 cups water

2 tablespoons salt

2 cups yellow cornmeal

2–4 ounces unsalted butter

2 cloves garlic, minced

½ medium onion, finely minced

2 tablespoons dried herbs, or 1 tablespoon each: chopped fresh basil, rosemary, and parsley

½ cup freshly grated Parmesan cheese

Freshly ground black pepper, to taste

The Staple of Lombardy

Polenta has been the staple food of Lombardy, at the foot of the Italian Alps, for three centuries. Polenta is a staple in Italy, and it's hard to ruin it. You can use polenta wherever you'd use pasta, serving it with tomato, vegetable, or cream sauces, or with brown gravy and mushrooms. You can make it soft, to mound on a plate or platter, or firm and then fry it in squares.

1. Bring the water to a boil.

2. Add salt, and using your hand to drop the cornmeal into the boiling water, let the cornmeal slip slowly between your fingers to make a very slim stream. You should be able to see each grain. Don't dump the cornmeal into the water or you will get a mass of glue.

3. Stir constantly while adding the cornmeal. Reduce heat to a simmer and keep stirring for about 20 minutes as it thickens.

4. Stir in the butter, garlic, onion, herbs, Parmesan cheese, and pepper. If you're making soft polenta, serve immediately. If you're making firm polenta, spread in a 9" × 13" lasagna pan that has been prepared with nonstick spray. Chill for 3 hours or overnight. Cut into sections and either fry, broil, or grill.

Sweet Potato Gratin with Leeks and Onions

This dish is the perfect choice when you want a sweet and savory, delicious combination.

INGREDIENTS | SERVES 4–6

2 leeks, white part only, rinsed and chopped

2 large sweet onions, such as Vidalia, sliced

2 cloves garlic, minced

2 stalks celery with tops, finely chopped

4 tablespoons extra-virgin olive oil or butter

4 large sweet potatoes, peeled and sliced thinly

1 teaspoon dried thyme

Salt and pepper, to taste

Milk to cover

1½ cups wheat-free corn bread crumbs

Butter or margarine, for topping

1. Preheat the oven to 325°F. Prepare an oval metal or pottery gratin pan with nonstick spray.

2. In a large pan over medium heat, sauté the leeks, onions, garlic, and celery in olive oil or butter.

3. Layer the sweet potato slices in the gratin pan with the vegetables. Sprinkle with thyme, salt, and pepper as you go along.

4. Finish with a layer of potatoes. Add the milk until it meets the top layer of potatoes. Then add the corn bread crumbs. Dot with extra butter or margarine.

5. Bake until the potatoes are soft, about 1 hour. Add more milk if it starts to dry out.

Broccoli and Cheese-Stuffed Baked Potatoes

*The whole family will love this recipe. You can experiment
with a variety of vegetables and different cheeses too.*

**INGREDIENTS | SERVES 4 AS A MEAL, OR
8 AS A SNACK**

4 large Idaho or Yukon Gold potatoes

5 cups broccoli florets

1 cup sour cream

¼ teaspoon nutmeg

1 cup grated white American cheese

3 cloves garlic, chopped

1 large onion, finely chopped

Salt and pepper, to taste

½ cup shredded sharp Cheddar cheese

1. Preheat the oven to 350°F.

2. Bake the potatoes in the oven for 40 minutes. Then cool the potatoes and split them in half lengthwise.

3. Steam broccoli until tender, about 5 minutes. Drain, rinse, and chop.

4. Spoon out the insides of the potatoes and place in a bowl; add the broccoli. Stir in the sour cream and nutmeg. Add the American cheese, garlic, and onion. Season to taste with salt and pepper.

5. Restuff the potato skins. Arrange the Cheddar cheese on top. Bake for another 20 minutes and serve hot.

Potato Frittata with Cheese and Herbs

Use both nonstick spray and butter in this recipe, or the starch in the potatoes will stick.
Spinach would make a lovely addition to this.

INGREDIENTS | SERVES 4

1 large Yukon Gold potato, peeled

4 teaspoons butter

Salt and pepper, to taste

6 eggs

½ cup grated Parmesan cheese

½ small green onion, finely minced

1 teaspoon dried parsley

6 sage leaves, minced

Fresh herbs, extra cheese, sour cream, for garnish

Striking Yukon Gold

Yukon Gold potatoes were developed in the 1970s at the University of Guelph, Ontario, Canada. They were initially slow to capture the market but are now widely popular, and particularly suited for baking, and in salads and soup.

1. Using a mandoline, slice the potato as thinly as possible. Prepare a heavy 12" pan, first with nonstick spray, then with butter.

2. Add the potatoes, making a thin layer, and season with salt and pepper. Cook over medium heat for 10 minutes—this will be the crust.

3. In a large bowl, beat the eggs well. Add the cheese, onion, parsley, and minced sage. Pour over the potatoes and turn down heat to the lowest possible setting. Cook for 10 minutes.

4. When the eggs have set, run the frittata under the broiler until golden brown on top. Cut into wedges and serve at once with garnishes.

Stuffed Eggplant with Ricotta and Spices

This dish is also known as Eggplant Sicilian. It freezes beautifully and is very delicious.

INGREDIENTS | SERVES 4

2 medium eggplants, peeled, cut into 16 round slices (8 slices each) and salted

1 cup rice or corn flour

Freshly ground black pepper, to taste

¼ cup extra-virgin olive oil, or as needed

1 clove garlic, chopped

2 cups tomato sauce

1 pound ricotta cheese

1 cup grated Parmesan cheese, divided

2 eggs

1 teaspoon dried basil

1 tablespoon dried oregano

1 cup shredded mozzarella cheese

Smaller Is Sweeter

The smaller eggplants now available are much sweeter and not old enough to have grown bitter. Also, many have few seeds. They come in pale cream, lavender, and purple, all the way from egg-sized to long and skinny. All are good!

1. Stack the salted eggplant slices on a plate and put another plate with a weight on top to press the brown liquid out of them.

2. Mix the flour and pepper and use it for dredging the eggplant slices. Fry the slices in the olive oil and garlic, removing to paper towels as they are browned.

3. Preheat oven to 325°F. Prepare a 2-quart casserole dish or a 10" × 10" glass pan with nonstick spray and spread with a thin layer of tomato sauce.

4. In a large bowl, mix the ricotta cheese, ½ cup of the Parmesan, eggs, basil, and oregano. Place a tablespoon of the egg-cheese mixture on each slice of eggplant and roll, placing seam-side down in the baking dish.

5. Spread with remaining tomato sauce, sprinkle with the rest of the Parmesan cheese and the mozzarella cheese, and bake for 35 minutes.

Sweet Pepper and Feta Omelet

This omelet has a delightful flavor from the feta cheese melting into the eggs.
A nonstick pan takes all of the guesswork out of making omelets.

INGREDIENTS | SERVES 2

2 teaspoons unsalted butter

4 eggs, well beaten

2 ounces crumbled feta cheese

4" × 2" strips roasted red pepper

Salt and hot red pepper flakes, to taste

Extraordinary Eggs

Eggs are a versatile, all-purpose protein. Omelets can solve any number of nutritional problems, providing something that's really easy to digest and great for finicky appetites. Various vegetables, cheeses, and herbs make perfect fillings for omelets. The more creative the combination, the more interesting the omelet.

1. Heat a 10" nonstick pan over medium-high heat. Melt the butter and swirl to coat. Add the eggs and swirl to distribute evenly in pan.

2. Place the cheese and pepper strips on one side of the omelet. Season with salt and pepper flakes.

3. Cook until just set, when it has the consistency of custard (soft and creamy but not liquid or runny). Flip the plain side over the side with the cheese and peppers. Cut in half and serve on a warmed plate.

Brown Rice Pilaf with Toasted Almonds

For best results, soak the brown rice overnight to help make it softer and lighter. This can be served as a side dish or paired with beans to create a perfect meal.

INGREDIENTS | SERVES 6

⅓ cup almonds, slivered
1 large onion, finely chopped
3 garlic cloves, minced
1 tablespoon extra-virgin olive oil
1½ cups long grain brown rice
1 teaspoon dried parsley
3½ cups vegetable broth
2 teaspoons dried marjoram, minced
Salt and pepper, to taste

1. Place the almonds in small dry skillet over medium heat, stirring constantly for 3–4 minutes, until lightly browned. Place almonds in a small bowl.

2. In the small skillet, sauté the onion and garlic in oil. Cook until onion is translucent, about 5 minutes.

3. Add the rice and stir until thoroughly mixed, about 1 minute.

4. Add parsley, broth, and marjoram, cover and reduce heat to low.

5. Simmer until all the water is absorbed and the rice is fully cooked, about 45–50 minutes.

6. Uncover, fluff with fork, and let stand for a few minutes. Stir in toasted almonds and season with salt and pepper.

Classic Italian Risotto

Risotto should be very creamy on the outside, yet firm on the inside of each grain of rice.

INGREDIENTS | SERVES 4

5 cups canned or homemade vegetable broth
2 tablespoons butter
2 tablespoons extra-virgin olive oil
½ cup finely chopped sweet onion
2 cloves garlic, minced
2 stalks celery, finely chopped
¼ cup celery leaves, chopped
1½ cups arborio rice
⅓ cup dry white wine
1 teaspoon salt, or to taste
⅔ cup freshly grated Parmesan cheese
¼ cup chopped parsley
Freshly ground black pepper, to taste

Parmesan Cheese

Always grate Parmesan cheese yourself as you need it. Buy it in 1-pound blocks and keep well sealed with plastic wrap in the refrigerator. Try using a box grater for a coarse cheese with lots of body.

1. Bring the broth to a slow simmer over low heat and keep it hot.

2. Place the butter and oil in a heavy-bottomed pot, melt butter, and add the onion, garlic, celery, and celery leaves. Cook for 8–10 minutes.

3. Add the rice and stir to coat with butter and oil. Add white wine and salt.

4. In ¼-cup increments, start adding hot broth. Stir until the broth has been absorbed into the rice. Add another ¼ cup, stirring until all of the broth is absorbed. Repeat this process until all of the hot broth is gone. It must be stirred constantly and takes about 35 minutes.

5. When all of the broth is gone, taste the rice for desired consistency. If it needs more broth or water, add it and keep stirring. Add the cheese, parsley, and pepper. Serve immediately.

Vegetable Lasagna Primavera with Pasta Substitute

This vegetarian dish takes very little time and is excellent for a big family dinner or a holiday.

INGREDIENTS | SERVES 6–8

4 eggs, divided

½ teaspoon table salt or sea salt, or to taste

¼ teaspoon pepper, or to taste

1½ cups milk or water

1 cup corn flour (masa harina)

Butter or oil for greasing the griddle

1 pound ricotta cheese

2 garlic cloves, chopped

½ cup Parmesan cheese

2 cups chopped raw mixed fresh vegetables, such as scallions, zucchini, fresh spinach, and young peas

½ cup finely chopped fresh parsley

1½ cups Spicy Marinara Sauce (see Chapter 11)

1 cup shredded mozzarella cheese

1. Mix 2 of the eggs, salt, pepper, milk or water, and corn flour in the blender and process until smooth.

2. Using a well-greased griddle, pour the batter, fry until firm, and cut into 10" strips that are 2" wide. Turn using an extra-large, long spatula. As you finish, place the strips on a baking dish that has been prepared with nonstick spray. When the bottom of the pan is covered, fry the rest of the batter in the same way and save it for topping.

3. In a bowl, mix the ricotta, other 2 eggs, garlic, Parmesan, vegetables, and parsley. Spread in tablespoonfuls over the base in the pan. Cover with more of the pasta strips.

4. Add the marinara sauce to the pan and cover with shredded mozzarella. Bake for about 12 minutes. Serve hot.

A Versatile Pasta

Any sauce that you would use on wheat pasta can be used on rice pasta—from a rich Alfredo sauce to a robust marinara sauce.

Spinach, Kale, and Mushroom Pizza

This pizza goes beyond the typical red sauce and mozzarella cheese.
Goat cheese makes a wonderful addition to this sauceless pizza.

INGREDIENTS | SERVES 4

2 cups kale

2 cups spinach

1 cup sliced mushrooms

1 tablespoon grapeseed oil

2 cloves garlic, chopped

½ medium onion, chopped

Cauliflower Pizza Crust (see recipe in this chapter)

½ cup goat cheese, crumbled

Handful of fresh basil, torn

1. Preheat broiler. Place kale, spinach, and mushrooms in a skillet with grapeseed oil, garlic, and onion. Sauté for 3–4 minutes, until mushrooms soften and the greens wilt.

2. Place the vegetables on top of pizza crust. Next top with goat cheese and fresh basil.

3. Place under the broiler for 2 minutes until cheese is melted. Serve hot.

Pizza Is a Family Affair

Making pizzas can be a fun and easy family activity. Let the kids sprinkle the cheese, add the vegetables, or tear the basil. Doing simple prep work is an easy way to expose "future chefs" to the joy of cooking.

CHAPTER 9

Kids

Parmesan-Flax-Crusted Chicken Tenders

These tenders are so tasty, the whole family will love them.
Kids love to dip, so experiment with different dipping sauces too.

INGREDIENTS | SERVES 4

2 egg whites and 1 whole egg, beaten
1 cup ground flax seed
1 teaspoon dried basil
1 teaspoon dried oregano
1½ teaspoons red pepper flakes
2 cloves garlic, minced
½ teaspoon salt
½ teaspoon ground black pepper
⅓ cup Parmesan cheese, freshly grated
1 (16-ounce) package organic chicken tenderloins

Homemade Is Better

Chicken tenders you find in the grocery store can have a lot of preservatives and ingredients in them that you may not expect. This recipe is a perfect example of how easy they are to make at home.

1. Preheat the oven to 350°F. Spray 9" × 13" casserole dish with cooking spray.

2. Place egg whites and egg in a large bowl.

3. In a separate large bowl, place ground flax seed, basil, oregano, red pepper flakes, garlic, salt, pepper, and cheese. Stir until mixed.

4. Start by placing each chicken tender in egg mixture, then coat with flax mixture, and make sure it is thoroughly coated on both sides. Place in prepared casserole dish.

5. Place casserole dish in the oven and cook for 35 minutes, making sure to turn tenders over halfway through cooking time. Serve with your favorite dipping sauce!

Grilled Cheese

*This recipe is one of the hundreds of goodies you can make with the
No Grain Bread (see Chapter 3). Feel free to add some sliced tomatoes in there too.*

**INGREDIENTS | MAKES 32 SMALL
SQUARES**

1 loaf No Grain Bread (see Chapter 3),
cut into squares

½ cup soft butter

1 cup cubed Monterey jack cheese

½ cup grated Parmesan cheese

½ cup red roasted peppers (jarred is
fine)

½ cup chopped sweet red onion

Stuffing and Spreads

Making spreads and stuffing for any
number of things is a great way to use
leftovers. You can take a chunk of leftover
Brie cheese and put it in the food processor with some chopped onion and a bit of
butter or margarine and have a whole new
experience. Leftover chicken is excellent
for making many different spreads, filling
for stuffed celery, or a little sandwich.

1. Arrange bread squares on a baking sheet that you have prepared with nonstick spray. Preheat the oven to 350°F.

2. Process the rest of the ingredients in the food processor until mixed. Don't worry about making the cheese mixture smooth. Using a teaspoon, place a small mound of cheese/butter mixture on each bread square.

3. Bake until the cheese melts, about 10 minutes. You can vary this recipe by adding different herbs, chopped garlic, or any of your favorite flavors.

Popcorn with Parmesan Topping

There is no need to add butter to this popcorn.
Parmesan cheese adds a delightful flavor to your typical, ordinary popcorn.

INGREDIENTS | SERVES 8

1 tablespoon grapeseed oil
1 cup popcorn kernels
½ teaspoon sea salt
½ cup Parmesan cheese, grated

Get Creative with Your Popcorn!

There are so many different seasonings you can add to your popcorn that won't add calories, fat, or additives. Chili powder, curry, garlic powder, lemon pepper, or even sugar and cinnamon are among the many options you have. This is a perfect opportunity for children to experiment with new flavors too.

1. Place grapeseed oil in bottom of a large pot.

2. Place popcorn kernels on top of the oil in the pan. Do NOT turn stove on yet. Stir kernels to make sure they are evenly coated with the oil.

3. Place heat on medium and, and with the pot uncovered, shake the kernels around in the pot until the first kernel pops. Quickly place the lid on top and wait until all the kernels pop.

4. Once done, remove from heat and add salt and Parmesan cheese. Stir to mix thoroughly. You can store popcorn in an airtight container for up to 6 months.

Baby Back Ribs

You can use any kind of barbecue sauce you wish for this recipe.
The trick is to cook the ribs in the sauce.

INGREDIENTS | SERVES 4–6

4 pounds baby back ribs, cut into 1-rib servings

½ cup vegetable oil

1 cup Easy Barbecue Sauce (see recipe in this chapter)

1 teaspoon garlic powder

1 cup tomato juice

½ cup orange juice

1. Fry the ribs in vegetable oil over medium-high heat until lightly brown, about 3–4 minutes each side.

2. Add the rest of the ingredients and cover. Cook over very low heat for 1 hour.

3. Remove the ribs and continue cooking the sauce until it is reduced to 1 cup, about 5–8 minutes. Serve sauce with ribs for dipping.

Easy Barbecue Sauce

You will never want store-bought barbecue sauce again after you make this.
This zesty sauce is perfect for chicken, pork, or beef. You can keep this in
an airtight container in the refrigerator for a few weeks.

INGREDIENTS | MAKES 8 SERVINGS (1 CUP)

1 tablespoon cider vinegar

½ cup ketchup

1 tablespoon honey

2 tablespoons brown sugar

1 teaspoon garlic powder

½ tablespoon onion powder

1 tablespoon red pepper flakes

1 teaspoon Dijon mustard

2 tablespoons wheat-free Worcestershire sauce

¼ teaspoon salt

1. Place all the ingredients in a small saucepan over medium heat.

2. Bring to a boil, turn heat to low, and simmer on low for a few minutes, stirring.

3. Allow to cool before brushing onto meat.

Chili Bean Dip with Dipping Vegetables

This is the perfect after-school snack for hungry children.
Feel free to eliminate the jalapeño if it's too spicy for the little ones.

INGREDIENTS | MAKES 1 QUART

½ pound ground beef

1 medium onion, chopped

2 jalapeño peppers, or to taste, cored, seeded, and chopped

2 cloves garlic, chopped

1 tablespoon extra-virgin olive oil

¼ teaspoon ground pepper

4 teaspoons chili powder, or to taste

1 (13-ounce) can crushed tomatoes with juice

1 (13-ounce) can red kidney beans

½ cup flat beer

Cheddar cheese, shredded, for topping (optional)

Assortment of carrots, celery pieces, radishes, broccoli, spears of zucchini, etc.

1. Sauté the beef with the onion, peppers, and garlic in the oil in a large skillet, breaking up any clumps with a spoon.

2. When the vegetables are soft, add the rest of the ingredients (except the cheese and vegetables for dipping). Cover and simmer for 1 hour.

3. Serve warm. Top with shredded cheese if desired. Or cool, and turn this into a dip by pulsing it in the food processor. Do not make it smooth. Serve alongside veggies.

Chili and Beans

There are endless variations of the chili-and-bean combination. Some people use turkey, others add dark chocolate and cinnamon and vary the amounts of beans and tomatoes. Some forms of chili don't have any beans. Different regions use various amounts of spice, heat, and ingredients.

Deviled Eggs

This protein-packed recipe is a perfect afternoon snack for children and adults alike.

INGREDIENTS | MAKES 10 DEVILED EGGS

5 hard-boiled eggs

½ cup whole or low-fat mayonnaise

1 teaspoon Dijon mustard

1 teaspoon Tabasco sauce or other hot red pepper sauce

½ bunch chives, snipped finely

2 teaspoons capers, the smallest available

Paprika, for garnish (optional)

1. Peel eggs, cut them in half, and remove the yolks to your food processor. Arrange the whites on a platter.

2. Add the mayonnaise, mustard, Tabasco or pepper sauce, chives, and capers to the food processor and process until blended.

3. Stuff the egg whites with the yolk mixture, and sprinkle with paprika, if desired.

Grilled Chicken Wings

Traditional Buffalo wings are generally fried. This recipe, done with a rub and some olive oil, is a lot less fattening. Double the recipe and refrigerate half for delicious cold snacks.

INGREDIENTS | SERVES 4–8

4 pounds chicken wings, split at the joint, tips removed

1 tablespoon onion powder

1 tablespoon garlic powder

¼ teaspoon cinnamon

2 teaspoons dark brown sugar

½ teaspoon paprika

½ teaspoon ground black pepper

¼ cup freshly squeezed lime juice

¼ cup extra-virgin olive oil

1 teaspoon salt

Ground black pepper, to taste

1. Rinse the wings, and set them on paper towels to dry.

2. In a large bowl, mix the rest of the ingredients together. Coat the chicken with the spice mixture, cover, and refrigerate for 1 hour.

3. Grill over medium-hot coals or broil at 350°F for 20 minutes, turning every few minutes, or until well browned.

Olive Oil in Spray Bottles

This is a very easy and economical way to use olive oil. Just buy a bottle used for spraying plants with water and fill it with olive oil instead. Use it for spraying your food, salads, and so on. Or you can get olive oil–flavored nonstick spray at the supermarket. The nonstick spray, however, is not suitable for salads.

Spaghetti Squash with Marinara Sauce

*Spaghetti squash holds endless possibilities for a nutritious, wheat-free diet.
It's delicious and so easy to prepare.*

INGREDIENTS | SERVES 6–8

1 (4-pound) spaghetti squash, rinsed

1 cup freshly grated Parmesan cheese

1 clove garlic, minced

Garnish of fresh herbs such as parsley, basil, and oregano

2 cups of your favorite jarred, wheat-free marinara sauce

Freshly Grated Cheese

Blocks of Parmesan cheese will keep for a week, tightly wrapped, in the refrigerator. It is so easy to grate exactly the amount you need, when you need it, and it tastes 100 percent better than the grated cheese you get in a box or jar. Use a box grater and place a piece of waxed paper on a cutting board. Grate away, then remove the grater, make a funnel of the paper, and slide the cheese into a bowl or add it to what you are preparing. You can also use Romano, fontina, or Cheddar cheese in this way and enjoy them so much more.

1. Preheat oven to 275°F.

2. Make a boat of aluminum foil and place the squash in the center and place on a baking sheet. Pierce the squash in several places with a knife to let the steam escape. Sprinkle with water. Tent with more foil and roast for 2 hours. The squash is done when you can insert a fork easily.

3. Cool the squash so you can handle it. Cut it in half and scoop out the seeds. Using a fork, run it through the flesh and it will turn into "spaghetti."

4. Mix the squash and most of the cheese together in a medium bowl and reheat. Sprinkle with the remaining cheese, garlic, and herbs, toss with marinara, and serve.

Homemade Sweet Potato Chips

Sweet potatoes are loaded with vitamin A and very delicious when fried and salted.
(You can substitute plantains for a taste of the islands.)

INGREDIENTS | MAKES ABOUT 3 DOZEN CHIPS

2 large sweet potatoes, peeled
3 cups canola oil
Salt and pepper, to taste
1 teaspoon cinnamon (optional)

Veggie Chips!

These "chips" can be prepared with a variety of different vegetables. You can make eggplant, zucchini, or even parsnip chips. The kids won't even suspect they are healthy!

1. Slice the potatoes thinly with a mandoline.

2. Heat the oil in a deep-fat fryer to 375°F.

3. Fry potato slices for about 3–4 minutes, depending on the thickness of the chips. When the chips are very crisp, remove from the oil and drain.

4. Add salt, pepper, and cinnamon if desired. Serve with dip or eat plain.

Maple Corn Cakes

This is a wonderful quick meal for the kids. Serve with bacon, sausages, or ham and eggs, if you are really hungry.

INGREDIENTS | MAKES 12 MEDIUM-SIZED PANCAKES

2 cups rice flour
5 teaspoons wheat-free baking powder
1 teaspoon salt
2 tablespoons maple syrup
2 cups milk
2 eggs
1 tablespoon butter, melted
1½ cups corn kernels (fresh or frozen)
Butter or oil for the griddle

1. Mix the dry ingredients together in a bowl.

2. Slowly add the syrup, milk, eggs, and butter, whisking to keep it light. Fold in the corn.

3. Heat the skillet or griddle to medium. Drop the cakes on the buttered griddle using a ladle. Fry until little bubbles form on the tops of the cakes. Turn and fry on the reverse side until golden brown. Serve with maple syrup, or fresh berries and whipped cream.

Parmesan-Kale Chips

Low calorie and nutritious, these make the perfect snack for the little ones.
Just like potato chips, you can eat the whole bowl in one sitting.

INGREDIENTS | SERVES 6

1 bunch kale (the curly kind is less bitter)

1 tablespoon extra-virgin olive oil in Misto sprayer

1 teaspoon salt

1 tablespoon finely grated Parmesan cheese

1. Preheat oven to 350°F. Line a noninsulated cookie sheet with parchment paper.

2. With a knife or kitchen shears, carefully remove the kale leaves from the thick stems and tear into bite-sized pieces. Wash and thoroughly dry kale with a salad spinner.

3. Spray the kale with olive oil from Misto sprayer and sprinkle with salt and Parmesan.

4. Bake until the edges brown, but are not burnt, 10–15 minutes.

Tropical Fruit Salsa

The sweet blend of fruits and vegetables makes a wonderful and unique salsa. Try it with pork, lamb, or any kind of fish. It is also great eaten with Brown Rice Chips (see recipe in this chapter).

INGREDIENTS | MAKES ABOUT 1½ CUPS

1 large mango, peeled, seeded, and diced

1 cup fresh pineapple, diced

½ red bell pepper, seeded and diced

¼ cup minced red onion

½ teaspoon freshly grated lime zest

Juice of ½ lime

Salt, to taste

Mix all ingredients in a bowl and cover. Refrigerate for 2 hours. Serve at room temperature.

Does Slicing Onions Make You Cry?

Place peeled and unsliced onions in a bowl of water for a few minutes before slicing. This little water soaking helps reduce some of the onion's harsh acids, which can cause tearing.

Brown Rice Chips

These chips will be a favorite in your house. They will stay fresh in an airtight container for up to a week.

INGREDIENTS | SERVES 8

1 12-ounce package brown rice tortillas
1 tablespoon cinnamon
1 tablespoon turbinado sugar
½ teaspoon ground cloves
½ teaspoon allspice

1. Preheat oven to 350°F. Cut the tortillas into slices.

2. In a small bowl combine the cinnamon, sugar, and spices together.

3. Lay tortilla slices out in a single layer on a baking sheet and sprinkle with cinnamon spice/sugar mixture.

4. Bake 8–12 minutes, until chips start to lightly brown. Repeat with remaining tortilla slices. Let cool 10 minutes and serve with chilled Tropical Fruit Salsa (see recipe in this chapter).

Roasted Pink Pepper Nuts

These will keep for up to one week in a tight plastic or tin container.
You can also substitute black or white pepper with only slightly different results.

INGREDIENTS | MAKES 2½ CUPS

¼ cup unsalted butter
¾ cup golden brown sugar (not "Brownulated")
4 teaspoons water
½ teaspoon ground cloves
⅛ teaspoon ground nutmeg
¼ teaspoon cinnamon
2 teaspoons salt
1 tablespoon freshly ground pink peppercorns
2½ cups blanched almonds

1. Preheat the oven to 350°F. Line a cookie sheet with aluminum foil and treat with nonstick spray.

2. In a saucepan over medium heat, melt the butter, add sugar and water, mix well.

3. Add the spices, salt, and peppercorns. When well blended, add the almonds and coat.

4. Transfer the nuts to the cookie sheet. Bake for about 10 minutes, until well browned. Cool and store in airtight container.

Apple and Pear Nachos

Children will not only love eating these, but they will have so much fun preparing them too.

INGREDIENTS | SERVES 4

1 sliced apple

1 sliced pear

2 tablespoons raw almond butter, slightly heated

2 ounces pecans, walnuts, almonds, or nuts of choice

Chocolate chips, to taste

Golden raisins, to taste

Shredded coconut

1. Arrange sliced apples and pears on a plate.

2. Pour the melted nut butter over the top. Then add nuts, chocolate chips, raisins, coconut, or any other of your favorite toppings, and serve immediately.

Banana-Nutter Sandwich

Move over PB & J, there's a new sandwich in town.
This one is wheat-free and uses bananas instead of jelly.

INGREDIENTS | SERVES 6

1 loaf No Grain Bread (see Chapter 3)

½ cup natural peanut butter

3–4 large bananas, sliced

1. Slice loaf of bread into 12 slices.

2. Spread peanut butter on 6 slices, then add sliced bananas. Place remaining bread slices on top to make a sandwich.

Wrap It Up!

These sandwiches are just as delicious when you use wheat-free wraps. Simply spread peanut butter on wrap, top with banana slices and wrap it up! Feel free to substitute other nut butters as well.

Sweet Cherry–Quinoa Granola Bars

Your kids will be asking for these granola bars over and over again.
Feel free to use whatever dried fruits you have in the house as a substitute for cherries.

INGREDIENTS | MAKES 18 BARS

1½ cups puffed rice cereal

1 cup rolled oats (make sure they are wheat-free)

1 cup cooked quinoa

½ cup dried cherries, unsweetened

⅓ cup sunflower seeds

⅓ cup sliced walnuts

¼ cup pumpkin seeds

2 tablespoonsground flaxseed

2 tablespoons chia seed, ground

1 teaspoon ground cinnamon

½ teaspoon sea salt

⅓ cup sunflower seed butter

6 tablespoons pure maple syrup

1. Preheat the oven to 325°F. Line a baking sheet with parchment paper and set aside.

2. In a large mixing bowl, combine all ingredients, *except* the sunflower seed butter and maple syrup.

3. In a small saucepan, heat the sunflower seed butter and syrup over medium-low heat until it becomes liquefied and smooth.

4. Pour the liquid ingredients over the dry ingredients and mix together until fully combined and everything is coated evenly.

5. Spread the granola out on the parchment-lined baking sheet, into a thin ¼" layer. Bake in the center of oven for 25 minutes, until the granola is browned and slightly crispy. (Don't cook any longer, it may not look burnt but it will be.)

6. Let the granola cool for about 10 minutes on the baking sheet.

7. Transfer to a flat surface and cut into bars and finish cooling on a wire rack. Enjoy either in bar form or crumble as granola pieces. Store in an airtight container, for up to 5 days.

Pepperoni Pizza Quesadillas

What happens when pizza meets a wheat-free tortilla?
You get Pizza Quesadillas that your whole family will love.

INGREDIENTS | SERVES 4

8 corn or brown rice flour tortillas

2 cups Easy Pizza Sauce (see recipe in this chapter), plus extra for dipping

8 ounces shredded mozzarella cheese

⅓ pound pepperoni

Sliced mushrooms, peppers, onions (optional)

1. Brush each tortilla with a thin layer of pizza sauce (so thin that if you turned it over, none would drip).

2. Sprinkle cheese on top of 4 tortillas. Top with pepperoni and other toppings, if desired. Sprinkle with another layer of cheese and place another tortilla on top (sauce side in).

3. Lay out tortilla and place it on a griddle or in a pan sprayed with cooking spray and cook for 3–5 minutes on each side, until cheese is melted and tortillas are crispy.

4. Slice into quarters and serve with a little bowl of pizza dipping sauce.

Easy Pizza Sauce

This delicious sauce will enhance the flavor of any type of pizza you make.
This also makes a wonderful dipping sauce for quesadillas, chicken tenders, or even French fries.

INGREDIENTS | MAKES 2¾ CUPS

1 teaspoon extra-virgin olive oil

1–2 cloves garlic, finely chopped

½ medium onion, finely chopped

1 (15-ounce) can tomato sauce

1 (6-ounce) can tomato paste

1 tablespoon ground oregano

1 teaspoon ground basil

½ teaspoon turbinado sugar

½ teaspoon salt

1. In a skillet over medium heat, place the oil, garlic, and onions. Simmer until they soften, about 2–3 minutes.

2. In a medium bowl, mix together tomato sauce and tomato paste until smooth. Stir in oregano, basil, sugar, and salt. Add the cooked garlic and onions. Makes sauce for about 4 (10") pizzas.

Fruit Kebabs with Yogurt Dipping Sauce

This is a really fun way to get the little ones to eat fruit. Be sure to cut the ends off the skewers for safety.

INGREDIENTS | MAKES 4–6 KEBABS

1 (16-ounce) container strawberries, sliced

1 kiwi, sliced

¼ cantaloupe, scooped out with melon baller

1 apple, cut into squares

¼ honeydew, scooped out with melon baler

Juice of ½ lemon

Yogurt Dipping Sauce (see recipe in this chapter)

1. Place sliced fruit in any order on skewers with ends cut off.

2. Sprinkle with fresh lemon juice to ensure the fruit stays fresh.

3. Serve with yogurt dipping sauce, or even melted chocolate or nut butter.

It's a Marshmallow World

Why not add some mini marshmallows to these fun kebabs? Marshmallows turn this delicious snack into a wonderful dessert.

Yogurt Dipping Sauce

The thickness of Greek yogurt and the sweetness of the honey make this a perfect dip for any fruit out there.

INGREDIENTS | MAKES 2 CUPS

2 cups vanilla Greek yogurt

½ cup honey

¼ teaspoon lemon juice

½ teaspoon cinnamon

Mix all the ingredients in a small bowl. Serve immediately or store, covered, in the refrigerator.

Why Greek Yogurt?

Greek yogurt adds significantly more protein than regular yogurt. The thick texture of Greek yogurt is perfect for any type of dipping sauce.

Corn Dog Muffins

The whole family will love these. These make a delicious kid-friendly meal or a simple appetizer.

INGREDIENTS | MAKES 24 MUFFINS OR 48 MINI MUFFINS

1 (16-ounce) package hot dogs (beef, turkey, chicken, or veggie)
1 cup all-purpose wheat-free flour
1 cup yellow cornmeal
¼ cup turbinado sugar
2 teaspoons wheat-free baking powder
½ teaspoon salt
1 cup milk or buttermilk
2 eggs
¼ teaspoon wheat-free vanilla extract
¼ cup butter, softened
¼ cup unsweetened applesauce

Additional Goodies

Feel free to add whatever extras you'd like to these corn muffins. Sweet peppers, jalepeño peppers, broccoli, onions, basil, cilantro, and shredded cheese all make wonderful additions.

1. Preheat the oven to 425°F. Spray muffin tins with nonstick cooking spray or line with muffin liners.

2. Cut hot dogs into ¼" pieces.

3. In a medium-sized bowl, mix together flour, cornmeal, sugar, baking powder, and salt.

4. Stir in milk, eggs, vanilla, butter, and applesauce, and mix until smooth.

5. Pour chopped hot dogs into corn bread batter. Stir well. Fill ¾ of each muffin tin with corn bread/hot dog batter.

6. Bake until muffins become light brown and center is thoroughly cooked, about 12–15 minutes. Cool for a few minutes before serving.

Sneaky Kiwi-Pineapple Smoothie

This smoothie is a terrific way to "sneak" vegetables into your kids' smoothie! If they are suspicious of the bright green color, tell them that it's the kiwi that turned the smoothie green.

INGREDIENTS | MAKES 2 SMOOTHIES

1 cup pineapple chunks, fresh or frozen

2 kiwis, peeled and chopped

½ banana

6 ounces plain Greek yogurt

½ cup pineapple juice

Ice (you can use less if you use frozen pineapple)

2 tablespoons chia or flax seed (optional)

1 cup spinach or kale (optional)

Place all the ingredients in a blender. Blend until smooth. Serve immediately.

Almond Delight Yogurt Dip

This dip is a favorite of kids and grown-ups alike.
This dip goes wonderfully with sliced apples, bananas, carrots, or celery.

INGREDIENTS | SERVES 4

4 tablespoons almond butter

16 ounces vanilla Greek yogurt

½ teaspoon cinnamon

1 tablespoon honey

½ teaspoon wheat-free vanilla extract

¼ cup wheat-free chocolate chips (optional)

1. Place all ingredients (except chocolate chips if you are adding them) in a medium-sized bowl and stir until well combined.

2. Serve with sliced fruits and vegetables immediately. Top with chocolate chips if desired.

Dippers

This dip is super easy and can be used with a wide variety of foods besides fruits and vegetables. You can also dip sliced pancakes, waffles, graham crackers, or even pretzels for a sweet/salty snack. Feel free to also substitute peanut, cashew, or sunflower seed butter for the almond butter. This is a great snack for kids' lunchboxes as well.

CHAPTER 10

Quinoa

Double Chocolate-Quinoa Muffins

Quinoa adds a wonderful texture and a good amount of protein to these delicious chocolate muffins.

INGREDIENTS | MAKES 12 MUFFINS

1¾ cups buckwheat flour

¼ cup unsweetened cocoa powder

½ cup fine sugar

1½ teaspoons wheat-free baking powder

1 teaspoon sea salt

1 teaspoon cinnamon

¼ cup grapeseed oil

1 large egg

1 cup reduced-fat buttermilk

1¼ teaspoons wheat-free vanilla extract

2 cups cooked quinoa, cooled

⅓ cup semisweet chocolate chips

¼ cup chopped almonds or whatever nuts you like

Boost the Antioxidant Power

Why not add some ground flax seed to increase your fiber and antioxidants? Simply add 2 tablespoons ground flax seeds to the second step and add omega-3 fatty acids, antioxidants, fiber, and protein.

1. Preheat the oven to 350°F. Line muffin tins with cupcake liners or spray with baking spray.

2. Combine all the dry (the first 6) ingredients in a bowl and mix with a wire whisk.

3. In a separate, larger bowl, combine the wet ingredients (including the chocolate chips and nuts) and mix thoroughly.

4. Carefully fold in the dry ingredients and mix just until they are combined.

5. Fill muffin tins ¾ full with batter. Bake for 25 minutes, or until cooked through by inserting toothpick in the center and it comes out clean. Let cool slightly before removing from the pan.

Quinoa "Mac and Cheese" in Tomato Bowls

These yummy broiled tomatoes make delicious little bowls for this tasty quinoa dish.

INGREDIENTS | SERVES 4

¼ cup uncooked quinoa, rinsed and drained

1 tablespoon grapeseed oil

2 tablespoons pine nuts

2 cloves garlic, minced

1 cup fresh spinach leaves

Juice of ½ fresh lemon

¼ cup grated cheese of your choice

4 organic beefsteak tomatoes, top 1" sliced off, pulp and seeds scooped out

Quinoa's Superpowers

Quinoa has been popular lately because it is so versatile and can be used in so many different ways. Quinoa is actually a seed that is loaded with magnesium, iron, and calcium. Quinoa is just like a grain, but it is the only one to have all nine essential amino acids, which also makes it the only one to be a complete protein. It is low calorie, has a lot of fiber and is also wheat- and gluten-free.

1. Bring a pot of lightly salted water to a boil over high heat. Add the quinoa, and cook until the quinoa is tender, 15–20 minutes. Drain in a mesh strainer, and rinse until cold; set aside.

2. Heat the grapeseed oil in a skillet over medium heat, stir in pine nuts, and cook until lightly toasted, about 2 minutes.

3. Stir in the garlic, and cook until the garlic softens, about 2 minutes. Stir in the quinoa and spinach; cook and stir until the quinoa is hot, and the spinach has wilted, about 3–4 minutes. Stir in the lemon juice and the cheese.

4. Meanwhile, place tomatoes in a baking dish and place sliced top back on top of the tomato. Place under preheated broiler for 5 minutes until they soften slightly but still remain intact.

5. Take tomatoes out and place the quinoa mixture inside the tomato, using them like bowls. The juices of the tomato will combine with the quinoa mixture and taste delicious.

Tricolor Quinoa Salad with Vegetables, Cranberries, and Almonds

This salad is perfect for cookouts or potlucks when you want to have something a little different than your typical pasta or potato salad. This is definitely a crowd-pleaser!

INGREDIENTS | SERVES 4

1 cup uncooked tricolor quinoa, rinsed well and drained

¾ teaspoon kosher salt, divided, plus more for seasoning

2 tablespoons extra-virgin olive oil, divided

½ cup shredded carrots

1 (8.5-ounce) can artichokes, rinsed, drained well and sliced

½ cup cherry tomatoes, sliced

1 cup baby spinach

2 tablespoons coarsely chopped toasted almonds

½ lemon

¼ teaspoon basil

¼ teaspoon ground cumin

¼ teaspoon sweet paprika

1 medium firm-ripe avocado, pitted, peeled, and cut into ½" chunks

1 medium scallion, white and light green parts only, thinly sliced

2 tablespoons cranberries

Freshly ground black pepper, to taste

1. In a 2-quart saucepan, bring 2 cups water, the quinoa, and ½ teaspoon salt to a boil over high heat. Cover, reduce the heat to medium low, and simmer until the water is absorbed and the quinoa is translucent and tender, about 10–15 minutes. Immediately fluff the quinoa with a fork, and allow it to cool to room temperature.

2. In a sauté pan, place 1 tablespoon of oil with the carrots, artichokes, tomatoes, and spinach. Sauté until the vegetables soften, about 3–4 minutes. Add sliced almonds, and stir for 1 minute, until well mixed. Remove from heat.

3. Finely grate the zest from the lemon and then squeeze 1 tablespoon juice. In a small bowl, whisk the lemon zest and juice with the remaining tablespoon of olive oil, basil, cumin, paprika, and remaining ¼ teaspoon salt.

4. In a large bowl, toss the lemon juice mixture with the quinoa, avocado, scallions, and cranberries.

5. Add the vegetable mixture, season to taste with salt and pepper, and serve.

Vegetarian Quinoa–Black Bean Cakes

*These are so light and tasty that they can be made with a green salad
for an entrée or even served as an appetizer.*

INGREDIENTS | MAKES 8 CAKES

3 tablespoons grapeseed oil (or extra-virgin olive oil), divided

½ cup finely chopped green bell pepper

3 cloves garlic, chopped

1 medium onion, finely chopped

½ cup finely chopped plum tomatoes

1 (15-ounce) can organic black beans, thoroughly rinsed and drained

2 cups quinoa, cooked in vegetable broth

1 tablespoon fresh cilantro leaves

½ teaspoon cumin

½ teaspoon red pepper flakes

Salt and pepper, to taste

1 egg white, beaten

1 cup wheat-free bread crumbs

Fresh cilantro and diced tomatoes, for garnish (optional)

1. Heat 2 tablespoons of grapeseed oil in skillet, add the green pepper and sauté until soft, about 3 minutes.

2. Add the garlic, onion, and tomatoes, and continue to sauté until soft, about 3–4 minutes.

3. Remove from heat, combine with black beans, quinoa, cilantro, cumin, and red pepper flakes. Allow to cool for a few minutes. Add salt and pepper to taste. Place in food processor and pulse until chunky but not completely smooth.

4. Add the beaten egg white and mix well. Form into patties, dredge in bread crumbs and place in heated skillet with remaining 1 tablespoon grapeseed oil. Sauté at least 5 minutes on each side. Garnish with fresh cilantro and diced tomatoes.

Quinoa-Avocado Salad

This dish makes a hearty meal in itself or can be made as a side dish for chicken or fish. It tastes best when it is prepared the night before. Just make sure to save a little extra dressing to toss right before serving.

INGREDIENTS | SERVES 8

1½ cups uncooked quinoa, rinsed and drained

3 cups water

2 (15-ounce) cans black beans, rinsed and drained

1 (14-ounce) box of frozen corn, defrosted

2 avocados, peeled and cut into ½" pieces

2 pints grape tomatoes, halved

Cilantro-Lime Vinaigrette (see recipe in this chapter)

1. Cook the quinoa with the water according to package directions. Let cool to room temperature.

2. In a medium bowl, combine the beans, corn, avocado, and tomatoes. Toss with cooled quinoa.

3. Pour Cilantro-Lime Vinaigrette over the salad. Refrigerate for several hours or even overnight.

Cilantro-Lime Vinaigrette

This dressing is so wonderful you will want to make more of it and keep it in your refrigerator. It's perfect for all kinds of salads or even as a marinade.

INGREDIENTS | MAKES 8–10 SERVINGS

1 clove garlic, minced

¼ cup grapeseed oil

¾ teaspoon minced fresh gingerroot

¼ cup fresh lime juice

Zest of 1 lime

2 teaspoons balsamic vinegar

¼ cup fresh packed cilantro leaves

Salt, to taste

Mix all ingredients together in a small bowl. Refrigerate until ready to serve. Store in an airtight container in the refrigerator for several days.

Cilantro, Love It or Hate It?

If you are among those that do not like cilantro, you are not alone. Feel free to substitute Italian parsley, mint, basil, or any other herb for cilantro in a recipe.

Easy Breakfast Quinoa

Move over oatmeal, breakfast just got a little healthier!
Quinoa has more protein and fiber than oatmeal and other hot breakfast options.

INGREDIENTS | SERVES 2

½ cup uncooked quinoa
1 cup milk of choice
1 tablespoon chopped walnuts
1 teaspoon cinnamon
1 tablespoon almond butter
¼ cup fresh blueberries

Variations

This recipe has so many options. You can use different kinds of milks, nuts, fruits, or nut butters to get creative with. To save time on busy mornings, keep cooked quinoa in the refrigerator. Simply reheat quinoa with desired toppings and enjoy.

1. Place the quinoa in a fine mesh strainer. Rinse and drain quinoa. Combine quinoa and milk in a medium saucepan. Bring to a boil. Cover and reduce heat to a gentle simmer. Cook 10–15 minutes until the milk is absorbed and the quinoa is tender.

2. Add walnuts, cinnamon, and almond butter. Mix thoroughly. Let cool. Add fresh blueberries on top.

Balsamic Quinoa Salad with Sweet Peppers and Feta Cheese

This really should be prepared the night before because the quinoa soaks up the dressing wonderfully.

INGREDIENTS | SERVES 8

1½ cups uncooked quinoa, rinsed and drained
1 (15-ounce) can chickpeas, thoroughly rinsed and drained
1 yellow pepper, chopped
1 red pepper, chopped
½ medium red onion, minced
½ large cucumber, chopped
1 (6-ounce) container crumbled feta cheese

1. Cook the quinoa according to instructions on the box. Place in large bowl when it is completely cooked.

2. Add the chickpeas, peppers, onion, cucumber, and feta to the quinoa as it is cooling off and mix well.

3. Add Chia-Balsamic Vinaigrette from Chapter 8 and mix to combine. Chill for several hours, or overnight, before serving.

Quinoa Granola with Dried Cranberries

This granola is the perfect breakfast, snack, or dessert.

INGREDIENTS | SERVES 8

1 cup wheat-free whole rolled oats

1 cup buckwheat groats

⅓ cup uncooked quinoa, rinsed and drained

2 tablespoons ground chia seeds

¾ cup raw chopped pecans

¼ cup raw pumpkin seeds

¼ cup raw sunflower seeds

¼ cup raw chopped walnuts

½ cup shredded coconut, unsweetened

2 teaspoons cinnamon

1 teaspoon ground ginger

1 teaspoon allspice

½ cup real maple syrup

1 tablespoon wheat-free vanilla extract

¼ cup organic coconut oil, melted

⅓ cup chopped dates

⅓ cup dried cranberries, unsweetened

1. Preheat the oven to 225°F.

2. In a large bowl, combine the dry ingredients (first 4 ingredients). Add the nuts, seeds, and coconut. Mix well.

3. Stir to combine thoroughly while adding in the cinnamon, ginger, and allspice.

4. Mix in maple syrup, vanilla, melted coconut oil, dates, and cranberries. Make sure everything is evenly distributed and coated well.

5. Spoon and press mixture onto baking sheet lined with waxed paper or parchment paper. Bake for 60 minutes.

6. Let cool after removing from oven, then pull corners of waxed paper together to crumble granola. Store in airtight container when cooled for up to 3 days.

Asiago Quinoa with Portobello Mushrooms

This dish can be kept vegetarian, or you can also include diced shrimp or chicken to add some protein. In addition, you can throw in whatever fresh vegetables you have on hand to add some color.

INGREDIENTS | SERVES 6

2 tablespoons extra-virgin olive oil, divided

1 shallot, chopped

2 cloves garlic, minced

1 cup sliced portobello mushrooms, wiped clean, stems removed

1 teaspoon thyme

1 teaspoon oregano

1½ cups uncooked quinoa, rinsed and drained

2½ cups vegetable broth

2 tablespoons fresh basil, torn

⅓ cup Asiago cheese, grated

1. Heat 1 tablespoon of oil in a large skillet. Add the shallot, garlic, and mushrooms. Top with the thyme and oregano and cook until browned, about 5 minutes. Set aside.

2. Heat the remaining tablespoon of oil in a pot over medium-high heat. Add quinoa and let it brown, about 2–3 minutes. Pour in the vegetable broth and bring it to a boil. Cover and reduce heat to low. Simmer for 15–20 minutes, until all the liquid is absorbed.

3. Stir in mushroom mixture and top with basil and cheese.

Are Shallots the Same as Green Onions?

No, they are not. Shallots are often confused for green onions or scallions. They are, however, members of the onion family but have their own mild taste. Shallots look like small onions, which when peeled, have divided cloves like garlic. When a recipe calls for 1 shallot, they generally mean the entire shallot, not just one clove.

Quinoa Pilaf with Lentils and Spinach

This dish is loaded with protein; it makes the perfect vegetarian dish.

Watch the Dates on Your Lentils

Try not to mix older lentils with fresh ones. Older lentils may take longer to cook than the newer ones because they have lost moisture. This will leave the fresh lentils overcooked and mushy.

1. Place butter in large skillet over medium heat. Add onion and garlic and cook 3–4 minutes, until onion is translucent.

2. Add rinsed quinoa and let sit for 1 minute until brown. Add broth and bring to a boil. Reduce heat, cover, and let simmer on low heat until all broth is absorbed, about 15–20 minutes.

3. While quinoa is cooking, place dried lentils and olive oil in a small skillet. Add water, carrots, oregano, and basil. Bring water to slight boil over medium-high heat, then reduce heat to low. Cook lentils for 20–30 minutes, until tender.

4. When quinoa is finished cooking, stir in baby spinach. Add salt and pepper.

5. Combine lentil mixture and quinoa together. Garnish with toasted almonds if desired.

Quinoa Pudding with Fresh Raspberries

Who said you can't make pudding a little healthier? This tastes similar to tapioca pudding, with a slightly nutty taste and thicker texture.

INGREDIENTS | SERVES 4–6

2 cups uncooked quinoa

2 cups reduced-fat milk (the more fat in the milk, the creamier the consistency)

½ cup half-and-half

3 tablespoons sugar

2 tablespoons maple syrup

1½ teaspoons cinnamon, divided

2 teaspoons wheat-free vanilla extract

Fresh raspberries, to top pudding

Why Do You Have to Rinse Quinoa Before Cooking?

Rinsing quinoa is important for its outer coating, called saponin. Saponin has a bitter taste and can be unpleasant after it's cooked. You can also soak the quinoa if you'd like, but usually rinsing it for a minute or two does the trick.

1. Place the quinoa in a fine mesh sieve and rinse under cold water for 1 minute.

2. In a large saucepan, whisk together the milk, half-and-half, sugar, maple syrup, 1 teaspoon of the cinnamon, and vanilla extract. Bring to a simmer over medium heat. Cook for 25 minutes, stirring occasionally, until creamy.

3. Add quinoa and remaining ½ teaspoon cinnamon. Turn heat down to low and allow to simmer for 20 minutes, or until desired consistency is reached. Stir every few minutes to prevent a film from forming on the top of the pudding or on bottom of the pan.

4. Serve chilled, topped with raspberries (or fruit of your choice).

Black Bean–Quinoa Chili

This comforting dish can be made in a slow cooker or on the stove in a Dutch oven. This also freezes well.

INGREDIENTS | SERVES 10

1 cup uncooked red quinoa, rinsed and drained

2 cups vegetable broth

1 tablespoon canola oil

1 green onion, chopped

5 cloves garlic, chopped

1 tablespoon chili powder

1 tablespoon cumin

1 teaspoon coriander

2 cups plum tomatoes, diced

2 (14.5-ounce) cans black beans, rinsed and drained

1 green bell pepper, chopped

1 jalepeño pepper, seeded and chopped (optional)

1 tablespoon dried chipotle pepper

1 zucchini, chopped

1 teaspoon dried oregano

½ teaspoon dried cinnamon

Salt and ground black pepper, to taste

1 cup frozen corn

1 cup portobello mushrooms, chopped

¼ cup fresh cilantro, chopped

Sliced avocado, plain Greek yogurt, and shredded Cheddar cheese, for topping

1. Place quinoa and broth in a saucepan over high heat and bring to a boil. Cover, reduce heat to medium-low and let simmer for 15–20 minutes, until all the broth is absorbed. Set aside.

2. Heat oil in a large skillet. Add the onion and garlic, and sauté for 3–4 minutes, until soft. Add the chili powder, cumin, and coriander. Stir to combine.

3. Add the tomatoes, beans, peppers, zucchini, oregano, and cinnamon. Mix well and season with salt and pepper. Bring to a boil over high heat, reduce to low heat, cover and let simmer for 20 minutes.

4. After 20 minutes, add the quinoa, corn, and mushrooms, and cook for an additional 5 minutes to soften corn and mushrooms. Remove from heat.

5. Top with sliced avocado, a dollop of plain Greek yogurt, cilantro, and shredded cheese.

Slow Cook It!

This dish can be made easily in the slow cooker. Sauté onion and garlic in a skillet for 3–4 minutes, until soft. Add chili powder, cumin and coriander and mix thoroughly. Add all the other ingredients except the corn and mushrooms. Cook on low for 5–6 hours. Add corn and mushrooms in the last hour and garnish with toppings.

Quinoa Meat Loaf

You won't miss the bread crumbs in this recipe.
Quinoa adds protein and texture to your typical meat loaf.

INGREDIENTS | SERVES 6

¼ cup uncooked quinoa, rinsed and drained

½ cup chicken broth

1 teaspoon extra-virgin olive oil

1 small onion, chopped

2–3 cloves garlic, chopped

1 (20-ounce) package ground chicken (or turkey or lean ground beef)

1 tablespoon tomato paste

2 teaspoons wheat-free Worcestershire sauce

1 egg and 1 egg white

½ teaspoon salt

1 teaspoon ground black pepper

1 teaspoon ground rosemary

1 teaspoon ground basil

¾ teaspoon red pepper flakes

2 tablespoons Parmesan cheese, grated

1. Bring the quinoa and broth to a boil in a saucepan over high heat. Reduce heat to medium-low, cover, and simmer until the quinoa is tender and the broth has been absorbed, about 15–20 minutes. Set aside to cool.

2. Preheat the oven to 350°F.

3. Heat the olive oil in a skillet over medium heat. Add in the onion; cook and stir until the onion has softened and turned translucent, about 5 minutes. Add the garlic and cook for another minute; remove from heat to cool.

4. In a large bowl add the chicken, cooked quinoa, onions, garlic, tomato paste, Worcestershire sauce, egg and egg white, salt, pepper, seasonings, and Parmesan cheese. Mix until well combined. The mixture will be very moist. Shape into a loaf on a foil-lined baking sheet.

5. Bake until no longer pink in the center, 50–60 minutes. An instant-read thermometer inserted into the center should read at least 160°F. Let the meat loaf cool for 10 minutes before slicing and serving.

Quinoa Meatballs with Creamy Pesto Dipping Sauce

These meatballs make the perfect appetizer or main dish.
Serve with zucchini noodles or wheat-free pasta.

INGREDIENTS | SERVES 6

¼ cup uncooked quinoa, rinsed and drained

½ cup chicken broth

1 teaspoon extra-virgin olive oil

1 small onion, chopped

2–3 cloves garlic, chopped

1 (20-ounce) package ground chicken (or turkey or lean ground beef)

1 tablespoon tomato paste

2 teaspoons wheat-free Worcestershire sauce

1 egg and 1 egg white

1 teaspoon ground rosemary

1 teaspoon ground basil

¾ teaspoon red pepper flakes

2 tablespoons Parmesan cheese, grated

½ teaspoons salt

1 teaspoon ground black pepper

Creamy Pesto Dipping Sauce (see recipe in this chapter)

1. Preheat the oven to 350°F.

2. Bring the quinoa and broth to a boil in a saucepan over high heat. Reduce heat to medium-low, cover, and simmer until the quinoa is tender and the broth has been absorbed, about 15–20 minutes. Set aside to cool.

3. Heat the olive oil in a skillet over medium heat. Stir in the onion; cook and stir until the onion has softened and turned translucent, about 5 minutes. Add the garlic and cook for another minute; remove from heat to cool.

4. In a large bowl, combine the chicken, cooked quinoa, onions, garlic, tomato paste, Worcestershire sauce, egg and egg white, seasonings, Parmesan cheese, salt, and pepper. Mix until well combined. The mixture will be very moist.

5. Roll into 1½" balls. Place on a baking sheet lined with parchment paper.

6. Bake until no longer pink in the center, 20–25 minutes. Serve with pesto dipping sauce.

Creamy Pesto Dipping Sauce

This sauce is perfect for dipping chicken or other meat in, or use on top of wheat-free pasta.

INGREDIENTS | SERVES 10–12

½ cup extra-virgin olive oil

3 garlic cloves

1½ ounces pine nuts

2 ounces Parmesan cheese

2 ounces fresh basil leaves, torn

½ cup half-and-half

1. Add all the ingredients to food processor or high-powered blender in the order listed.

2. Blend for 2–3 minutes, until smooth. Serve immediately, or store in the refrigerator until ready to serve.

Pepperoni Pizza Quinoa Cups

These make fun appetizers or a great entrée. The whole family will love these.
They also freeze really well, so feel free to double this recipe and put half in the freezer.

INGREDIENTS | MAKES 12 QUINOA CUPS

1 cup cooked quinoa

3 cloves garlic, minced

½ cup pepperoni, diced

1 medium onion, finely chopped

1 cup shredded mozzarella cheese

¼ cup finely minced mushrooms

1 teaspoon oregano, dried

1 teaspoon basil, dried

½ teaspoon paprika, dried

½ teaspoon rosemary, dried

½ teaspoon fennel seed

2 large eggs

½ cup grape tomatoes, diced

1 teaspoon tomato paste

Easy Pizza Sauce, for dipping (see Chapter 9)

1. Preheat oven to 350°F. Spray a muffin tray with nonstick cooking spray.

2. Place all the ingredients except pizza sauce in a medium-sized mixing bowl. Stir thoroughly to combine.

3. Pour the quinoa mixture into muffin tins. Bake for 15–20 minutes, until cheese is melted.

4. Let stand for 5–10 minutes to cool before serving. Serve with Easy Pizza Sauce for dipping.

Autumn Root Vegetables and Quinoa

*This really does taste better the next day. Don't be alarmed
if your quinoa turns pink because of the beets!*

INGREDIENTS | SERVES 4–6

2 medium sweet potatoes, peeled and diced

2 medium red potatoes, peeled and diced

3 small beets, peeled and chopped

3 large carrots, peeled and chopped

½ medium red onion, chopped

4 garlic cloves, chopped

Juice of ½ lemon

1 teaspoon basil, dried

1 teaspoon parsley, dried

½ teaspoon thyme, dried

2 tablespoons extra-virgin olive oil

2 cups chicken broth

1 cup uncooked quinoa, rinsed and drained

1 cup chickpeas, rinsed and drained (optional)

Salt and pepper, to taste

1. Preheat the oven to 375°F.

2. Place chopped vegetables, lemon juice, seasonings, and olive oil in sealable plastic bag. Close the bag and shake vigorously to make sure the vegetables are evenly coated.

3. Spread the vegetables on a baking sheet evenly, making sure they are in one layer. Roast in the oven for 40 minutes, stirring occasionally.

4. Place broth in a small saucepan and bring to a boil. Add quinoa and cover and reduce heat to low. Cook for 15–20 minutes until all broth is absorbed. Fluff with a fork when done.

5. Mix roasted vegetables with quinoa mixture. Add chickpeas if desired. Season with salt and pepper if desired. Serve warm or cold.

Quinoa, Kale, and Roasted Tomato Salad with Feta Cheese

The roasted tomatoes bring out a magnificent flavor in this salad.
The feta melts wonderfully when placed over the warm vegetables and quinoa.

INGREDIENTS | SERVES 4

1 pint grape or cherry tomatoes, halved

1 tablespoon honey

4 sprigs of fresh thyme, chopped and stems removed

1 tablespoon extra-virgin olive oil

Salt and pepper, to taste

2 cups vegetable broth

1 cup uncooked quinoa, rinsed and drained

4 cups kale, stems removed and chopped

½ cup feta cheese, crumbled

2 tablespoons fresh parsley, chopped, for garnish (optional)

1. Preheat the oven to 350°F.

2. In a large resealable bag, place the tomatoes, honey, thyme, olive oil, salt, and pepper. Seal the bag and shake to combine.

3. Place tomato mixture on a baking sheet lined with parchment paper and roast for 1 hour, until the tomatoes become wrinkled and shriveled.

4. While the tomatoes are roasting, place vegetable broth and quinoa in a saucepan and bring to a boil. Cover, reduce heat to low, and continue to cook 15–20 minutes, until all the broth is absorbed. Fluff with a fork.

5. Immediately add the roasted tomatoes, kale, and feta cheese to the hot quinoa. The kale will soften and the feta will melt. Garnish with fresh parsley.

Spicy Quinoa Bean Burgers

*Even meat lovers will love these burgers! The patties can be made
ahead of time and then refrigerated until ready to cook.*

INGREDIENTS | MAKES 6 BURGERS

½ cup uncooked quinoa, rinsed and drained

1 cup vegetable broth

1 (15-ounce) can black beans, rinsed and drained

1 (15-ounce) can red kidney beans, rinsed and drained

1 cup baby spinach

¾ cup cornmeal or wheat-free bread crumbs

¼ cup red bell pepper, chopped

¼ cup frozen corn, defrosted

¼ cup mushrooms, finely diced

1 shallot, minced

1 clove garlic, minced

1 teaspoon chili powder

½ teaspoon red pepper flakes

1 teaspoon cumin

1 teaspoon paprika

1 teaspoon fresh cilantro, chopped

1 teaspoon wheat-free hot sauce

1 egg

Juice of ½ fresh lime

Fresh avocado slices and tomato slices, for topping

1. Preheat the oven to 375°F.

2. Place the quinoa and broth in a small saucepan and bring to a boil. Cover, reduce heat to low, and simmer for 15–20 minutes, until all the broth is absorbed.

3. Place the beans and spinach in blender or food processor and process for 1 minute, allowing some pieces of whole beans to remain.

4. Place the quinoa in a medium-sized bowl. Add the beans/spinach mixture, cornmeal, bell pepper, corn, mushrooms, shallot, garlic, seasonings, cilantro, hot sauce, egg, and fresh lime juice. Thoroughly mix with your hands to combine. If you have time, sit bowl in the refrigerator for a few minutes. This allows for easier forming of the patties.

5. Form the quinoa/bean mixture into 6 patties. Line baking sheet with aluminum foil and place patties on top. Bake for 30 minutes, making sure to turn them over after first 15 minutes.

6. Serve on top of rice or sautéed spinach and top with avocado and tomato slices. You can also eat these burgers with a wheat-free bun, in a wheat-free wrap or wrap each one in a giant lettuce leaf.

No Wheat-Free Bread Crumbs in the House?

Ground rolled oats are a wonderful substitution for wheat-free bread crumbs. Just make sure you read your labels to guarantee your rolled oats are wheat-free!

Greek Quinoa Salad

This is a wonderful recreation of a classic Greek salad.

INGREDIENTS | SERVES 4–6

2 cups low-sodium chicken broth

1 cup uncooked quinoa, rinsed and drained

½ cup grape or cherry tomatoes, halved

½ cup chopped red or yellow sweet bell pepper

¼ cup chopped cucumber

2 teaspoons chopped pitted kalamata olives

1 tablespoon extra-virgin olive oil

½ teaspoon lemon zest

1 teaspoon fresh lemon juice

1 teaspoon red vinegar

½ teaspoon basil, ground

½ teaspoon oregano

1 tablespoon garlic, minced

¼ cup crumbled feta cheese

1. Heat the broth in a medium saucepan until it comes to a boil. Add quinoa and cover. Cook for 15–20 minutes, until all broth is absorbed. Remove from heat. Fluff with a fork.

2. Place the tomatoes, pepper, cucumber, and olives in large bowl. Set aside.

3. In a small bowl, combine the olive oil, lemon zest, lemon juice, vinegar, basil, oregano, and garlic. Mix thoroughly.

4. Add the quinoa to the vegetables and cover with the dressing. Top with feta cheese; stir to combine.

Spicy Black Quinoa, Sausage, and Goat Cheese

This recipe may be called spicy, but you can always adjust the spices and seasonings according to your taste. You can also use sweet sausage if chorizo is too spicy. Black quinoa makes a lovely presentation too.

INGREDIENTS | SERVES 4

2 cups chicken broth

1 cup uncooked black quinoa, rinsed, and drained

1 tablespoon extra-virgin olive oil

½ green onion, diced

2 cloves garlic, minced

2 links Mexican chorizo

1 red or yellow pepper, seeded and chopped

1 green pepper, seeded and chopped

½ cup grape or cherry tomatoes, halved

¼ teaspoon cumin

⅛ teaspoon red pepper flakes

¼ cup crumbled goat cheese

Salt and pepper, to taste

1. Place the chicken broth into a medium saucepan and bring to a boil over high heat. Add quinoa and cover. Reduce heat and let simmer 15–20 minutes, until all liquid is absorbed. Remove from heat. Fluff with a fork and place into a large bowl.

2. While the quinoa cooks, place the oil in a large skillet along with onion and garlic. Cook over medium heat for 3–4 minutes, until they soften.

3. Add the chorizo and cook until browned and no longer pink inside, about 8–10 minutes. Remove from the skillet and cut into ½"-thick rounds. Place chorizo in the bowl with the quinoa.

4. In the same skillet, add the peppers, tomatoes, cumin, and red pepper flakes. Stir well and cook over medium heat for about 5 minutes, until vegetables soften.

5. Add the cooked vegetables to the bowl with the quinoa and chorizo. Top with goat cheese and stir to combine. Add salt and pepper to taste if desired.

Mushroom and Squash Quinoa Risotto

This dish has a unique twist on traditional risotto made with rice.
This can be left vegetarian or would also taste wonderful with sliced sweet sausage added to it.

INGREDIENTS | SERVES 4–6

1 cup uncooked quinoa, rinsed and drained

1½ cups vegetable broth (can also use chicken broth)

1 tablespoon butter

2 cloves garlic, minced

½ onion, minced

2 cups diced butternut squash

2 cups sliced mushrooms

1 tablespoon dried oregano

½ teaspoon dried marjoram

½ teaspoon dried sage

½ teaspoon cinnamon

½ cup dry white wine

¼ cup grated Parmesan cheese

1. Place quinoa and broth into a pot. Bring to a boil over medium heat. Cover and reduce heat to low. Simmer for 15–20 minutes until all liquid is absorbed.

2. Meanwhile while quinoa is cooking, place the butter, garlic, and onions into large skillet. Cook over medium heat 3–4 minutes until onions are translucent.

3. Add squash and let cook for 10 minutes or until squash softens.

4. Add mushrooms and seasonings; stir to combine.

5. Pour in the white wine and mix. Let cook for a few minutes until all the wine is absorbed. Add cooked quinoa to skillet and thoroughly combine.

6. Top with grated cheese and serve immediately.

CHAPTER 11

Pasta Dishes and Sauces

Asparagus, Mushrooms, and Yellow Tomatoes with Brown Rice Pasta

Fresh vegetables work best in this dish. This dish is packed with flavor and full of color.

INGREDIENTS | SERVES 6

1 (16-ounce) package brown rice pasta
1 tablespoon extra-virgin olive oil
2 cloves garlic, chopped
1 pound fresh asparagus, cut in half
1 pint yellow tomatoes, sliced in half
1 organic yellow pepper, sliced in strips
1 organic orange pepper, sliced in strips
1 cup mushrooms, sliced
½ cup vegetable broth (or broth of your choice)
1 tablespoon fresh Parmesan cheese, grated
Salt and pepper, to taste

1. Prepare the brown rice pasta according to the instructions on the package. This pasta should be prepared al dente. Rinse thoroughly with cool water to stop the cooking process and drain.

2. Place the oil, garlic, and vegetables in a skillet and sauté for 3–4 minutes, until they soften. Add vegetable broth and stir until well blended. Let cook for another 2–3 minutes, until the vegetables are tender.

3. Place the vegetables on top of the brown rice pasta and top with freshly shaved Parmesan cheese. Season with salt and pepper to taste if desired.

Brown Rice Pasta

Make sure you cook your brown rice pasta according to the instructions. If it is over-cooked, it becomes mushy and hardly palatable. If it is undercooked, it becomes chewy. It may take a few times to get the perfect, al dente brown rice pasta.

Sun-Dried Tomato–Artichoke Pasta with White Beans

Although this dish is vegetarian, cooked chicken or sausage would be a nice addition.

INGREDIENTS | SERVES 6

1 tablespoon grapeseed oil

3 cloves garlic, finely chopped

1 cup sun-dried tomatoes, sliced

2 cups chopped mushrooms

1 (9-ounce) box frozen artichoke hearts, rinsed and drained

1 (15-ounce) can small white beans, rinsed thoroughly and drained

2 cups vegetable broth

3 cups arugula

1 (16-ounce) package brown rice pasta

2 tablespoons fresh shaved Parmesan cheese (optional)

1. Place the oil and garlic in large skillet and let simmer for 1–2 minutes, until the garlic softens.

2. Add the sun-dried tomatoes, mushrooms, artichoke hearts, and beans, and let simmer for 3–4 minutes, until they soften.

3. Add broth and let simmer for 3–4 minutes. Add arugula, mix well and remove from heat. You do not want the arugula to get too soft.

4. Cook the brown rice pasta according to instructions. Rinse pasta with cool water and drain.

5. Mix pasta with broth and veggie mixture. Top with shaved Parmesan if desired.

Corn Pasta in Rich Cream Sauce with Prosciutto, Gorgonzola, and Walnuts

This is a delicious variation on the basic cream sauce.
Feel free to lighten this up using half-and-half instead of the cream.

INGREDIENTS | MAKES 2½ CUPS

1 (10-ounce) package corn pasta

3 tablespoons unsalted butter

3 tablespoons corn flour

2 cups medium cream, warmed

2 tablespoons minced prosciutto

½ cup crumbled Gorgonzola or blue cheese

¼ teaspoon ground nutmeg

½ cup walnut pieces, toasted

Salt and pepper, to taste

1. Cook corn pasta according to instructions on the package.

2. Melt the butter in a large skillet and stir in the flour. Sauté, stirring for 4–5 minutes over medium-low heat. Add the warm cream, whisking constantly until thickened to desired consistency.

3. Remove from the heat and stir in the prosciutto, cheese, nutmeg, walnuts, and salt and pepper. Toss with pasta. Serve immediately.

Rich Cream Sauces Are Versatile

You can add herbs, stock, or even bacon to a rich cream sauce. You can add cheese such as mascarpone or some prosciutto. Mushrooms add body and flavor too! You can adapt a cream sauce to loads of fish, meat, and vegetable dishes and benefit from the lush flavors.

Carbonara Sauce

*This is not for someone on a diet; however, it's very delicious and easy to make.
You can lighten this up by using half-and-half instead of heavy cream and cut the cheese to ¼ cup.*

INGREDIENTS | MAKES 1½ CUPS

4 strips bacon

4 shallots, minced

2 teaspoons coarsely ground black pepper

1 cup heavy cream

2 eggs, beaten

½ cup grated Parmesan cheese

¼ cup chopped fresh parsley

1 tablespoon fresh rosemary or 1 teaspoon dried, crumbled

1 teaspoon cracked black peppercorns, or to taste

Carbonara Fan

The origins of carbonara are found in Italy, but whether it comes from Rome or the Lazio region is uncertain. Food writer Calvin Trillin, author of *The Tummy Trilogy*, is such a fan of carbonara sauce that he suggested it replace turkey as the American holiday dish on Thanksgiving Day.

1. Cook the bacon over low heat until it is fried crisp, then remove it to paper towels to drain. Let it cool and crumble it. Reserve the fat.

2. Sauté the shallots in the bacon fat. Add the black pepper and cream. Bring to a boil and cook over medium-low heat until thick, about 4–5 minutes.

3. In a medium bowl, mix the eggs and cheese. Whisk in a tablespoon of sauce. Continue to add sauce slowly, whisking constantly. Add the parsley, crumbled rosemary, crumbled bacon, and peppercorns.

4. Pour over rice noodles, quinoa pasta, or spaghetti squash. (You probably won't need salt because there's salt in the bacon.)

Rice Pasta in Spicy Spinach and Lobster Sauce

Rice pasta is found in Asian markets and some specialty supermarkets.

INGREDIENTS | SERVES 4

1 (16-ounce) package rice pasta

1 (1½-pound) lobster

2 tablespoons butter

2 tablespoons cornstarch

1 cup chicken or clam broth, heated

1 cup heavy cream

3 cups fresh baby spinach, rinsed and stems trimmed

1 tablespoon dry sherry

Pinch ground nutmeg

1 teaspoon hot red pepper flakes or cayenne pepper

Salt and pepper, to taste

1. Cook rice pasta according to instructions.

2. Plunge the lobster into plenty of boiling salted water. Cook for 15 minutes. Cool; crack the shell and remove the meat. Set the meat aside.

3. In a large saucepan, melt the butter and add the cornstarch, stirring until smooth. Whisk in the broth. Add the cream and heat.

4. Stir in the spinach and cook until wilted. Add the sherry, nutmeg, red pepper flakes, and reserved lobster. Sprinkle with salt and pepper. Serve over the rice pasta.

Zucchini Pasta with Parmesan and Spicy Marinara Sauce

This is such a fun substitution for regular noodles or pasta.
This dish is also a perfect way to get more vegetables into your diet.

INGREDIENTS | SERVES 4

4 large zucchini

1 tablespoon grapeseed oil

2–3 cloves garlic, minced

Salt and black pepper, to taste

3 tablespoons Parmesan cheese, grated

Spicy Marinara Sauce (see recipe in this chapter)

1. Cut the zucchini into thin, noodle-like strips using a peeler or mandoline.

2. Heat the oil in a large skillet over medium-high heat. Add zucchini and garlic; cook and stir until just tender, about 5 minutes. Season to taste with salt and pepper.

3. Sprinkle with Parmesan cheese. Top with Spicy Marinara Sauce.

Spicy Marinara Sauce

This sauce is perfect for many various dishes. You can adjust the spiciness by increasing or decreasing the red pepper flakes.

INGREDIENTS | SERVES 10

3 tablespoons extra-virgin olive oil

1 medium onion, finely chopped

6 garlic cloves, minced

1 teaspoon oregano, dried

1 teaspoon parsley, dried

¾ teaspoon rosemary, dried

1 cup fresh basil leaves, torn

¾ teaspoon marjoram

½ teaspoon crushed red pepper flakes

2 (28-ounce) cans crushed tomatoes

1 red bell pepper, seeded and finely chopped

½ cup dry white wine

Salt and pepper, to taste

1. Heat the olive oil in a large pan. Add onion, garlic, and spices. Cover and cook for 10 minutes.

2. Add all other ingredients and simmer gently for 75 minutes.

Spaghetti Squash with Creamy Vodka and Shrimp Sauce

The squash can be prepared a day in advance. Spaghetti squash is extremely versatile and tastes wonderful in many sauces, from a tomato-filled marinara to a meaty Bolognese.

INGREDIENTS | SERVES 6

1 large (4–5 pounds) spaghetti squash, cooked

2 minced shallots

1 clove garlic, minced

2 tablespoons extra-virgin olive oil

1 tablespoon butter

1 tablespoon cornstarch

½ cup vodka

1 (28-ounce) can crushed tomatoes

1 cup heavy cream

1½ pounds shrimp, peeled and deveined

Salt and plenty of freshly ground pepper, to taste

½ cup each chopped fresh parsley and basil

¼ cup prosciutto, minced, for garnish

1. Place the cooked squash in a large bowl and keep warm while you make the sauce.

2. Sauté the minced shallots and garlic in a mixture of oil and butter in a large skillet for 2–3 minutes. When soft, add the cornstarch. Cook and stir over low heat until well blended, for 3–4 minutes.

3. Add the vodka and tomatoes. Cover and simmer gently for 20 minutes.

4. Stir in the cream and heat slowly, then add the shrimp. Do not boil after the cream has been added. When the shrimp turns pink, about 2–3 minutes, pour over the spaghetti squash, and add salt and pepper to taste. Garnish with parsley, basil, and prosciutto.

Greek Eggplant and Olive Sauce

Here you have many of the flavors of Greece without the travel.
Touches of garlic and mint do not overwhelm. Goes great over wheat-free pasta or rice.

INGREDIENTS | SERVES 4

2 tablespoons flax meal

½ cup rice flour mixed with 1 teaspoon salt

1 medium eggplant, peeled and cubed

⅓ cup extra-virgin olive oil

2 cloves garlic, minced

½ cup kalamata or other black, Greek olives, pitted and chopped

10 mint leaves, coarsely chopped

½ cup finely snipped chives

Juice of ½ lemon

Extra olive oil if sauce seems dry

1. Mix the ground flax with the flour and salt. Dredge the eggplant cubes in flour mixture.

2. In a saucepan, heat the olive oil over medium-high heat. Sauté the eggplant until brown.

3. When brown, lower heat and add the garlic; sauté for another 3 minutes.

4. Add the rest of the ingredients and serve.

Confetti and Rice Pasta with Chicken

This is fun to eat and pretty to look at. The "confetti" is minced vegetables.
Lots of Parmesan cheese completes the dish.

INGREDIENTS | SERVES 4

½ cup extra-virgin olive oil

½ cup finely chopped sweet red pepper

½ cup finely chopped yellow summer squash

½ cup zucchini squash, finely chopped

1 bunch scallions, finely chopped

2 cloves garlic, finely chopped

½ cup rice or corn flour

1 teaspoon salt

½ teaspoon pepper, or to taste

½ teaspoon dried thyme

¾ pound boneless, skinless chicken breast, cut into bite-sized pieces

½ cup chicken broth

8 ripe plum (Roma) tomatoes, chopped, or 1½ cups canned

1 teaspoon dried oregano

1 teaspoon dried basil

1 tablespoon red pepper flakes, or to taste

1 pound rice pasta, cooked

1 cup freshly grated Parmesan cheese

1. In a large skillet over medium heat, heat the olive oil and add the pepper, squash, scallions, and garlic. Sauté, stirring frequently, for 3–4 minutes.

2. While the vegetables are sautéing, mix the flour, salt, pepper, and thyme on a piece of waxed paper.

3. Dredge the chicken in the flour mixture and add to the pan along with the vegetables.

4. Add the broth, tomatoes, oregano, basil, and plenty of red pepper flakes. Cook, uncovered, for 10 minutes to make sure the chicken is done.

5. Add the rice pasta to the pan of sauce and mix. Sprinkle with plenty of Parmesan cheese and serve.

Rice Pasta

Rice pasta is available online and at Asian markets. Many supermarkets also carry it. Soba—Japanese noodles—have both buckwheat flour and wheat flour in them and sometimes the contents are listed in Japanese characters.

Creamy Mushroom and Cognac Sauce

This goes great over wheat-free pasta, polenta, or rice.
Add an extra 1½ cups of broth to the recipe to turn it into soup.

INGREDIENTS | SERVES 4

½ cup cognac

1 (4-ounce) package dried porcini or Asian black mushrooms

3 tablespoons unsalted butter

3 tablespoons chestnut flour

4 shallots, minced

10 ounces button mushrooms, bases of stems removed

¼ teaspoon nutmeg

1 cup beef broth

1 cup heavy cream

1 tablespoon fresh thyme

Salt and freshly ground black pepper, to taste

1. Place the cognac and dried mushrooms in a saucepan and add water to cover. Simmer over low heat for 10 minutes. Remove from the stove and cool. Purée in the blender until very smooth.

2. Melt the butter in a saucepan, and stir in the chestnut flour, stirring until well blended. Add the shallots and button mushrooms, stirring constantly for 3–4 minutes.

3. Whisk in the rest of the ingredients, including the puréed mushroom-and-cognac mixture. (At this point you can add 1½ cups extra broth if making soup.)

Spring Vegetables with Pesto and Pasta

This dish is so easy to prepare and tastes wonderful with grilled chicken, shrimp, or steak.

INGREDIENTS | SERVES 4

½ medium onion, sliced

1 tablespoon extra-virgin olive oil

1 bunch asparagus, trimmed and cut into 1" pieces

3 large carrots, peeled and sliced

1 cup arugula

½ cup shelled English peas

Wheat-free pasta of your choice

Classic Pesto Sauce (see Chapter 8)

1. Place the onion in a large skillet with oil. Sauté for a few minutes until translucent, 3–4 minutes.

2. Add asparagus and carrots. Let cook for 5 minutes, until their colors brighten and they become tender.

3. Add arugula and peas, and stir to combine for 1 minute until arugula wilts. Remove from heat and place in a large bowl.

4. Cook pasta according to instructions. When finished cooking, toss vegetables and pasta together. Add the amount of pesto to your liking.

Quinoa Angel Hair with Bolognese Sauce

Quinoa pasta has become more popular for its added protein and wonderful texture.
Most grocery stores and specialty markets carry quinoa pasta.
If you can't find it, feel free to substitute with another wheat-free pasta or rice.

INGREDIENTS | SERVES 4–6

1 tablespoon extra-virgin olive oil
2 cloves garlic, chopped
½ medium onion, chopped
1 pound lean ground beef, turkey, or chicken
2 ounces diced pancetta
½ cup ground pork
½ cup chopped mushrooms
½ cup chopped carrots
Spicy Marinara Sauce (see recipe in this chapter)
1 (8-ounce) package quinoa pasta
Parmesan cheese, for topping (optional)

1. In a large skillet over medium heat, place the oil, garlic, and onion. Sauté for 3–4 minutes, until onions are translucent and tender.

2. Add the ground beef, pancetta, and ground pork and brown over medium heat until no longer pink, about 5–8 minutes.

3. Once the meat is cooked, add mushrooms and carrots and cook for 3–4 minutes, until they soften.

4. Add Spicy Marinara Sauce (you can adjust the spices, when preparing the Spicy Marinara Sauce, according to your tastes) and let simmer over low heat for 20–25 minutes, stirring occasionally.

5. Cook quinoa pasta according to package instructions. Place Bolognese sauce on top. Add grated Parmesan cheese if desired.

Pasta Primavera with Summer Vegetables

This dish can be served over brown rice pasta, quinoa pasta, rice or even quinoa.
Feel free to add some shrimp or chicken to it if you'd like.

INGREDIENTS | SERVES 6

16 ounces pasta of your choice

3 tablespoons extra-virgin olive oil

½ green onion, chopped

2 garlic cloves, minced

1 large carrot, peeled and diced

1 large zucchini, peeled and diced

1 summer squash, peeled and diced

½ medium green bell pepper, seeded and diced

½ medium red bell pepper, seeded and diced

½ cup chopped green beans

½ small eggplant, sliced into ¼" slices, peeled and cut crosswise

½ cup sliced plum tomatoes

½ cup Spicy Marinara Sauce (see recipe in this chapter)

Grated Parmesan cheese, for topping (optional)

Salt and pepper, to taste

1. Cook pasta according to package instructions. Rinse with cool water and set aside.

2. In a large skillet over medium heat, add the oil, onion, and garlic. Cook for 2–3 minutes, until onions and garlic become tender.

3. Add the vegetables and stir to combine. Cook vegetables about 10 minutes, until they soften. Remove from heat.

4. Add the marinara sauce to the vegetables and stir to combine. Add pasta and stir once again. Top with grated Parmesan cheese and salt and pepper to taste if desired.

Shrimp Fra Diavolo

This dish is spicy, but you can easily adjust the spices according to your taste.

INGREDIENTS | SERVES 6

2 tablespoons extra-virgin olive oil

6 cloves garlic, chopped

½ medium onion, minced

4 medium tomatoes, chopped

1 tablespoon ground basil

1 tablespoon ground oregano

½ cup dry white wine

1 teaspoon salt

½ teaspoon crushed red pepper flakes

16 ounces small shrimp, peeled and deveined

½ pound pasta of choice, cooked according to instructions

1 tablespoon fresh parsley, chopped

1. In a large skillet over medium heat, heat oil, garlic, and onion. Cook for 3–4 minutes, until tender and aromatic.

2. Add the tomatoes, basil, oregano, white wine, salt, and red pepper flakes. Lower heat and cook 25 minutes, stirring occasionally.

3. Add shrimp to tomato mixture and cook 5–8 minutes, until cooked through.

4. Pour shrimp sauce over cooked pasta. Top with chopped parsley.

Fra Diavolo

"Fra Diavolo" means "brother devil" in Italian, named for its spicy taste. If you like it even spicier, increase the red pepper flakes to 1 teaspoon. You can also use any type of shellfish in this dish for variety.

Pasta and Sausage in Garlic–White Wine Sauce

This light, simple dish is loaded with flavor.
Vermouth is a perfect substitution for dry white wine if you don't have any.

INGREDIENTS | SERVES 6

1 pound pasta of your choice

3 garlic cloves, minced

2 tablespoons extra-virgin olive oil, divided

1 pound asparagus, ends trimmed and cut into ¼" pieces

1 pint organic grape tomatoes, halved

1 (8-ounce) package mushrooms, cleaned and sliced

1 (6-ounce) package baby spinach

1 tablespoon oregano, dried

1 teaspoon rosemary

1 tablespoon basil, dried

Pinch of salt and pepper

½ cup dry white wine

½ cup low-sodium chicken stock

1 (16-ounce) package pork sausage (you can also use turkey or chicken sausage)

1 tablespoon fresh Parmesan cheese, shaved

1. Cook pasta according to package instructions.

2. Place chopped garlic and 1 tablespoon of olive oil in large skillet and let simmer for 1–2 minutes over low-medium heat.

3. Add chopped asparagus, tomatoes, and mushrooms and cook for 3–4 minutes until they get tender.

4. Add baby spinach and cook 2–3 more minutes until spinach is soft. Sprinkle with seasonings and stir until well blended.

5. Add wine and chicken stock, stir, and lower heat. Let simmer for 3–4 minutes.

6. While the veggies are simmering, take out a grill pan. In remaining 1 tablespoon olive oil, grill sausages until no longer pink. Remove casings if you like.

7. Add vegetable mixture to cooked pasta. Add sliced sausage and stir until well blended. Sprinkle Parmesan cheese on top.

Creamy Cheddar Sauce with Ham and Sherry

This is excellent over vegetables, spaghetti squash, or rice.
You can also use prosciutto if you don't have smoked ham.

INGREDIENTS | MAKES 2½ CUPS

3 tablespoons unsalted butter

3 tablespoons corn flour

2 cups milk or cream, warmed

⅔ cup grated sharp Cheddar cheese

¼ cup minced smoked ham

2 teaspoons sherry

Salt and pepper, to taste

1. In a skillet over medium-low heat, melt the butter and stir in the flour. Sauté, stirring for 4–5 minutes.

2. Add the warm milk or cream, whisking constantly, until thickened to desired consistency, about 3–5 minutes.

3. Remove from the heat and stir in the cheese, ham, sherry, salt, and pepper. Serve.

Sherry as a Flavoring

There are several kinds of sherry used in cooking, dry and sweet. Sweet sherry is often called cream sherry, as in Harveys Bristol Cream. Really good sherry is made in Spain by British companies who export it all over the world. The Chinese love it in sauces and soups, and it does add a wonderful flavor. It's also good in shrimp bisque, lobster Newburg, and other seafood dishes.

Roasted Garlic Sauce with Cheese

If you haven't tried roasted garlic yet, now is the time!
Roasting garlic is simple and makes the garlic milder, softer, and sweeter.

INGREDIENTS | MAKES ¾ CUP

1 head garlic, unpeeled, dampened
1 tablespoon unsalted butter
1 teaspoon cornstarch
½ cup milk
¼ cup chicken broth
2 tablespoons minced Italian flat-leaf parsley
2 tablespoons extra-virgin olive oil
1 teaspoon vinegar or lemon juice
Salt and pepper, to taste
2 tablespoons Parmesan cheese

1. Preheat the oven to 300°F.

2. Wrap the dampened garlic in aluminum foil and roast in oven for 60 minutes. Cool until you can handle it. Cut off the tip ends and squeeze garlic out of the shells; set aside.

3. In a saucepan, melt butter over low heat and stir in the cornstarch. Continue to cook for 3–4 minutes over low heat. Whisk in the milk, chicken broth, parsley, and olive oil.

4. Add vinegar or lemon juice, salt, pepper, cheese, and reserved garlic.

5. Place mixture in the blender and process until smooth. Pour into a serving bowl and use with vegetables, spaghetti squash, salads, rice, or tomatoes.

Sautéed Vegetables with Pumpkin Seed Pesto

Pumpkin seeds make a wonderful alternative to classic pesto made with pine nuts.
They are also packed with vitamins, minerals, antioxidants, and fiber, which make it even more healthy.

INGREDIENTS | SERVES 6

Pesto

½ cup extra-virgin olive oil
½ cup torn fresh basil
½ cup raw pumpkin seeds
¼ cup grated Parmesan cheese
2 large cloves garlic

Vegetables

1 teaspoon extra-virgin olive oil
1 clove garlic, diced
1 medium yellow squash, chopped
1 medium zucchini, chopped
1 orange pepper, chopped
½ cup sliced mushrooms
1 teaspoon dried basil
½ cup low-sodium vegetable broth
2 cups fresh spinach

1. Place all the pesto ingredients in a high speed blender or food processor. Blend for 2–3 minutes until smooth. Add additional olive oil if the pesto gets stuck in the blender. Set pesto aside.

2. In a large skillet, place the oil and garlic and cook for 2 minutes. Add squash, zucchini, pepper, mushrooms, and basil and stir to combine. Cook for 4–5 minutes until vegetables become tender.

3. Add vegetable broth and spinach. Stir well until spinach wilts and remove from heat.

4. Place pesto over vegetables and serve with pasta, quinoa, or rice.

CHAPTER 12

Dairy-Free and Wheat-Free

Brown Rice with Baby Spinach, Tomatoes, and Grilled Turkey Sausage

This dish will be a family favorite. It's so simple to make and can be made ahead of time.

INGREDIENTS | SERVES 6

1½ cups brown rice, uncooked
1 (16-ounce) package turkey sausage
¼ teaspoon grapeseed oil
2 garlic cloves, chopped
2 cups organic baby spinach
½ pint grape or cherry tomatoes, sliced in half
1 yellow pepper, cut in 1" slices
¼ cup chicken broth
½ teaspoon sea salt
Pepper, to taste
½ teaspoon oregano
1 tablespoon fresh basil, torn

1. Cook rice according to package instructions.

2. Grill sausage in a grill pan or on the grill for 5–8 minutes, until browned and no longer pink. Set aside.

3. In a saucepan over medium heat, place oil and garlic, and sauté for 1–2 minutes, until garlic softens.

4. Add the spinach, tomatoes and pepper and cook for 3–4 minutes, until vegetables are tender.

5. Add the chicken broth, salt, pepper, and oregano, turn heat to low and let simmer for 3–4 more minutes.

6. Add cooked sausage and stir to combine. Pour sausage/vegetable mixture over rice and serve immediately. Top with fresh basil.

Southern Fried Green Tomatoes

*Use tomatoes that are very firm. They usually aren't very large,
so count on two per person. Serve with thick slices of country ham or Irish bacon.*

INGREDIENTS | SERVES 4

1 cup corn flour

Salt and coarsely ground black pepper, to taste

1 cup cornmeal

2 whole eggs whisked in a large flat soup bowl

8 green tomatoes, cores trimmed, cut in ⅓" slices

Oil for frying

1. Spread the flour mixed with salt and pepper on one sheet of waxed paper and the cornmeal on another. Place the whisked eggs in a bowl between the two.

2. Dip the tomato slices first in the flour, then in the egg, and coat them with cornmeal.

3. Heat ½" of oil in a frying pan and heat to 350°F. Slide the tomato slices in and fry for 4 minutes or until well browned. Turn and finish frying, about 3–4 minutes.

4. Drain on paper towels. Serve as a side dish with eggs and bacon. This dish is perfect for brunch.

Avocado-Chia-Chocolate Pudding

*Those who are dairy free can now eat pudding again.
You would never know the creaminess in this pudding comes from avocado and not milk or cream.*

INGREDIENTS | SERVES 2

1 ripe avocado, peeled and diced

2 tablespoons unsweetened cocoa powder

½ ounce unsweetened baking chocolate

½ cup almond milk

1 teaspoon ground chia seeds

2 tablespoons honey

1 teaspoon wheat-free vanilla extract

Place all ingredients in blender or food processor; mix until smooth. This will be thick and creamy just like a regular pudding. Can be refrigerated in an airtight container for several days.

Avocados Are Good for You!

Don't be afraid to eat avocados. Though this fruit is high in fat, it is the healthy kind of fat that actually helps raise your good cholesterol. Avocados are also high in protein and loaded with vitamins and minerals.

Stuffed Peppers with Veggie-Burger Filling and Spices

Veggie burgers are typically well seasoned and quite delicious. They can be a great alternative to regular meats, although this recipe can also be prepared using ground beef, chicken, or turkey.

INGREDIENTS | SERVES 4

4 large garlic cloves, minced

1 large onion, minced

¼ cup extra-virgin olive oil

1 tablespoon Asian sesame oil

1 pound wheat-free veggie burgers

Salt and pepper, to taste

4 large green or red bell peppers

Dry Veggie Burgers?

You can do several things to keep veggie burgers moist. Mixing a bit of chopped fresh tomato into the mix is one option. Another is to add olive oil, milk, or cream before grilling. A bit of cooked, mashed potatoes also adds bulk and moisture. Add about a tablespoon of tomato, oil, milk, or mashed potato per burger.

1. In a skillet over medium heat, sauté the garlic and onion in the olive and sesame oils until soft, about 3–4 minutes.

2. Add the veggie burgers, break them up into pieces with a wooden spoon and stir. Add salt and pepper.

3. Preheat oven to 350°F. Prepare a baking sheet with nonstick spray.

4. Cut the peppers in half lengthwise and scoop out seeds and cores. Fill with the burger mixture. Place on the baking sheet.

5. Bake for 25 minutes. Serve hot.

Persian Rice with Saffron and Sour Cherries

This is excellent with duckling, turkey, or chicken. It has a slight bite to it and a nice tang. It's a simple recipe, but most delicious, and quite different from other side dishes.

INGREDIENTS | SERVES 6–8

1 tablespoon extra-virgin olive oil

1½ cups basmati or other short grain rice

2½ cups chicken broth

1 teaspoon saffron threads

1 (8-ounce) jar imported Iranian sour cherries, blanched, with juice

1 tablespoon butter

1 teaspoon salt

Freshly ground pepper, to taste

½ cup slivered almonds, toasted, for garnish

Rice and Fruit

You can also use a 15-ounce can unsweetened sour cherries or 1 pound sour red pie cherries, but do not use sweetened pie cherries in this recipe. Interestingly, you can use summer fruit, tropical fruit, dried fruit, and just about any kind of nut with white rice or wild rice.

1. Heat the oil in a large skillet and add the rice; cook, stirring, for 6 minutes.

2. Add the chicken broth and bring to a boil. Reduce heat to low and add all remaining ingredients, except the almonds.

3. Cover and simmer for 25 minutes, or until the rice is tender. Check the rice every 10 minutes to make sure it does not dry out. If the rice is stubbornly tough, add more broth or water.

4. Place in a warm serving bowl and sprinkle with almonds.

Beef-Flavored White Rice with Asian Spices

This is the perfect side dish to complement any Asian-style stir-fry or grilled meat or fish.
Five-spice powder is available at some supermarkets and at most Asian markets.

INGREDIENTS | SERVES 4

½ cup wheat-free soy sauce
¼ cup dry white wine or sake
1 tablespoon freshly grated gingerroot
1 tablespoon Asian sesame seed oil
1 teaspoon Asian five-spice powder
2 cloves garlic, minced
4 scallions, minced
⅔ cup beef broth
3 cups hot, cooked white rice

Mix together all ingredients except the rice to make a sauce. Boil to reduce for 3 minutes. Then mix in the rice, and serve hot.

Asian-Style Soup with Rice Noodles

This can be served in small bowls as a first course or in large bowls as lunch.
The contrast between soft and crunchy, spicy and sweet, makes this interesting and delicious.

INGREDIENTS | SERVES 4

1 quart chicken broth
2 cloves garlic, minced
1" piece fresh gingerroot, peeled and minced
1 bunch scallions, thinly sliced
12 canned water chestnuts
1 cup bean sprouts, well rinsed
½ cup dry sherry
½ cup wheat-free soy sauce
½ pound satin tofu
2 cups rice noodles, cooked
12 snow peas, sliced on the diagonal, for garnish

1. Bring the chicken broth to a boil and add all but the tofu, noodles, and snow peas. Cover and simmer for 10 minutes. Add the tofu.

2. Stir gently and add the cooked noodles. Garnish with the snow peas and serve.

Spanish-Style Rice

*This is an excellent side to pair with a steak. Perfect for entertaining,
it can be made in advance and then reheated just before serving time.*

INGREDIENTS | SERVES 4

3 cups water

2 teaspoons salt

1 cup white rice, uncooked

½ cup extra-virgin olive oil

1 large onion, chopped

1 clove garlic

½ teaspoon oregano, dried

2 jalapeño or poblano peppers, cored, seeded, and chopped

1 roasted red pepper, from a jar or your own, chopped

4 ripe plum tomatoes, cored and chopped

1 teaspoon lemon zest

10 black olives, sliced

Freshly ground black pepper, to taste

1. Bring the water to a boil, and add the salt and the rice. Reduce the heat to low, cover, and simmer until tender, about 25 minutes.

2. While the rice is cooking, heat the oil in a large frying pan.

3. Add the onion, garlic, oregano and hot peppers. Sauté over low heat for 8–10 minutes.

4. Mix in the rest of the ingredients and simmer for 10 minutes.

5. Add to the hot rice and serve.

Ground Pepper

You can get pink, white, and black peppercorns. Some cooks like to mix them. Some say there is a taste difference among the three. Other cooks use white pepper in white food so you won't see the black specks. Try a coarsely ground pepper in recipes like the one above. To coarsely grind, place 6–8 peppercorns between two pieces of waxed paper. Use a heavy frying pan to press down on the corns until they are cracked and in coarse pieces. Don't just lay them on a board and hit them with the pan or they will fly all over the kitchen.

Rice Flour Crepes

Use 1½ cups of rice milk instead of water if you want a richer crepe.

INGREDIENTS | SERVES 4

2 eggs

1½ cups water or rice milk

½ teaspoon salt

¼ teaspoon freshly ground white pepper

1 cup rice flour

Peanut or canola oil

Crepes, Pancakes, and Tortillas—Ripe for the Stuffing

While gluten-free flours can be a disaster under certain circumstances, they are a great success when it comes to crepes, pancakes, and corn tortillas, which are made like crepes. You can stuff them like wontons, make tubes and fill them, or fold them and dip them into a spicy sauce. Experiment.

1. Place the eggs, water or rice milk, and salt in a blender and process them together. Add pepper and flour, stopping once to scrape the sides of the container.

2. Oil a nonstick pan, set heat to medium, and slowly pour or ladle small amounts (about ¼ cup) of the batter into the pan, lifting and tipping to spread the batter.

3. When the edges start to get brown, after about 3 minutes, flip the crepe. Cook for only 1 minute on the reverse side or it will become crisp and not pliable.

4. Cool and stack between sheets of waxed paper.

Stir-Fried Shrimp and Vegetables in Rice Crepe Wraps

*These are wonderful as an appetizer or as an entrée. Feel free
to dip them in teriyaki sauce (but read the label to make sure it is wheat-free).*

INGREDIENTS | SERVES 4

1 tablespoon sesame seed oil

¼ cup peanut oil

4 scallions, sliced

4 garlic cloves, minced

1 zucchini squash, finely chopped

1 medium onion, finely chopped

⅔ pound raw shrimp, shelled and deveined

½ cup almonds, chopped

1 tablespoon fish sauce

¼ cup dry sherry

1 teaspoon wasabi powder mixed with 2 teaspoons water to make a paste

Rice Flour Crepes (see recipe in this chapter)

1 egg, beaten

1. Heat the sesame and peanut oils in a wok or frying pan and add the vegetables and shrimp. Stir and cook until the shrimp turn pink, about 2–3 minutes.

2. Add the rest of the ingredients except for the crepes and the egg. Mix well. Place the shrimp and vegetables in a bowl and cool.

3. Put a spoonful of filling on half of a crepe. Paint the rim of the circle with the beaten egg. Fold over and press to seal.

4. Broil on high heat or steam the filled crepes for 10 minutes, or until they are steaming hot. Serve hot.

Stuffed Artichokes with Lemon and Olives

*Artichokes have a way of making everything around them taste delicious.
They can be eaten with just a little lemon juice.*

**INGREDIENTS | SERVES 4 AS AN ENTRÉE,
OR 8 AS AN APPETIZER**

4 large artichokes, trimmed and split
lengthwise

4 quarts water

½ lemon

1 cup cooked rice

10 green olives, chopped

10 kalamata olives, chopped

2 tablespoons minced parsley

3 tablespoons grapeseed oil

1 teaspoon garlic salt

Pepper, to taste

1 egg (optional)

1. Boil the artichokes in 4 quarts of water with squeezed lemon, and including rind, for 20 minutes. Drain and lay on a baking sheet, cut-side up.

2. Preheat the oven to 350°F.

3. Mix the rest of the ingredients (including the egg, if using) together in a large bowl.

4. Spoon the filling over the artichokes, pressing between the leaves. Bake for 15 minutes, until hot.

Curried Lamb Grilled on Skewers

*Try grilling these and serving with the your favorite dipping sauce.
These were a huge crowd-pleaser at my wedding reception!*

INGREDIENTS | SERVES 4

½ cup peanut oil

1 teaspoon curry powder

2 tablespoons lemon juice

4 cloves garlic, minced

½ teaspoon ground coriander

2 teaspoons hot sauce, or to taste

1 pound bite-sized lamb chunks, from
the leg or shoulder

1. Soak 8–10 wooden skewers in water for at least 40 minutes.

2. Mix the peanut oil, curry, lemon juice, garlic, coriander, and hot sauce together in a bowl.

3. Add the lamb and turn to coat with the marinade. Cover and refrigerate for 2 hours.

4. String the lamb on the skewers and grill over hot coals for 4 minutes per side. Serve hot.

Coconut-Almond Ice Cream

Even those who are not on a wheat- and dairy-free diet will love this ice cream!
You can also add dairy-free carob chips (instead of chocolate chips) to this ice cream.

INGREDIENTS | SERVES 6

4 cups coconut milk (full fat)
½ cup honey
1 tablespoon wheat-free vanilla extract
½ cup slivered almonds, toasted

1. Combine all the ingredients in a large mixing bowl. You might have to whisk to get the milk and honey to combine.

2. Prepare following your ice cream maker instructions. Store in the freezer for up to 2 weeks.

No Ice Cream Maker?

What happens if you don't have an ice cream maker? Don't fret. You can easily make this without one. Add all the ingredients except almonds in a blender or food processor and blend for 2–3 minutes, until thoroughly mixed. Make sure you stop to scrape the sides of the blender too. Take the mixture out of blender and pour into an airtight freezer-safe container. Toss in almonds and stir to combine. Freeze for 6–8 hours, until it hardens.

Mixed Berry Smoothie

This smoothie is ideal for breakfast or as a snack. You can substitute
different frozen fruits if you do not have frozen berries in your house.

INGREDIENTS | SERVES 2–3

2 cups unflavored almond milk or milk of your choice
1 tablespoon pure maple syrup
1 teaspoon wheat-free vanilla extract
½ cup frozen raspberries
½ cup frozen strawberries
1 tablespoon coconut oil
½ teaspoon cinnamon
½ cup blueberries, frozen

1. Place all ingredients into a blender container in the order listed.

2. Blend until smooth, about 1 minute. Pour into glasses and serve.

Pumpkin-Spice Muffins

You will love these muffins, as they will leave you satisfied, and you will never miss wheat or dairy.

INGREDIENTS | MAKES 18–24 MUFFINS, DEPENDING ON THEIR SIZE

1 (15-ounce) can puréed pumpkin
2 eggs
¼ cup canola oil
1 teaspoon wheat-free baking powder
½ cup turbinado sugar
½ cup 100% maple syrup
¼ teaspoon salt
1 tablespoon pumpkin pie spice
1 teaspoon ground cinnamon
½ teaspoon ground cloves
⅛ teaspoon ground ginger
1¼ cups flax seed, ground
1 cup all–purpose, wheat-free flour

1. Preheat the oven to 375°F. Spray muffin tins with baking spray or line with cupcake liners.

2. In a large bowl, mix all the ingredients together except for the ground flax seed and the flour until thoroughly combined.

3. Add the ground flax seed and flour slowly and mix to combine. Pour batter into muffin cups.

4. Bake for 35–40 minutes, until toothpick comes out clean when inserted in the middle of muffin.

White Chicken Chili

This is the perfect comfort food any time of the year.
Wheat-free corn bread would go perfectly with this dish.

INGREDIENTS | SERVES 6

1 tablespoon grapeseed oil

1 medium onion, chopped

4 cloves garlic, chopped

1 cup mushrooms, chopped

1½ cups frozen corn

½ cup chopped green bell pepper

1 (4-ounce) can chopped green chili peppers

1½ teaspoons ground cumin

¼ teaspoon ground cayenne pepper

½ teaspoon chili powder

1 teaspoon oregano

3 (15-ounce) cans navy white beans, rinsed and drained

2 (14.5-ounce) cans chicken broth

1½ pounds cooked skinless, boneless chicken breast, chopped

1 tablespoon cilantro, chopped

Chopped scallions or chopped cilantro, for garnish

1. Heat oil in a large pot or Dutch oven over medium-low heat, and add onion and garlic. Cook for 3–4 minutes, until onions become translucent.

2. Add mushrooms, corn, and bell pepper, and cook until they soften a bit, about 2–3 minutes.

3. Add chili peppers, cumin, cayenne pepper, chili powder, and oregano. Stir to combine.

4. Take 1 can of white beans and place in a blender or food processor until completely blended. You might need to add a bit of water if it becomes too thick.

5. Pour blended bean mixture into pot along with chicken broth, remaining 2 cans of beans, cooked chicken, and cilantro, and stir. Reduce heat to low and continue to simmer about 10–15 minutes, stirring occasionally.

6. Top with chopped scallions or chopped cilantro.

Spice It Up

Do you like your chili a little spicier? Just add a fresh jalapeño (seeded and diced), or increase the cayenne pepper and chili powder. This dish can be made to suit your taste.

Almond Butter–Raisin Cookies

These cookies are so easy to make. You can use other nut butters if you'd like. They also freeze very well.

INGREDIENTS | MAKES 24 COOKIES

1 cup unsalted almond butter, stirred well

¾ cup coconut sugar or sugar of your choice

1 large egg

½ teaspoon baking soda

¼ teaspoon sea salt, omit if the almond butter is salted

1 teaspoon wheat-free vanilla extract

½ teaspoon cinnamon

3 ounces raisins (you can also use dried cranberries, apricots, dates, cherries, or dried fruit of your choice)

1. Preheat oven to 350°F.

2. In a medium bowl, stir together all ingredients except raisins until blended.

3. Stir in raisins.

4. Drop dough by tablespoonfuls onto parchment-lined baking sheets. Bake for 10–15 minutes or until lightly browned.

5. Let cool on baking sheets for 5 minutes. Remove to a wire rack and let cool for 15 more minutes.

Strawberry-Blueberry Coulis

This is wonderful not only on crepes but on ice cream and pancakes as well. You can also mix it into Easy Breakfast Quinoa (see Chapter 10) for some added sweetness in the morning.

INGREDIENTS | MAKES 1½ CUPS

½ pint fresh blueberries, rinsed

½ pint fresh strawberries, rinsed, stems removed, quartered

¼ cup water

¼ cup sugar

½ teaspoon wheat-free vanilla extract

1" × ½" strip orange rind

Place all of the ingredients in a saucepan and bring to a boil. Remove from heat and cool. Whisk until smooth. Serve warm or cool.

Fresh Three-Berry Granita

Delicious and refreshing as is, or mixed with vanilla ice cream—this is the perfect light summer treat.

INGREDIENTS | MAKES 1 QUART

1½ cups sugar

⅔ cup water

1 pint strawberries, rinsed, stems removed, and halved

1½ pints fresh raspberries, rinsed

½ pint fresh blueberries, rinsed

¼ cup lemon juice

1. Mix the sugar and water together in a large saucepan and bring to a boil. Reduce heat and simmer until all of the sugar is dissolved.

2. Add the rinsed and stemmed berries and cook for 6 minutes. Add the lemon juice.

3. Place in your freezer in ice cube trays. Occasionally, break up the granita with a fork so that it does not turn into a block of ice. Or use an ice cream maker to make your granita. The ice cream maker will increase the shelf life of the granita, making it a sorbet. Soften slightly before serving.

CHAPTER 13

Side Dishes

Balsamic Roasted Vegetables

This is the perfect side dish that can be made with any vegetable you have on hand. You can make double the amount and add roasted vegetables to omelets or pizza—or even on top of sandwiches.

INGREDIENTS | SERVES 12

1 head broccoli crowns, chopped

2 red bell peppers, seeded and diced

1 large sweet potato, peeled and cubed

4 large carrots, peeled and chopped

1 bunch asparagus, ends trimmed and chopped

1 medium red onion, quartered

1 tablespoon chopped fresh thyme

2 tablespoons chopped fresh rosemary

3 tablespoons olive or grapeseed oil

3 tablespoons balsamic vinegar, divided

Salt and freshly ground black pepper, to taste

1 tablespoon fresh lemon juice

1. Preheat oven to 475°F.

2. In a large bowl, combine the broccoli, red bell peppers, sweet potatoes, carrots, and asparagus.

3. Separate the red onion quarters into pieces, and add them to the mixture.

4. In a small bowl, stir together the thyme, rosemary, oil, 2 tablespoons of the balsamic vinegar, salt, and pepper. Toss with vegetables until they are coated.

5. Spread vegetables evenly on a large roasting pan. Roast for 25–30 minutes, stirring every 10 minutes, or until vegetables are cooked through and browned.

6. Drizzle with fresh lemon juice and remaining 1 tablespoon balsamic vinegar.

Simple Zucchini-Parmesan Sticks

This is an easy, delicious side dish that complements any entrée.
These are also perfect for a light, healthy snack.

INGREDIENTS | SERVES 4

Nonstick cooking spray

1 cup zucchini, sliced into 2–3" sticks

Misto sprayer filled with extra-virgin olive oil

1 tablespoon shaved Parmesan cheese

Salt and pepper, to taste

1. Preheat oven to broil. Line baking sheet with aluminum foil. Spray nonstick cooking spray on aluminum foil to prevent sticking.

2. Place sliced zucchini sticks on aluminum foil and spray lightly with olive oil sprayer.

3. Sprinkle Parmesan cheese on top. Season with salt and pepper.

4. Broil for a few minutes until cheese melts and turns light brown, about 2 minutes.

Delicious Garlic Butternut Squash

The name says it all! This is perfect, simple, and delicious. Butternut squash is low in calories and rich in vitamins and minerals. It's a wonderful alternative to potatoes.

INGREDIENTS | SERVES 6

2 tablespoons minced fresh parsley

1 tablespoon grapeseed oil

2 garlic cloves, minced

¼ cup grated Parmesan cheese

½ teaspoon rosemary, dried

½ teaspoon kosher salt

½ teaspoon pepper

3½ pounds butternut squash, peeled and cut into 1" cubes

1. Preheat oven to 400°F.

2. In a large bowl, combine the parsley, oil, garlic, cheese, rosemary, salt, and pepper. Add the squash and toss to coat.

3. Transfer to an ungreased shallow 2-quart baking dish. Bake, uncovered, for 50–55 minutes or until squash is just tender.

Cutting Butternut Squash

First, cut off ¼" from both ends. Use a sharp vegetable peeler and peel the outer layer of squash. Once completely peeled, slice squash in half from top to bottom. Next, scoop out the seeds and gummy pulp inside the squash. Cut each half in half, making quarters. Then chop each quarter into strips. Finally, slice each strip into cubes.

Lemon Rice with Toasted Pine Nuts

This dish can easily be made into a meal by simply adding chicken or sausage.
The lemon flavor is so light and can easily go alongside most entrées.

INGREDIENTS | SERVES 4

1 cup arborio rice
4½ cups water, divided
1 tablespoon grapeseed oil
Juice from ½ lemon
1 clove garlic, finely chopped
Salt and pepper, to taste
Zest from 1 lemon
¼ cup fresh parsley
1 tablespoon pine nuts, toasted
1 tablespoon Parmesan cheese (optional)

Arborio Rice

Arborio rice cooks much differently than other varieties of rice. Arborio rice is typically used in risotto dishes, which require a creamier texture. By slowly adding the water and continuously stirring, the rice releases starches, which make the texture much more creamy.

1. In a large saucepan, combine the rice with 1½ cups of the water over high heat and bring to a boil. Reduce heat to medium, stirring continuously until the water is absorbed.

2. In ¼-cup increments, add remaining 3 cups water to the saucepan. Continue to stir constantly while adding the water and until all 3 cups of water have been absorbed. Drain well, but do not rinse.

3. In a small bowl, mix the oil and lemon juice.

4. Transfer the rice to a medium-sized serving bowl. Add garlic, lemon juice mixture, and season with salt and pepper.

5. Add the lemon zest, parsley, and pine nuts, and toss. Top with Parmesan cheese if desired.

Spicy Corn Bread, Stuffed with Chilies and Cheese

This is perfect with soup, fried chicken, stews, and chowders.
You can easily adjust the spices according to your taste.

INGREDIENTS | SERVES 6–8

1 cup cornmeal (yellow or white)

1 cup corn or rice flour

¼ cup light brown sugar

3 teaspoons wheat-free baking powder

1 teaspoon salt

¼ teaspoon cumin

1 teaspoon dried red pepper flakes, or to taste

½ cup buttermilk

½ cup sour cream

2 eggs, beaten

2 tablespoons unsalted butter, melted

½ cup chipotle chilies, chopped

½ cup grated pepper jack or Cheddar cheese

1. Preheat oven to 400°F. In a large bowl, mix together the cornmeal, flour, sugar, baking powder, salt, cumin, and red pepper flakes.

2. Mix in the buttermilk, sour cream, eggs, and melted butter.

3. Prepare an 8" square baking pan with nonstick spray. Place half of the batter in the pan. Sprinkle with peppers and cheese. Cover with the rest of the batter. Bake for 20–25 minutes.

The Word on Chipotle

Chipotle chilies are jalapeño chili peppers that have been smoked and preserved in brine or vinegar. They are useful in cooking and baking, adding a smoky zing to recipes.

Polenta with Sun-Dried Tomatoes and Basil

The fascinating thing about polenta is that you can change the seasonings and/or toppings and fry, grill, or broil and have a different dish, still based on polenta, time after time.

INGREDIENTS | MAKES 12 SQUARES

8 ounces sun-dried tomatoes in oil, chopped finely

20 basil leaves, rinsed

2 cloves garlic

½ teaspoon oregano, dried

Additional extra-virgin olive oil, if necessary 1 batch Classic Polenta with Herbs and Parmesan (see Chapter 8), prepared firm

1 cup grated mozzarella cheese

Polenta: A Fancy Name for Good Old Cornmeal

You can buy polenta by the ounce in the market. It is expensive and less nourishing than making it yourself. You can make polenta by the pound cheaply. It can be elegant but usually is simply fried or served in a soft, creamy mound, like mashed potatoes. It's good with any sauce or gravy; it's so very bland that you really need to spice it up.

1. Preheat oven to 350°F.

2. Blend the tomatoes, basil, garlic, and oregano in a food processor. This should be chunky, not puréed. Add extra olive oil if too dry to process. Spread the tomato mixture over the polenta and cut into squares.

3. Place the squares on a cookie sheet that you have buttered or sprayed with nonstick spray. Bake for 20 minutes.

4. At the last minute, sprinkle the mozzarella cheese over the top and bake until melted. Serve immediately.

Indian Corn Cakes

This is delightful as a side dish or as an easy snack.

INGREDIENTS | MAKES ABOUT 12 CAKES

7 cups water

1 tablespoon salt, or to taste

2 cups cornmeal

½ teaspoon freshly ground black pepper, or to taste

1 teaspoon molasses

4 tablespoons butter

Corn Lore

Native Americans saved early settlers in this country with their stores of corn. Native Americans taught the colonists how to grow, dry, and mill corn into meal. Interestingly, corn, as a crop, started in ancient Mexico and Central America. The valuable crop went all the way to Canada, indicating tribal movement and sharing.

1. Bring the water to a boil and add salt. Stir in the cornmeal and cook for about 20 minutes, stirring occasionally. Add the pepper and molasses.

2. Prepare an 11" × 13" glass lasagna pan with nonstick spray. Spread the corn mixture in the pan and cover. Refrigerate for 1–2 hours, or until very stiff.

3. Heat butter in a large frying pan. Cut the corn cakes into 12 squares and fry until golden on both sides, about 3–4 minutes per side.

Guacamole

There are many recipes for guacamole. This a delicious recipe where the flavors unite wonderfully. Serve with Baked Corn Tortilla Chips (see Chapter 2).

INGREDIENTS | MAKES 1–1½ CUPS

3 medium Hass or 2 large, smooth-skinned avocados, peeled and seeded

Juice of 2 limes

½ cup finely minced sweet onion

½ cup grape or cherry tomatoes, halved

½ teaspoon Tabasco sauce, or to taste

½ teaspoon salt, or to taste

2 tablespoons finely chopped fresh cilantro

⅛ teaspoon cayenne pepper (optional)

1. In a large bowl, using a fork, mash the avocados.

2. Mix in the rest of the ingredients until well blended.

Choosing Avocados

Most store-bought avocados are as hard as stones. That's fine; if you buy ripe ones, they generally have many blemishes. Just buy them a few days before you plan to serve them. Place them on a sunny windowsill or in a brown paper bag or wrap them in a newspaper. The paper seems to hasten ripening. The avocado should not have oily black spots in it when you cut it open but should be a uniform green. One or two black spots can be cut out, but don't use an avocado that is full of black spots or gray-brown areas.

Risotto with Spinach and Gorgonzola Cheese

This is a wonderful complement to any poultry or seafood dish.

INGREDIENTS | SERVES 4

5 cups canned or homemade chicken, fish, or vegetable broth

2 tablespoons butter

2 tablespoons extra-virgin olive oil

½ cup finely chopped sweet onion

1½ cups arborio rice, uncooked

Salt and freshly ground black pepper, to taste

10 ounces fresh spinach, rinsed and chopped finely

¼ cup crumbled Gorgonzola cheese

Roasted red pepper strips and chopped parsley, for garnish

1. Bring the broth to a slow simmer in a saucepan and keep hot.

2. Heat the butter and oil in a large, heavy pan; add the onion and sauté until softened, about 8 minutes. Add the rice and stir. Add salt and pepper.

3. Add the broth, ¼ cup at a time, until it is all gone, stirring constantly. This will take about 35 minutes. If the rice is still not done, add water, ¼ cup at a time. When rice is cooked, add spinach, one handful at a time. Stir to combine.

4. Stir in the Gorgonzola cheese and garnish with strips of roasted red pepper and parsley. Serve hot.

Corn Soufflé

This is a tasty side dish with roast turkey or pork. Just make sure the oven is very hot. The herbs and seasonings can be adjusted to suit your tastes.

INGREDIENTS | SERVES 4–6

½ cup corn or rice flour

¼ cup milk or light cream

3 eggs, separated

3 teaspoons wheat-free baking powder

2 tablespoons finely grated Parmesan cheese

1 clove garlic, minced

Salt, pepper, and 1 teaspoon of your favorite herbs, to taste

1 cup fresh corn, cut off the cob, or frozen

1. Preheat the oven to 375°F.

2. Place the flour, milk, egg yolks, baking powder, cheese, garlic, salt, pepper, and herbs in a food processor and blend together. Place in a bowl and add the corn.

3. Beat the egg whites until stiff and fold them into the corn mixture.

4. Grease or use nonstick spray on a 2-quart soufflé mold. Pour the mixture into the mold, and place in the middle of the oven for 25–30 minutes, until brown and puffed. Serve hot.

Winter Cranberry-Orange Corn Bread

Don't let the title fool you; this is wonderful any time of the year. This corn bread can also be chopped and used as stuffing.

INGREDIENTS | SERVES 8–10

1 cup cornmeal (yellow or white)

1 cup corn or rice flour

3 tablespoons light brown sugar

3 teaspoons wheat-free baking powder

1 teaspoon salt

1 tablespoon honey

1 cup milk

2 eggs, beaten

3 tablespoons unsalted butter, melted

½ cup dried cranberries

Zest of 1 orange

½ cup chopped walnuts (optional)

1. Preheat the oven to 400°F. Spray an 8" square baking pan with nonstick spray.

2. In a large bowl, mix all of the dry ingredients together. Slowly stir in the rest of the ingredients.

3. Turn into the pan and bake for 20–25 minutes. Cool for a few minutes before cutting into squares and serving.

Crispy Corn Fritters

Fritters are really fun to make and to eat. They can be as plain or as interesting as you want.
The idea is to make them really creamy on the inside and crispy on the outside.

INGREDIENTS | MAKES 12–14 FRITTERS

1 egg

⅓ cup milk or beer

⅔ cup cornstarch or corn flour

1½ teaspoons wheat-free baking powder

½ teaspoon salt

Red pepper flakes and/or ground black pepper, to taste

⅛ teaspoon freshly grated nutmeg

1 cup fresh corn, cut off the cob, or frozen

Peanut, canola, or other cooking oil (not olive oil)

1. Starting with the egg and milk, place everything but the corn and oil in a food processor and blend until smooth. Scrape into a bowl; fold in the corn.

2. Heat about 1" of oil to 350°F in a large frying pan.

3. Drop the fritters by the tablespoonful into the hot oil and cook for 3–5 minutes. Drain on paper towels and serve hot.

Frittering Away

You can vary your fritters by using chopped clams instead of corn. They are fine with eggs for breakfast or as a side dish with chicken or steak. They are good with syrup or herb-savory with gravy. You can also use them as hors d'oeuvres to dip in salsa.

Sweet Potato and Black Bean Hash

This is a wonderful side dish and leftovers can easily be wrapped up in wheat-free tortillas.
Feel free to add chorizo or any kind of sausage to make a complete meal.

INGREDIENTS | SERVES 4

2 tablespoons extra-virgin olive oil

1 medium onion, thinly sliced

2 cloves garlic, minced

1 small yellow pepper, chopped

2 medium sweet potatoes, peeled and diced into ½" cubes

1 jalepeño pepper, seeded and minced (optional)

1½ teaspoons cumin

1 teaspoon coriander

⅛ teaspoon cayenne pepper

½ teaspoon chili powder

¾ cup vegetable broth

1 (15-ounce) can black beans, rinsed thoroughly and drained

2 tablespoons minced fresh cilantro

Salt and pepper, to taste

Sliced avocado, lime wedges, diced scallions, and sour cream, for garnish (optional)

1. Heat the olive oil over medium heat in a large skillet. Add onions and garlic and cook for 3–4 minutes.

2. Add the yellow pepper and cook another 2 minutes until they all start to brown.

3. Add the sweet potatoes and continue to stir while they brown. Cook for another 5 minutes. Add jalepeño pepper (if using), cumin, coriander, cayenne pepper and chili powder. Stir to combine.

4. Add broth and continue to stir for 3–4 minutes, until liquid is absorbed.

5. Add beans and continue to stir, making sure everything is completely mixed. Add cilantro, and season with salt and pepper.

6. Can be served warm or cold. Garnish with sliced avocado, lime wedges, diced scallions, or sour cream, if desired.

Garlicky Parmesan Roasted Potatoes

This side dish is a perfect companion to any meat or poultry dish. These potatoes also make a wonderful accompaniment to eggs for breakfast or brunch. Using fresh herbs and Parmesan cheese is definitely better when roasting.

INGREDIENTS | SERVES 4

2 tablespoons extra-virgin olive oil

2 cloves garlic, minced

1 medium onion, finely chopped

1 teaspoon chopped fresh basil

1 teaspoon fresh rosemary, chopped

1 teaspoon fresh parsley, chopped

2 tablespoons fresh Parmesan cheese, grated

⅛ teaspoon crushed red pepper flakes

½ teaspoon salt

4 large red potatoes, scrubbed clean and sliced into cubes

1. Preheat oven to 450°F.

2. Place all the ingredients in a large resealable plastic bag. Close the bag and shake to evenly coat potatoes.

3. Spray a baking sheet with nonstick cooking spray. Spread potato mixture in an even layer on baking sheet. Place in oven for 40 minutes, making sure to stir potatoes occasionally.

4. Place oven on broil and cook potatoes 1–2 minutes, until they become browned and crispy. Remove from oven. Serve immediately.

Dried Herbs

If you would like to use dried herbs or don't have fresh herbs on hand, remember that less is more. Dried herbs are usually stronger than fresh ones. Typically, you can cut the amount in half when using dried herbs.

Snow Peas with Ginger and Water Chestnuts

This is a lovely side dish that would go perfectly over a bed of rice. You can add tofu if you would like to add protein and keep it vegetarian. You can also add cooked beef or chicken.

INGREDIENTS | SERVES 4

1 cup snow peas, washed

1 tablespoon butter or sesame oil

½ cup water chestnuts, rinsed and drained

2 teaspoons fresh gingerroot, chopped

1 clove garlic, minced

Juice from ½ lemon

1 tablespoon sesame seeds

1 tablespoon wheat-free soy sauce

1. Remove strings and ends of snow peas.

2. Melt butter over high heat in large skillet, add peas, water chestnuts, gingerroot, garlic, lemon juice, sesame seeds, and soy sauce.

3. Continue to cook over high heat, while stirring, until peas are crisp and tender. Serve immediately.

Kale, Squash, and Bean Medley

This makes a wonderfully well-balanced vegetarian meal.
This can also be a lovely addition to a hearty steak or poultry dish.

INGREDIENTS | SERVES 6–8

¾ pound butternut squash, peeled and cut into 1" cubes (about 1 cup)

¼ cup vegetable broth

1 teaspoon minced fresh gingerroot

1 teaspoon rosemary, dried

2 tablespoons butter

3 cups kale, trimmed and washed

¼ cup dried cranberries

¼ cup chopped pecans, toasted

½ cup white beans, rinsed and drained

1 teaspoon salt

1. In a large skillet, cook squash with vegetable broth, gingerroot, and rosemary over medium-low heat for about 8–10 minutes, until squash becomes tender.

2. Stir in butter, kale, cranberries, pecans, beans, and salt. Toss to coat. Serve immediately.

Cheesy Broccoli Rice

You will find that many other broccoli rice casseroles use canned creamed soups.
Be careful cooking with those as they contain a lot of sodium and fat.

INGREDIENTS | SERVES 10

2 cups water

1 cup uncooked jasmine rice, rinsed

1 teaspoon butter

4 slices bacon

4 cups broccoli florets and stems, cleaned and trimmed, finely chopped

1 medium onion, chopped

2 cloves garlic, minced

½ cup mushrooms, diced

1 tablespoon cornmeal

1½ cups milk

2 cups shredded Gouda cheese (you can also use Cheddar, Swiss, or provolone), divided

Flavoring with Bacon

Bacon is an excellent garnish. It also can add flavor to soups and stews, and fat for sautéing vegetables, mushrooms, and so on. A little goes a long way. If you are watching your diet, just drain the bacon well on paper towels and crumble it. Then, sprinkle it on soups, salads, vegetables, pasta, and rice.

1. Preheat oven to 350°F.

2. In a large saucepan, place the water and rice over high heat and bring to a boil. Cover, reduce heat to low and simmer about 10 minutes, until all the liquid has been absorbed and rice is tender. Remove from heat and fluff with fork. Cover again and let sit 5 minutes.

3. In a large skillet, melt butter over medium-high heat. Add bacon and cook until crisp while turning over several times. Remove bacon from skillet and place on paper towels to drain.

4. Place broccoli in large saucepan; add water to cover broccoli. Bring to boil over high heat and reduce heat to medium. Cook for 3–4 minutes, until broccoli is bright green and tender. Remove from heat, drain, and place broccoli in a 1½-quart casserole dish. Crumble bacon into small pieces.

5. In same skillet that you cooked bacon, add onion, garlic, and mushrooms. Cook for 2–3 minutes more, until mushrooms are softened.

6. Add cornmeal and mix to combine. Slowly add milk and continue stirring until sauce thickens, about 4 minutes.

7. Add 1½ cups of the cheese and crumbled bacon. Stir.

8. Combine rice and cheese sauce with broccoli in casserole dish. Top with remaining ½ cup cheese. Bake for 20 minutes, or until cheese is completely melted and golden brown.

Garlic and Parmesan Mashed Potatoes

These mashed potatoes are so flavorful you don't need any gravy. This dish goes wonderfully with fish, steak, meat loaf, chicken, or turkey. The possibilities are endless.

INGREDIENTS | SERVES 6

4 cloves garlic, minced and divided

2½ pounds Yukon Gold potatoes, scrubbed clean, unpeeled and quartered

2 tablespoons butter, softened

½ cup buttermilk

2 tablespoons sour cream

½ teaspoon sage

1 teaspoon salt

¼ cup Parmesan cheese, grated

Chopped green onion, for garnish

Be Creative with Potatoes

Let your imagination go wild with potatoes! Gone are the days when you think of boring, lumpy, instant potatoes. Making your own mashed potatoes is easy. You can add whatever seasonings and additions you'd like.

1. Place 2 cloves of garlic and the potatoes in a large saucepan. Cover with water and bring to a boil over high heat. Once boiling, cover and reduce heat to low and simmer 20–25 minutes, until the potatoes are fork tender.

2. Drain the potatoes thoroughly and place back into saucepan.

3. In a small bowl, add butter, 2 remaining cloves minced garlic, buttermilk, sour cream, sage, and salt. Stir to combine.

4. Add cheese and stir well. Place garlic sauce over potatoes and mix well. Mash with potato masher or hand mixer on medium-high speed until desired consistency. Top with chopped green onions. Serve immediately.

Cheddar and Bacon Mashed Potatoes

Another lovely variation of typical mashed potatoes, this side dish will surely impress your guests.

INGREDIENTS | SERVES 6

1 tablespoon butter

4 slices applewood smoked bacon

2½ pounds russet potatoes, unpeeled, scrubbed clean and cut into quarters

1 clove garlic, minced

1 cup sharp Cheddar cheese, shredded

¾ cup milk

2 tablespoons sour cream

Salt and pepper, to taste

1 teaspoon chives, minced

1. Melt butter in large skillet over medium-high heat. Add bacon and cook until crisp while turning over several times. Remove bacon from skillet and place on paper towels to drain.

2. Place potatoes and garlic in a large saucepan. Cover with water and bring to a boil over high heat. Once boiling, cover and reduce heat to low, and simmer for 20–25 minutes, until potatoes are fork tender.

3. Drain potatoes thoroughly and place back into saucepan.

4. Crumble bacon into small pieces.

5. In a medium bowl, mix cheese, milk, crumbled bacon, and sour cream. Stir well and pour mixture on top of potatoes. Mix thoroughly and mash with potato masher of hand mixer on medium-high speed until desired consistency is reached.

6. Add salt and pepper to taste and serve with chives on top. Serve immediately.

Balsamic Roasted Brussels Sprouts

Even those who do not typically like Brussels sprouts will love these!
This is a simple and tasty dish, delicious enough for a holiday dinner.

INGREDIENTS | SERVES 6

3 tablespoons extra-virgin olive oil

2 tablespoons balsamic vinegar

1 clove garlic, minced

1 teaspoon sweet paprika

1½ pounds Brussels sprouts, bottoms trimmed, outer leaves removed, and halved

4 shallots, thinly sliced

Salt and pepper, to taste

The Many Benefits of Brussels Sprouts

Brussels sprouts are part of the cabbage family and actually look like little cabbages. Brussels sprouts were first grown in Brussels, Belgium, hence the name. These sprouts are packed with vitamins C, A, and B.

1. Preheat the oven to 400°F.

2. In a small bowl, mix together the oil, balsamic vinegar, garlic, and paprika.

3. Place Brussels sprouts, shallots, and oil/vinegar mixture in a large resealable plastic bag. Make sure the bag is closed and shake to coat sprouts evenly. Season with salt and pepper.

4. Place sprouts on a baking sheet that is coated with nonstick cooking spray. Roast sprouts for 35 minutes, shaking pan every 5–8 minutes to make sure they are evenly browning.

5. Remove from oven when finished; season with some more salt. Serve immediately.

Creamed Spinach

This recipe is wonderful and can easily be doubled to feed a larger group.
You can substitute half-and-half for the heavy cream to lighten this up.

INGREDIENTS | SERVES 10

3 (10-ounce) bags fresh spinach, chopped

¼ cup butter

3 cloves garlic, minced

½ teaspoon nutmeg

1 medium-sized shallot, minced

½ cup heavy cream

½ cup grated Asiago cheese

½ cup Parmesan cheese, grated

Salt and pepper, to taste

1. Place spinach in a large stock pot, cover with water and cook over medium-high heat until wilted, about 2–3 minutes. Remove from heat and drain in colander until most of the liquid is gone.

2. Place butter in large skillet and melt over medium heat. Add garlic, nutmeg, and shallot, and cook 3–4 minutes, until shallot is translucent.

3. Add spinach and slowly pour in heavy cream. Sprinkle in Asiago and Parmesan cheeses. Continue to stir until sauce thickens, about 4–5 minutes. Season with salt and pepper. Serve warm or hot.

CHAPTER 14

Soups and Stews

White Bean, Kale, and Turkey Sausage Stew

Who says comfort food has to be laden with fat and calories for it to be comforting? This dish is simple enough to prepare during the week.

INGREDIENTS | SERVES 6

1 tablespoon grapeseed oil

½ cup chopped onion

1 (16-ounce) package turkey sausage, cut into ½" slices

1 medium zucchini, quartered and cut into ½" slices

½ red bell pepper, chopped

3 cloves garlic, crushed

6 cups chopped, trimmed kale (about ½ pound)

½ cup fresh mushrooms, chopped

½ cup water

2 (15-ounce) cans cannellini beans or other white beans, rinsed and drained

3 Roma (plum) tomatoes

¼ teaspoon ground fennel

⅛ teaspoon dried chili flakes

½ teaspoon Italian seasoning

¼ teaspoon rosemary

¼ teaspoon salt

¼ teaspoon freshly ground black pepper

1. Heat oil in a large Dutch oven over medium-high heat. Sauté onion and sausage 5–6 minutes or until sausage is browned.

2. Add the zucchini, pepper, and garlic, and cook for 2 minutes.

3. Add kale and remaining ingredients; bring to a boil. Cover, reduce heat, and simmer 10 minutes or until thoroughly heated. Serve immediately.

Carrot-Ginger-Apple Soup

This wonderful, vegan soup can be served hot or cold.
The coconut milk and apples add a natural sweetness to this soup.

INGREDIENTS | SERVES 4–6

1 pound fresh carrots, chopped into 2" rounds

1 tablespoon coconut oil

1" piece fresh gingerroot, grated

2 cups organic vegetable broth

1 apple, cored and sliced, peel on

1. Place carrots, coconut oil, and grated gingerroot in a stock pot over medium heat and sauté until soft, about 3–4 minutes.

2. Add vegetable broth to stock pot and let simmer for 2–3 minutes.

3. Place cooked carrots, broth, and sliced apples into high-speed blender or use immersion blender to blend in the stock pot. Blend on low for 2–3 minutes to desired creaminess.

Shrimp Bisque with Scallops

This is an elegant first course or a delicious lunch. It's very easy to make in advance,
adding the cream at the last minute when heating.

INGREDIENTS | SERVES 4–6

2 minced shallots

1 clove garlic, minced

2 tablespoons butter

2 tablespoons cornstarch

1 tablespoon tomato paste

4 cups shrimp shell broth (see sidebar later in this chapter) or bottled clam broth

½ pound shrimp, cleaned and deveined

½ pound bay scallops

1 cup heavy cream

Salt and pepper, to taste

1 tablespoon dry sherry per bowl of soup

Chopped parsley, for garnish

1. In a stock pot, sauté the shallots and garlic in the butter for 2–3 minutes.

2. Blend in cornstarch and tomato paste. Add broth and bring to a boil. Then lower heat and simmer for 10 minutes.

3. Spoon in the shrimp and scallops and cook for 2–3 minutes.

4. Let cool for 5 minutes. Using blender, blend in batches until puréed. Return to the pot and add cream. Taste for salt and pepper, adding as necessary.

5. Spoon in the sherry. Garnish with parsley.

Harvest Corn Chowder with Bacon

For this soup, fresh corn is best. Frozen or canned corn just won't taste the same.
Fresh corn is sweet and crisp.

INGREDIENTS | SERVES 6

½ pound bacon

2 large sweet onions, chopped finely

2 large Idaho potatoes, peeled and chopped

½ large carrot, chopped

1 sweet red pepper, cored, seeded, and chopped

3 tablespoons cornstarch mixed with ¼ cup water until smooth

1 quart homemade or canned low-salt chicken broth

3 cups fresh corn removed from cob

1 tablespoon salsa

1 cup whole milk

1 cup heavy cream

¼ teaspoon ground nutmeg

1 bunch fresh parsley, washed, stems removed, chopped

Salt and pepper, to taste

1. Fry bacon in a large skillet until crisp and drain on paper towels; when cool, crumble and set aside, reserving grease in pan.

2. Sauté the onions, potatoes, carrots, and pepper in the bacon grease for 10 minutes, stirring often.

3. Add the cornstarch/water mixture, and stirring constantly, ladle in the chicken broth. Bring to a boil. Cover, lower heat, and simmer for 30 minutes.

4. Stir in the rest of the ingredients. Taste, and season with salt and pepper. Do not boil after adding the cream. Serve hot, sprinkling the top with the crumbled bacon.

Thick and Rich Cream of Broccoli Soup

This hearty soup is perfect on a cold, winter day.
Feel free to add diced chicken or turkey to make it more of a meal.

INGREDIENTS | SERVES 4–6

1 pound broccoli

1 tablespoon extra-virgin olive oil or butter

1 large sweet onion, chopped

2 cloves garlic, chopped

1 stalk celery, chopped

2 tablespoons cornstarch dissolved in ⅓ cup cold water

3 cups low-salt chicken broth

½ cup dry white wine

¼ teaspoon freshly grated nutmeg

Juice and rind of 1 lemon

Salt and freshly ground pepper, to taste

1 cup heavy cream

¾ cup minced prosciutto or other smoked ham

1. Rinse, trim, and coarsely chop the broccoli; set aside in a colander to drain.

2. In a large soup pot, heat the oil or butter, and add onion, garlic, and celery. Sauté until softened, about 3–4 minutes.

3. Stir in the cornstarch/water mixture and other liquid ingredients.

4. Mix in the broccoli, nutmeg, juice and rind of lemon, salt, and pepper.

5. Simmer the soup, covered, until the broccoli is tender, about 15 minutes.

6. Remove the lemon rind. In blender, purée in batches, or use immersion blender directly in soup pot. Stir in the cream and ham. Reheat but do not boil. Serve hot.

Adding Depth of Flavor to Soup

Adding sausage, ham, or bacon to a soup enriches the flavor of soup. The salt and smoke in the curing process of pork plus the herbs and spices used in sausage also add to the flavor of a soup or stew. Smoked ham hocks are a classical tasty touch in Southern cooking. They are inexpensive and meaty, but the skin and bones must be removed before the soup is served.

New England Clam Chowder

This delightful chowder will warm you up on the chilliest winter days.

INGREDIENTS | SERVES 4–6

2 dozen cherrystone clams (2" across)

2 cups water

3 ounces salt pork, chopped finely

1 large onion, chopped

1 medium carrot, peeled and chopped

2 stalks celery with tops, chopped finely

2 large Idaho potatoes, peeled and chopped

2 tablespoons cornstarch (more if you like it really thick), divided

2 bay leaves

½ teaspoon dried dill weed

1 teaspoon dried thyme

1 teaspoon celery salt

1 tablespoon wheat-free Worcestershire sauce

3 cups clam broth

1 cup whole milk

1 cup cream

Freshly ground black pepper, to taste

½ cup chopped fresh parsley for garnish

Is That Clam Alive or Dead?

Never use a dead clam. Always run them under cold water and scrub vigorously with a brush. To test for life, tap two clams together. You should hear a sharp click, not a hollow thud. If the clam sounds hollow, tap it again, and then, if still hollow-sounding, discard it.

1. Scrub the clams and place them in a large pot. Add the water, cover, and boil until the clams open. Remove them to a large bowl and let cool; reserve the juice. When cool, remove the clams, discard the shells, and chop the clams in a food processor.

2. In a soup pot, fry the salt pork until crisp. Drain on paper towels. Reserve 1 tablespoon salt pork grease to cook vegetables.

3. Add the vegetables to the pot, and over medium heat, sauté until soft, about 10 minutes. Blend in 1 tablespoon of the cornstarch and cook for 2 more minutes, stirring continuously.

4. Add the reserved clam juice, bay leaves, dill weed, thyme, and celery salt to the pot.

5. Stir in the Worcestershire sauce, clam broth, the chopped clams, and the salt pork. Bring to a slow boil before adding the milk, cream, and remaining tablespoon of cornstarch. Reduce the heat, cover and simmer for ½ hour. After you add the milk and cream do not boil. If you do, your soup is likely to curdle.

6. Taste and adjust seasonings, if necessary. Before serving, remove bay leaves. Add black pepper to taste and garnish with chopped fresh parsley, and serve hot.

Manhattan Red Clam Chowder

With tender chunks of clam, this savory dish will satisfy the seafood lover in your family.

INGREDIENTS | SERVES 6

2 dozen cherrystone clams (2" across)

2 cups water

3 ounces salt pork, chopped finely

1 large onion, chopped

1 medium carrot, peeled and chopped

2 stalks celery with tops, chopped finely

2 large Idaho potatoes, peeled and chopped

1 tablespoon cornstarch (more if you like it really thick)

2 bay leaves

½ teaspoon dill weed, dried

1 teaspoon dried thyme

1 teaspoon celery salt

1 tablespoon wheat-free Worcestershire sauce

3 cups clam broth

1 (28-ounce) can chopped tomatoes with their juice

Freshly ground black pepper, to taste

Parsley, chopped, for garnish

Tomato or Cream in Your Clam Chowder?

Manhattan clam chowder, made with tomatoes, is a latecomer to the chowder arena. During the eighteenth and nineteenth centuries, tomato-based chowder was banned in New England. In fact, tomatoes were suspect for many years—it was the invention and distribution of ketchup in the early twentieth century that brought the tomato into its own in America.

1. Scrub the clams and place them in a large pot. Add the water, cover, and boil until the clams open. Remove them to a large bowl and let cool; reserve the juice. When cool, remove the clams, discard the shells, and chop the clams in a food processor.

2. In a soup pot, fry the salt pork until crisp. Drain on paper towels. Reserve 1 tablespoon salt pork grease to cook the vegetables.

3. Add the vegetables to the pot, and over medium heat, sauté them until soft, about 10 minutes. Blend in the cornstarch and cook for 2 more minutes, stirring continuously.

4. Add the reserved clam juice, bay leaves, dill weed, thyme, and celery salt to the pot.

5. Stir in the Worcestershire sauce, clam broth, the chopped clams, and the salt pork. Reduce the heat, cover and simmer for ½ hour. Add the tomatoes. Cover and simmer for another ½ hour.

6. Before serving remove bay leaves. Add black pepper to taste and garnish with chopped fresh parsley, and serve hot.

Shrimp and Coconut Soup

This can be served chilled or hot. You can add 1 cup of cooked rice or quinoa to this, but it is not necessary.

INGREDIENTS | SERVES 4

2 shallots, minced

2 teaspoons peanut oil or other vegetable oil

2 tablespoons cornstarch

1½ cups Shrimp Shell Broth (see sidebar), warmed

½ cup dry white wine

1 cup unsweetened coconut milk

1 cup cooked rice or quinoa (optional)

1 pound shrimp, shelled and deveined, chopped

Salt and freshly ground white pepper, to taste

1. Sauté the shallots in the oil until soft, about 10 minutes over medium heat. Stir in the cornstarch and cook until very thick.

2. Add the liquid ingredients and cook, covered, over very low heat for 30 minutes.

3. Stir in the rice or quinoa and the shrimp; heat until the shrimp turns pink. Add basil, salt, and white pepper, to taste, and serve hot or cold.

Shrimp Shell Broth

Shrimp Shell Broth makes a flavorful addition to seafood soup. Next time you are preparing shrimp, reserve the shells. Add 1 cup water, 1 cup wine, and a bay leaf to the shells from a pound of shrimp. Bring to a boil, lower heat, and simmer, covered, for 20 minutes. Strain and use as broth in your soup.

Thick and Hearty Lancashire Lamb Stew

This heartwarming stew freezes wonderfully ,so feel free to double the recipe and freeze half of it. You can also substitute canned cannellini beans for the bagged kind.

INGREDIENTS | SERVES 6

¼ cup extra-virgin olive oil

2 pounds lamb stew meat

½ cup potato flour

Salt and pepper, to taste

2 slices bacon, chopped

4 cloves garlic

2 large onions, chopped

2 medium carrots, peeled and chopped

2 celery stalks, chopped

2 bay leaves

2 cups chicken broth

1 cup dry white wine

½ bunch parsley

2 tablespoons dried rosemary

Juice and zest of ½ lemon

2 teaspoons wheat-free Worcestershire sauce

1 (1-pound) bag Great Northern beans, soaked overnight and then simmered for 5 hours, or 3 (15-ounce) cans white beans, rinsed and drained

1. Heat the olive oil in a big, heavy-bottomed stew pot.

2. Dredge the lamb stew meat with flour, salt, and pepper. Brown the meat, including the bacon, for 5–8 minutes.

3. Add the garlic, onions, carrots, celery, and bay leaves and cook for 4–5 minutes.

4. When the vegetables are soft, add the broth, wine, and herbs. Stir in the lemon juice, zest, and the Worcestershire sauce. Cover and cook for 3 hours.

5. Pour off the broth and put in the freezer to bring the fat to the top. When the meat is cool enough to handle, remove from the bones.

6. Return the meat and broth to the pot. If too thin, mix 2 tablespoons of cornstarch with 3 tablespoons water and stir into broth. Bring to a boil.

7. Stir in the beans. Cover and cook at a simmer for 20 minutes.

Wild, Wild Rice and Mushroom Soup

The beauty of this rich, extremely comforting soup is that you can add more vegetables or cooked sausage, turkey, or chicken at the end.

INGREDIENTS | SERVES 6

3 tablespoons butter

2 cloves garlic, minced

1 cup finely chopped sweet onion, such as Vidalia

10 each: shiitake, morel, porcini, and oyster mushrooms, brushed clean and chopped

2 tablespoons corn flour or cornstarch

5 cups low-salt beef broth, heated

2 cups cooked wild rice

1 cup heavy cream

¼ teaspoon dried rosemary, crumbled

⅛ teaspoon dried thyme, crumbled

Salt and pepper, to taste

½ cup dry sherry

6 fresh sage leaves

1. In a soup pot, melt the butter, and add the garlic and onion. Sauté for 5 minutes.

2. Add the mushrooms. Add the flour or cornstarch, and stir until thickened, cooking for another 5 minutes.

3. Slowly add the broth, stirring constantly. Mix in the wild rice. Add the cream, rosemary, thyme, salt, and pepper, and allow to cook for another 2–3 minutes.

4. Add the sherry and serve in heated bowls, with a sage leaf floating in each one.

Hot or Cold Asparagus Soup

This delightful soup tastes just as good served hot or cold.
This fresh, velvety soup has the most beautiful green color.

INGREDIENTS | SERVES 10–12

4 shallots, chopped

2 tablespoons extra-virgin olive oil

2 pounds fresh asparagus or 3 (10-ounce) packages frozen, cut into 1" pieces

2 quarts chicken broth

Salt and pepper, to taste

Juice of 1 lemon

1 teaspoon lemon zest

1 teaspoon Tabasco sauce, or to taste

1 cup heavy cream

1 cup reduced-fat milk

½ cup chopped fresh chives or mint leaves, for garnish

1. Using a large, heavy-bottomed soup pot, sauté the shallots in olive oil. When the shallots are softened after about 2–3 minutes, add the asparagus and toss for another 3–4 minutes.

2. Add the broth, salt, pepper, lemon juice and zest, and Tabasco sauce. Cover and cook until the asparagus is very tender, about 5 minutes.

3. Pour into a blender and process until very smooth, or use an immersion blender directly in soup pot. If you are going to serve it hot, reheat, add cream and milk, and serve. For a cold soup, chill, add cream and milk, and serve. Garnish with chopped fresh chives or mint leaves.

Summer Cucumber Soup

This is very refreshing on a hot day. This soup is so simple to prepare,
you can make an elegant and healthy summer soup in no time.

INGREDIENTS | SERVES 4

2 English cucumbers, peeled and chopped

2 cups reduced-fat buttermilk

1 cup Greek yogurt

2 teaspoons salt

Juice of 1 lemon

Zest of ½ lemon

⅔ tablespoon snipped fresh dill weed

½ cup snipped fresh chives (snipped to ¼" pieces)

Freshly ground pepper, to taste

Mix all ingredients in a nonreactive ceramic or porcelain bowl. Chill overnight. Serve in chilled bowls.

Fresh Tomato and Basil Soup

This taste is so fresh and delicious, you will want to serve it year-round.
This goes perfectly with grilled cheese using No Grain Bread (see Chapter 3).

INGREDIENTS | SERVES 4

4 tablespoons butter

¼ cup cornstarch

2 cups cherry or grape tomatoes

2 cups fresh basil leaves, stems removed

2 tablespoons fresh oregano leaves

2 cloves garlic, minced

1½ cups milk

1 cup cream or half-and-half

Salt and pepper, to taste

1. Make a roux with the butter and cornstarch in a large stock pot or Dutch oven; cook over medium heat for 5 minutes.

2. Place the tomatoes, basil, oregano and garlic in the blender and process until smooth. Stir the tomatoes into the hot butter mixture.

3. Bring to a boil, and add the milk and cream. Reduce heat and keep over low heat for 3–4 minutes; sprinkle with salt and pepper to taste.

Do Not Boil

When a recipe calls for cream, it's important to heat without boiling. If you boil it, you may get curdled soup. If it does get away from you, add a few tablespoons of boiling water and blend until the curds come back together.

Fresh Spring Soup with Baby Peas

This soup was lightened up by substituting reduced-fat milk for half the cream.
Garnish with a few cooked shrimp or a few tablespoons smoked ham or prosciutto, finely chopped.

INGREDIENTS | SERVES 4

1 cup chopped spring onions or scallions

2 cloves garlic, smashed

1 bunch sorrel (or 1 bunch watercress)

10 young dandelion greens (small leaves only)

¼ cup extra-virgin olive oil

¼ cup cornstarch

3 cups vegetable stock

⅛ teaspoon ground allspice

½ teaspoon fresh parsley, chopped

Zest of ½ lemon, minced

1½ cups fresh baby peas or 1 (10-ounce) package frozen peas

½ cup reduced-fat milk

½ cup cream

Salt and pepper, to taste

1. In a large stock pot, sauté the onions or scallions, the garlic, and the greens in olive oil for 5 minutes, until greens are wilted.

2. Whisk in the cornstarch and vegetable stock. Stir in the allspice, parsley and lemon zest.

3. When smooth, transfer the mixture to a blender and purée, or use immersion blender directly in stock pot. Return the soup to the pot and add the peas. Cook for 5–8 minutes, or until tender.

4. Add the milk, cream, salt, and pepper. Do not boil, but serve hot.

Springtime, Anytime!

You can enjoy spring flavors any time of year, thanks to California herbs and frozen *petit pois* (tiny peas). If you can get spring onions, fine; if not, use scallions. Don't leave out the lemon zest! The vitamin C in the lemon helps maintain the beautiful green color by preventing browning.

Spicy Mexican Black Bean Soup

This traditional soup is easy but takes quite a while to make. It freezes beautifully, so make a lot. If ham hocks are hard to find, add 1 teaspoon liquid smoke or smoked paprika at the end in place of the ham hocks.

INGREDIENTS | MAKES ABOUT 3 QUARTS

1 pound ham hocks, split

1 pound black beans, soaked in fresh water overnight

2 medium onions, chopped

4 cloves garlic, minced

2 cups beef broth

Juice of 1 fresh lime

1 large (½-pound) Idaho or Yukon Gold potato, peeled and chopped

2 medium carrots, peeled and cut up

2 jalapeño peppers, cored, seeded, and chopped

1 tablespoon ground cumin

½ teaspoon cayenne pepper

1 tablespoon ground coriander

Salt and freshly ground black pepper, to taste

½ cup chopped fresh Italian flat-leaf parsley or cilantro

1 cup golden rum

Sour cream and thinly sliced lemon or lime, for garnish

Soaking Beans: The Long and Short of It

Our fast-food culture has moved the packagers of many varieties of dried beans to tell the consumer to boil, then soak for a short period of time. Sounds like a good idea; however, this method soon separates the bean from its skin and it just does not make for a good texture, whether you are leaving the beans whole or puréeing them. If you are short on time, use canned beans.

1. In a large stock pot or Dutch oven, cover the ham hocks with cold water, bring to a boil, cover, and lower heat to simmer. Simmer for 4 hours.

2. Remove the meat from the pot and reserve the cooking liquid. Remove the meat from the bones, discard the skin and bones, chop the meat, and set aside. Drain the beans. Add the beans to the reserved cooking liquid from the ham.

3. Stir the onion, garlic, beef broth, lime juice, vegetables, spices, and salt and pepper into the pot with the beans and cooking liquid. Add enough water to make 3½ quarts. Cover and simmer for 5 hours.

4. Stir in parsley or cilantro, taste for seasonings, and add additional salt and pepper if necessary.

5. Place mixture in the blender and purée the soup in batches, or use an immersion blender directly in soup pot. Return to the pot to heat. Return the meat to the pot.

6. Either add all of the rum at once and serve, or you can add it to individual bowls of soup. Top each bowl of soup with sour cream and a slice of lemon or lime.

Onion Soup with Poached Eggs

This comforting soup is a wonderful addition to any brunch.
Everything but the eggs can be made in advance.

INGREDIENTS | SERVES 4

4 slices bacon

2 medium Vidalia onions, sliced thinly

2 medium red onions, sliced thinly

2 medium yellow onions, sliced thinly

4 tablespoons extra-virgin olive oil or unsalted butter

1 tablespoon chickpea flour

4 cups low-salt beef broth

¼ cup dry red wine

1 bay leaf

1 tablespoon thyme

1 tablespoon wheat-free Worcestershire sauce

Salt and pepper, to taste

4 eggs

¼ cup chopped fresh parsley, for garnish

1. Fry the bacon until crisp and drain on paper towels; when cool, crumble.

2. Sauté the onions in the olive oil for 2–3 minutes, stir in the flour, and cook for 3–4 minutes, stirring to get rid of the lumps.

3. Add the broth, wine, bay leaf, thyme, and Worcestershire sauce. Cover and simmer over low heat for 1 hour.

4. Just before serving, raise the heat, and add salt and pepper to taste. Swirl the soup and add the eggs directly to the soup, one at a time. Remove the eggs after 1 minute. Ladle soup and 1 egg each into 4 warm bowls and garnish with chopped parsley.

Steamy Oyster Stew

This elegant and satisfying stew is lovely enough for entertaining.

INGREDIENTS | SERVES 4

2 tablespoons unsalted butter

1 tablespoon shallots, minced

2 tablespoons wheat-free Worcestershire sauce

1 cup bottled or fresh clam broth

2 tablespoons cornstarch mixed with 3 tablespoons cold water

⅛ teaspoon cayenne pepper

1 quart shucked oysters, drained

2 cups milk

1 cup heavy cream or half-and-half

Sprinkle of celery salt and paprika

4 pats butter

Oyster crackers

1. Mix the butter, shallots, Worcestershire, and clam broth together in a saucepan over medium heat for 3–4 minutes. Whisk in the cornstarch/water mixture. Add the cayenne pepper, oysters, milk, and heavy cream.

2. Heat carefully over low heat until quite thick, stirring frequently for about 10 minutes.

3. Just before serving, sprinkle with celery salt and paprika, then float a pat of butter on top of each bowl. Serve with oyster crackers on the side.

Ostentatious Oysters

Oysters are loaded with zinc, iron, potassium, magnesium, and calcium as well as vitamins A and B_{12}. They are also low in calories and high in protein. These nutritional advantages remain whether oysters are consumed raw or cooked.

Italian Sausage, Bean, and Vegetable Soup

There's nothing like a bowl of good soup, especially when you are in a hurry.
This hearty soup can be made quickly and will not disappoint.

INGREDIENTS | SERVES 4–6

1 pound Italian sausage, either sweet or hot, cut into 1" pieces

1 large red onion, chopped

4 cloves garlic, minced

¼ cup extra-virgin olive oil

1 (28-ounce) can crushed tomatoes with their juice

1 bunch escarole, washed, base stems removed, chopped

2 (15-ounce) cans beef broth

2 (15-ounce) cans white beans

1 tablespoon fresh rosemary, crumbled

1 tablespoon dried oregano

⅓ cup grated Parmesan cheese

1. In a large skillet, sauté the sausage, onion, and garlic in the olive oil for 5–6 minutes.

2. When the onion and garlic are soft, add the rest of the ingredients, except the Parmesan cheese. Cover and simmer over very low heat for 30 minutes.

3. Garnish with Parmesan cheese and serve.

Tasty Taco Soup

This wonderful soup can be made into a chili if you reduce the amount of broth.

INGREDIENTS | SERVES 8

3 tablespoons extra-virgin olive oil, divided

1½ pounds lean ground beef (you can also use ground turkey or chicken)

1 medium onion, chopped

3 cloves garlic, minced

1 red or yellow bell pepper, chopped

1 cup diced tomatoes

1½ cups frozen corn

1 tablespoon chili powder

¼ teaspoon red pepper flakes

¼ teaspoon oregano, dried

½ teaspoon paprika

1 tablespoon cumin

2–3 tablespoons fresh cilantro, chopped

Salt and pepper, to taste

1 (15-ounce) can red kidney beans, thoroughly rinsed and drained

1 (4.5-ounce) can green chili peppers

3 cups chicken broth

1½–2 cups water (depending on how much liquid you want)

Juice of ½ lime

Cheddar cheese, sour cream, extra cilantro, for garnish

1. In a large stock pot or Dutch oven, heat 2 tablespoons of the oil and add the ground meat. Cook for 5–8 minutes, until completely browned and no longer pink. Remove from heat and place meat into a bowl.

2. In the same pot, heat the remaining tablespoon oil, onion and garlic for 3–4 minutes, until they soften.

3. Add the bell peppers, tomatoes, corn, spices, and cilantro. Season with salt and pepper and mix well.

4. Add the kidney beans and chili peppers and mix again.

5. Add the meat back to pot along with chicken broth, water, and lime juice. Mix well and bring to a boil.

6. Cover and reduce heat to low. Season with additional salt and pepper, if desired. Simmer for 30 minutes. Garnish with cheese, sour cream and extra cilantro, if desired.

Do You Love Sour Cream?

If you are looking for a healthier alternative, why not substitute plain Greek yogurt for sour cream? Greek yogurt is also thick and creamy but has much less fat and fewer calories. Greek yogurt is also much higher in protein.

Lentil-Spinach Soup

Nothing warms you up like a warm bowl of comforting soup loaded with healthy vegetables and beans. This freezes wonderfully so go ahead and double the recipe.

INGREDIENTS | SERVES 6

1 tablespoon extra-virgin olive oil

2 medium onions, finely chopped

4 cloves garlic, minced

3 large carrots, chopped

3 stalks celery, diced

1 medium zucchini, diced

2 teaspoons oregano, dried

2 teaspoons basil, dried

1 teaspoon cumin

1 cup grape or cherry tomatoes, halved

1½ cups brown lentils, dried

4 cups vegetable broth (you can also use chicken broth)

4 cups water

1 bay leaf

Rind of Parmesan cheese (optional)

3 cups spinach

1 tablespoon lemon juice

Salt and pepper, to taste (optional)

1. Heat the oil in a large pot over medium heat. Add the onions, garlic, carrots, celery, and zucchini and cook for 3–4 minutes, until vegetables soften.

2. Add oregano, basil, and cumin. Stir to combine and cook for 3–4 minutes.

3. Add tomatoes, lentils, vegetable broth, water, bay leaf, and Parmesan cheese rind, if using. Bring to a boil.

4. Reduce heat and let simmer 50–60 minutes, or until lentils are soft.

5. Right before ready to serve, add spinach and lemon juice. Stir well until spinach wilts.

6. Season with salt and pepper, if desired. Remove Parmesan cheese rind and bay leaf before serving.

For the Carnivores . . .

This is a delightful vegetarian soup. If you are a meat eater and are looking for a heartier soup, add some cooked bacon, ham, sausage, chicken, or turkey at the end. You can add some small wheat-free noodles, potatoes, or corn as well for a more substantial meal.

Hearty Beef Stew

This heartwarming stew will leave you asking for seconds.
If you like a thicker stew, add a bit more cornstarch.

INGREDIENTS | SERVES 10

2 pounds beef stew meat, cubed

¼ cup all-purpose wheat-free flour

4 cloves garlic, minced

1 teaspoon onion powder

½ teaspoon black pepper

2 tablespoons extra-virgin olive oil

3½ cups beef broth

2½ cups water

½ cup red wine

1 teaspoon wheat-free Worcestershire sauce

2 teaspoons marjoram, dried

1 teaspoon rosemary, dried

1 teaspoon parsley, dried

3 large red potatoes, peeled and cubed

4 large carrots, sliced and quartered

4 stalks celery, sliced

1 large onion, chopped

3 teaspoons cornstarch

2 teaspoons cold water

1. Place the beef in a resealable plastic bag along with flour, garlic, onion powder, and black pepper. Make sure the bag is closed and shake until meat is evenly coated.

2. In a large pot or Dutch oven, place olive oil and flour-coated beef and cook over medium heat until browned, about 5–6 minutes.

3. Add broth, water, red wine, and Worcestershire sauce. Stir well and add marjoram, rosemary, and parsley. Bring to boil. Reduce heat to low, cover and simmer for 1 hour.

4. Stir in potatoes, carrots, celery, and onion.

5. In a small bowl, mix together the cornstarch and water. Add mixture to pot and stir in well.

6. Cover again and simmer another 55–60 minutes, until potatoes soften. Serve immediately.

Cook It Slow

You can easily cook this stew in the slow cooker. Simply follow step #1, and then place beef and the remaining ingredients (except cornstarch and water) in slow cooker. Cook on low for 10–12 hours, or on high for 4–6 hours, adding the cornstarch and water mixture in the last hour.

Creamy Ham and Potato Soup

This is comfort food at its finest and is filling enough for an entrée.
This is a great way to use leftover ham too. Go ahead and add whatever vegetables
you'd like; cauliflower, asparagus, and corn would be delicious in this soup.

INGREDIENTS | SERVES 8

3½ pounds Yukon Gold potatoes, peeled and diced

2 medium onions, chopped

2 medium carrots, sliced

2 celery stalks, diced

1 cup smoked ham, diced

⅛ teaspoon cayenne pepper

½ teaspoon sage, dried

1 teaspoon parsley, dried

2 cloves garlic, minced

3 cups chicken broth

2 cups water

Salt and pepper, to taste

4 tablespoons butter

5 tablespoons wheat-free, all-purpose flour

1½ cups milk

¼ cup shredded Cheddar cheese, for garnish (optional)

Chopped fresh chives, for garnish

1. In a large stock pot, place the potatoes, onions, carrots, celery, ham, cayenne pepper, sage, parsley, garlic, broth, and water over high heat. Bring to a boil, then lower heat to medium, and cook for 15 minutes, until potatoes soften. Add salt and pepper to taste.

2. To make a roux, melt butter over medium-low heat in a medium saucepan. Slowly add flour, stirring continuously until thick, about 1 minute. Gradually add milk while continuing to stir. Continue stirring until thick and no lumps remain, about 4 minutes.

3. Stir the milk mixture into stock pot and mix well. Cook until thoroughly combined. Add shredded cheese, if desired, and garnish with chopped chives. Serve immediately.

What Is a Roux?

A roux is very simple to make and is crucial for thickening soups and sauces. A roux is prepared by using equal parts fat and flour and mixing them together until they are completely smooth.

Slow Cooker Thai Curried Chicken Soup

This soup is packed with flavor. If you like it less spicy, cut down on the curry paste.
Leftovers taste wonderful over a bed of rice or quinoa.

INGREDIENTS | SERVES 6

2 pounds boneless, skinless chicken, cubed

½ teaspoon salt

½ teaspoon pepper

4 cloves garlic, minced

1 tablespoon fresh gingerroot, minced

1 tablespoon peanut oil

2 teaspoons red curry paste

1 teaspoon curry powder

1 teaspoon turmeric

1 teaspoon cumin

1 (14-ounce) can coconut milk

4 cups chicken broth

1 tablespoon fish sauce (optional)

Juice of 1 lime

1 jalepeño pepper, sliced (optional)

1 cup mushrooms, sliced

1 medium onion, chopped

1 red pepper, chopped

Sliced green onions and lime wedges, for garnish

1. Sprinkle the chicken breasts with salt and pepper. Set aside.

2. Place the garlic, gingerroot, and peanut oil in a large skillet over medium-high heat and cook for 1–2 minutes, until tender.

3. Stir in the chicken and cook while stirring for 5–8 minutes, until browned and no longer pink.

4. Place the cooked chicken in the slow cooker. Add the remaining ingredients to slow cooker except vegetables. Stir to combine. Cook on low for 6 hours.

5. Add vegetables including jalapeño and let cook another 30 minutes, until they soften. Garnish with sliced green onions and lime wedges.

Lentil and Sausage Soup with Quinoa and Kale

This soup is hearty enough for a complete meal. It is packed with protein and can be easily frozen in an airtight container.

INGREDIENTS | SERVES 6–8

1 tablespoon grapeseed oil

3 cloves garlic, minced

1 pound turkey sausage, casings removed, can also use pork or chicken sausage

½ cup diced carrots

½ cup diced celery

½ cup diced onion

1 tablespoon dried basil

1 tablespoon dried oregano

1 teaspoon dried rosemary

½ teaspoon dried thyme

8 cups low-sodium chicken broth

16 ounces dried lentils, rinsed

1½ cups cooked quinoa

5 cups kale, rinsed and stems removed

4 tablespoons grated Parmesan cheese (optional)

1. Place oil and garlic in large stock pot or Dutch oven. Cook for 1–2 minutes until garlic softens.

2. Add sausage and cook over medium-low heat until browned and no longer pink inside, about 5–8 minutes. Break the sausages up into bite-sized pieces.

3. Add diced vegetables and seasonings. Stir well and slowly add the broth, lentils, and quinoa. Turn heat to high and bring to a boil. Cover soup and reduce heat to low. Simmer for 45–60 minutes until lentils become soft.

4. Add kale in the last 5–10 minutes. Serve immediately. Top with Parmesan cheese if desired.

CHAPTER 15

Desserts

Frozen Chocolate Covered Banana Bites

These are the perfectly portioned snack or dessert. Children and adults alike love these little treats.

INGREDIENTS | MAKES 30 BITES

2 ripe bananas (not too ripe or they won't work)

1 cup wheat-free baking chocolate

1 tablespoon milk

Shredded coconut, slivered almonds, or toffee bits for toppings (optional)

1. Line a baking sheet with waxed or parchment paper.

2. Cut bananas into ½"-thick slices and place them on the lined baking sheet. Place them in the freezer on the tray while you melt the chocolate.

3. Place the chocolate in a small saucepan and melt over low heat while stirring continuously. Add milk and continue to stir until completely melted. Remove from heat.

4. Place a toothpick (or you can use a fork) in each banana slice and dip into melted chocolate. Place on lined baking sheet.

5. You can pour some extra melted chocolate on top of banana slices. Sprinkle with shredded coconut, slivered almonds, or whatever topping you like.

6. Transfer tray to freezer for a minimum of 1 hour or until completely frozen. Store in an airtight container in the freezer.

Cranberry-Apple Granola Cookie Bars

These bars are like a cookie and a granola bar in one. There is no need to buy the packaged granola bars anymore. These are healthy and delicious.

INGREDIENTS | MAKES 25 BARS

3 cups wheat-free rolled oats

¾ cup walnuts, finely chopped

¾ cup ground flax seed

⅓ cup almond meal

½ cup shredded coconut

⅛ teaspoon kosher salt

1¼ cups honey

1 teaspoon wheat-free vanilla extract

2 ounces dried cranberries, unsweetened

2 ounces dried apple slices, unsweetened

1. Preheat the oven to 350°F.

2. In a large bowl, mix the oats, walnuts, flax, almond meal, coconut, and salt. Place on baking sheet and roast in the oven for 15 minutes, stirring occasionally.

3. Dissolve honey and vanilla in saucepan over low heat.

4. Remove dry ingredients from the oven and pour into a bowl. Lower oven to 300°F. Grease 9" × 13" glass dish with cooking spray.

5. Mix honey mixture into bowl with dry ingredients, then add the cranberries and apples.

6. Pour into greased dish and spread out evenly. Use rubber spatula to press down evenly. Bake for 30–40 minutes, until golden brown.

7. Let cool for at least 1½–2 hours to harden.

Strawberry-Vanilla Cheesecake with Walnut Crust

This is a fine combination with a delightful flavor and smooth consistency.

INGREDIENTS | SERVES 10–12

1½ cups ground walnuts

½ cup sugar

½ teaspoon cinnamon, ground

½ cup unsalted butter, melted

4 eggs, separated

3 (8-ounce) packages cream cheese

1 cup sour cream

2 teaspoons wheat-free vanilla extract

1 teaspoon salt

2 tablespoons rice flour

⅔ cup strawberry preserves, melted

Nut Crusts for Cheesecake

This recipe specifies walnuts because they are probably the least expensive shelled nut and work well in these recipes. However, you can substitute hazelnuts, almonds, or pecans. Pecans add a Southern touch and are really good (see the Pumpkin Pie with Pecan Crust recipe in this chapter). Grinding nuts is simple—just use your food processor.

1. Mix together the walnuts, sugar, cinnamon, and melted butter. Prepare a springform pan with nonstick spray and press the nut mixture into the bottom to form a crust. Chill for at least 1 hour.

2. Preheat oven to 350°F.

3. Beat the egg whites and set aside.

4. In a large bowl, using an electric mixer, beat the cream cheese, sour cream, vanilla, salt, and rice flour together.

5. Add the egg yolks, one at a time, while beating. When smooth, fold in the egg whites and mix in the strawberry preserves.

6. Pour into the springform pan and bake for 1 hour. Turn off oven and crack the door. Let cake cool for another hour. Chill before serving.

Raspberry-Blueberry Coulis

This is wonderful not only on crepes but on ice cream and pancakes as well. You can also mix it into Rice Pudding (see recipe in this chapter) for a different take on an old-fashioned dessert.

INGREDIENTS | MAKES 1½ CUPS

½ pint fresh blueberries, rinsed
½ pint fresh raspberries, rinsed
¼ cup water
¼ cup sugar
1" × ½" strip orange rind

Place all of the ingredients in a saucepan and bring to a boil. Remove from heat and cool. Remove orange rind. Whisk until smooth. Serve warm or cool.

Orange-Carrot Cake

This delicious cake has a nice zing with the addition of a little lemon juice and the grated orange rind. The gingerroot adds an appealing sophistication.

INGREDIENTS | SERVES 8–10

4 eggs, separated
½ cup brown sugar
1½ cups grated carrots
1 tablespoon lemon juice
Grated rind of ½ fresh orange
½ cup corn flour
1" piece fresh gingerroot, peeled and minced
1 teaspoon cinnamon
1½ teaspoons baking soda
½ teaspoon salt

1. Liberally butter a springform pan and preheat oven to 325°F.

2. Beat the egg whites until stiff and set aside.

3. Beat the egg yolks, sugar, and carrots together. Add the lemon juice, orange rind, and corn flour. Mix until smooth, then add the gingerroot, cinnamon, baking soda, and salt. Gently fold in the egg whites.

4. Pour the cake batter into the springform pan and bake for 1 hour. Test by plunging a toothpick into the center of the cake—if the pick comes out clean, the cake is done.

What's Up, Doc?

Carrot cake was created during World War II when flour and sugar were rationed. The sweetness of carrots contributed to this cake, and when oranges were available, it became a feast. Cooks used their fuel carefully too, baking and making stews and soups in the oven all at the same time. Sometimes, hard times make for sweet endings.

Crispy Chocolate-Mint Meringue Cookies

These are crisp and delicious. The nuts add a wonderful crunch.
Use either blanched almonds or hazelnuts.

INGREDIENTS | MAKES ABOUT 40 COOKIES

½ cup sugar, divided

¼ cup unsweetened cocoa powder

⅛ teaspoon salt

3 egg whites (from extra-large eggs)

⅛ teaspoon peppermint extract

⅛ teaspoon cream of tartar

½ cup hazelnuts, lightly toasted, skinned, and coarsely chopped

Ugly, But Good!

These cookies are known in Italy as "ugly but good"! Other, kinder descriptions include "kisses" and "crisps." They are a bit dumpy looking, but just try one. This recipe is a simplification of the original, far more time-consuming one.

1. Preheat the oven to 275°F. Line 2 cookie sheets with parchment paper.

2. Sift ¼ cup of the sugar and ¼ cup cocoa together in a bowl. Add salt.

3. In a separate bowl, beat eggs whites, mint extract, and cream of tartar. When peaks begin to form, add the remaining ¼ cup sugar, a teaspoon at a time. Slowly beat in the cocoa mixture. The meringue should be stiff and shiny.

4. Add chopped nuts. Drop by teaspoonfuls on the parchment paper. Bake for 45–50 minutes. Cool on baking sheets. You can place these in an airtight cookie tin or serve them the same day.

Apple Cobbler

This smells like autumn but tastes wonderful any time of the year.

INGREDIENTS | SERVES 10

8 large tart apples such as Granny Smiths, peeled, cored, and sliced

½ cup fresh lemon juice

1 teaspoon cinnamon, ground

1 cup sugar, divided

1 stick (½ cup) unsalted butter, melted

½ teaspoon salt

1½ cups rice flour or quinoa flour

1 tablespoon wheat-free baking powder

1 cup buttermilk

1. Preheat the oven to 375°F.

2. Place apples into a bowl and sprinkle with lemon juice, cinnamon, and ½ cup of the sugar. Mix well.

3. Prepare a 9" × 13" baking dish with nonstick spray. Spread the apples on the bottom.

4. Pour the melted butter into a large bowl. Add the remaining ½ cup sugar and salt, and whisk in the flour and baking powder. Add the buttermilk and stir; don't worry about lumps.

5. Drop the batter by tablespoonfuls over the fruit. Bake for 35–40 minutes. Cool for 25 minutes. Serve with vanilla ice cream or whipped cream.

Pumpkin Custard

You can substitute frozen winter (butternut) squash for the pumpkin with good results.
If you do use canned pumpkin, make sure the label says 100 percent pumpkin, not pumpkin pie filling.

INGREDIENTS | SERVES 6–8

2 cups cubed fresh pumpkin, steamed in 1 cup water, or 2 (12–ounce) packages frozen winter squash, thawed

½ cup brown sugar

¼ cup white sugar

½ teaspoon each: ground ginger, ground cloves, ground nutmeg

1 teaspoon ground cinnamon

3 eggs, beaten

1 cup heavy cream

1. Preheat the oven to 325°F.

2. Purée the pumpkin in your blender or food processor. Slowly add the rest of the ingredients.

3. Pour into a buttered casserole dish. Place a roasting pan of hot water in the middle of the oven. Put the bowl of pumpkin custard in the roasting pan and bake for 50–60 minutes. A nice variation is to add a cup of pecan pieces and let them bake right into the custard.

Chocolate Mousse

The classic darling of the French bistro, this is a fresh take on an old favorite.
If you'd like to lighten it up, substitute half-and-half for the heavy cream.

INGREDIENTS | SERVES 6–8

4 squares semisweet chocolate

¼ cup rum or cognac

½ cup sugar, or to taste

1 teaspoon instant coffee powder

¼ cup boiling water

5 eggs, separated

1 cup heavy cream, whipped stiff with 1 tablespoon sugar

Garnishes for Chocolate Mousse

Fresh raspberries are perfect garnishes for chocolate mousse, as are sprigs of mint. You can also pour a bit of peppermint schnapps over each serving for an added kick. Chambord, a black raspberry liqueur, would also be a wonderful substitution for rum or cognac when added to the mousse when you are making it.

1. Combine the chocolate, rum or cognac, and sugar in a heavy saucepan or the top of a double boiler.

2. Mix the coffee powder with boiling water and add to the chocolate mixture.

3. Cook over very low heat, stirring from time to time, until the chocolate melts. Remove from the heat and cool for 3 minutes.

4. Slowly beat in the egg yolks, one at a time. Let cool.

5. In a bowl, whip the egg whites untill stiff peaks form. Fold in the egg whites. Spoon into a serving bowl or dessert glasses. Chill for 4–6 hours. Serve with whipped cream.

Rice Pudding

This classic dessert is an extremely popular dessert in many restaurants.
You can save some calories and fat by using reduced-fat milk and cutting back on the sugar to ¼ cup.

INGREDIENTS | SERVES 6

1 tablespoon butter
1½ cups water
¾ cup arborio rice, uncooked
1 egg
2 cups milk, divided
⅓ cup turbinado sugar
¼ teaspoon salt
½ cup golden raisins
1 teaspoon cinnamon
½ teaspoon nutmeg
½ teaspoon wheat-free vanilla extract

Temper, Temper

What does it mean to "temper an egg"? It simply means to slowly add the beaten egg to the hot milk while stirring. If you just dump the egg mixture in, you could end up with scrambled eggs in the mixture, which wouldn't be tasty in a rice pudding.

1. Melt the butter in a medium saucepan. Add the water and bring to boil. Stir rice into boiling water. Reduce heat to low, cover, and simmer about 20 minutes, until all water has been absorbed.

2. Place the egg in a small bowl and beat. Slowly add ½ cup of milk to the egg. Set aside.

3. Add remaining 1½ cups milk, sugar, and salt to the cooked rice. Cook over medium heat about 30 minutes, until it begins to get thicker and creamier.

4. Slowly add in egg/milk mixture, making sure to stir constantly.

5. Add raisins, cinnamon, nutmeg, and vanilla. Continue to cook another 2 minutes, while stirring constantly. Serve warm or cold.

Peanut Butter Cookies

These are quite addicting; you might find it difficult to eat just one!
These are equally as delicious with or without chocolate chips.

INGREDIENTS | MAKES 2–3 DOZEN
COOKIES, DEPENDING ON
SIZE

1 cup natural peanut butter, well stirred

½ cup turbinado sugar

⅓ cup brown sugar

1 large egg, beaten

½ teaspoon wheat-free vanilla extract

½ teaspoon baking soda

1 cup wheat-free chocolate chips
(optional)

½ cup almonds or nut of your choice,
finely diced

1. Preheat oven to 350°F.

2. In a medium-sized mixing bowl, combine the peanut butter, sugars, egg, vanilla, and baking soda. Mix thoroughly. Add chocolate chips and diced nuts if desired.

3. Line a baking sheet with parchment paper. Spoon cookie dough by tablespoonfuls onto baking sheet. Bake for 12–15 minutes, until centers are cooked and edges are lightly browned. Let them cool on the sheet for 5–10 minutes before transferring to a wire rack to cool completely.

No Bake Peanut Butter–Flax Bites

These simple bars are an easy after-school snack for children or a quick treat.
These are so much healthier than other treats with a long list of ingredients.

INGREDIENTS | MAKES 20 BITES

1 cup dry old-fashioned wheat-free oats

½ cup dark chocolate chips

½ cup natural peanut butter

½ cup ground flax seed

⅓ cup honey

1 teaspoon wheat-free vanilla extract

1. Stir all ingredients together in a medium-sized bowl until thoroughly mixed. Spread in a 9" × 9" pan and place in the refrigerator to cool.

2. Cut the bites into small squares. Store in an airtight container and keep refrigerated for up to 1 week.

Recipe Alternatives

Try sunflower seed butter, cashew butter, or almond butter in place of the peanut butter. Or substitute chopped dried cranberries, raisins, cherries, or nuts for the chocolate chips. You can also roll them into little balls instead of cutting them into squares.

Chestnut Cookies

These cookies are delicious around the holidays.
They are so unique and delightful the whole family will love them.

INGREDIENTS | MAKE ABOUT 48 COOKIES

1 (2-ounce) can chestnuts, roasted, peeled, and packed in water

1½ cups chestnut flour

½ cup milk

2 egg yolks

1 teaspoon wheat-free vanilla extract

½ teaspoon nutmeg

1 teaspoon salt

2 teaspoons wheat-free baking powder

½ cup granulated sugar

½ cup unsalted butter, melted

3 egg whites, beaten stiff

1. Preheat the oven to 350°F.

2. Drain the chestnuts and chop in the food processor. Place in the bowl of an electric mixer. With the motor on low, add the chestnut flour, milk, egg yolks, vanilla, nutmeg, salt, baking powder, sugar, and melted butter.

3. Fold the egg whites into the chestnut mixture. Drop by the teaspoonful on cookie sheets lined with parchment paper.

4. Bake for 12–15 minutes. Cool and place on platters for immediate use, or store in tins for later use.

Chestnuts—Raw, Jarred, or Canned?

Preparing chestnuts can be a real pain! You have to make cross slits in each, then either boil or roast them, and get the shells off. Then, you have to peel off the skins. This process is time-consuming. However, you can buy prepared chestnuts in jars and cans and avoid all that work. Of course, your house won't smell like roasted chestnuts, but you'll have more time to enjoy them.

Pavlova with Chocolate and Bananas

Pavlova is a meringue dessert cake with a whipped cream topping. Place the whipped cream on the pavlova right before serving as it will become soft and doesn't usually hold for more than a few hours.

INGREDIENTS | SERVES 6

4 egg whites

1 teaspoon vinegar

½ teaspoon wheat-free vanilla extract

½ cup plus ⅓ cup sugar, divided

3 squares semisweet chocolate

½ cup unsalted butter

2 bananas, kept in the freezer for 20 minutes to firm

1 cup heavy cream, whipped with 2 teaspoons powdered sugar

1. Preheat the oven to 200°F.

2. Whip the egg whites, and as they stiffen, add the vinegar and vanilla extract and slowly add the ½ cup sugar. Pour into a 9" glass pie pan that you've treated with nonstick spray.

3. Bake the meringue for 2 hours. Then, turn off the oven and crack the door. Let the meringue rest for another hour. It should become very crisp and lightly browned. Do not prepare ahead of time if the weather is humid.

4. Melt the chocolate, butter, and remaining ⅓ cup sugar. Cool until it's still liquid but room temperature.

5. Peel and slice 1 banana in single layer into the meringue crust. Spoon half of the chocolate sauce over banana slices. Slice the other banana into another layer over chocolate sauce, then spoon the remaining sauce on top of bananas, and top with whipped cream.

Apple Brown Betty with Corn Bread

Now you know what to do with old, stale bread. You can make it into a delicious, homey baked pudding.

INGREDIENTS | SERVES 4

4 large tart apples, peeled, cored, and sliced

Juice of ½ lemon

2 cups corn bread cubes

2 eggs, lightly beaten

1½ cups milk

1 teaspoon wheat-free vanilla extract

¼ teaspoon ground nutmeg

¼ teaspoon ground ginger

1 teaspoon ground cinnamon

⅛ teaspoon ground cloves

½ teaspoon salt

½ cup dark brown sugar, or to taste

½ cup butter

1. Preheat the oven to 350°F. Liberally butter a 2-quart casserole dish or treat it with nonstick spray.

2. Put the apples in the casserole and sprinkle with lemon juice. Add the bread cubes. Mix well.

3. Beat together the eggs, milk, vanilla, spices, salt, and sugar. Mix with the apples and bread cubes. Dot with butter.

4. Bake for 45 minutes, or until brown on top and very moist inside. Serve warm with whipped cream or ice cream.

Why Not Use Canned Whipped Cream?

Whipped cream that comes in aerosol spray cans is much sweeter than the cream you would whip yourself. Also, there is more air than cream, so you are paying a premium for the spray convenience. When you do your own cream whipping, you will get a lot more flavor, no additives, and a healthier end product.

Lemon Clouds

Light and delicious—this is a delight, any time of year.

INGREDIENTS | SERVES 4–6

1½ teaspoons unflavored gelatin
2 tablespoons cool water
Juice of 1 fresh lemon
1 tablespoon minced lemon rind
½ teaspoon wheat-free vanilla extract
½ cup sugar, or to taste
1 cup boiling water
2 tablespoons unsalted butter
4 egg whites

1. In the container of a blender, sprinkle the gelatin over the water. Let rest for 4–5 minutes.

2. Add the lemon juice, lemon rind, vanilla, sugar, boiling water, and butter. Blend until well mixed. Cool.

3. Beat the egg whites until stiff. Fold them into the lemon mixture. Chill in the refrigerator, stirring every half hour. Place in individual glasses or bowls. Serve with lots of fresh berries.

Green Tea–Kiwi Popsicles

These are healthy and refreshing. If you are making these for children you can easily use decaffeinated green tea matcha powder.

INGREDIENTS | MAKES 4 POPSICLES

1½ teaspoons green tea matcha powder
1 tablespoon boiling water
2 kiwis, peeled and diced
12 ounces vanilla Greek yogurt
1 teaspoon fresh lemon juice
3 tablespoons honey

1. In a small bowl, combine matcha powder and boiling water. Stir to combine to create a smooth paste. Set aside.

2. In a large bowl, mix the diced kiwis, Greek yogurt, lemon juice, and honey. Stir in matcha paste, and make sure it is thoroughly combined.

3. Spoon mixture into Popsicle molds, making sure to only fill ¾ of the way. Place in the freezer until frozen.

Naturally Red Velvet Cupcakes
with Cream Cheese Frosting

There is no need for artificial colors in these cupcakes. Beets make these cupcakes a wonderful red color.

INGREDIENTS | MAKES 12 CUPCAKES

1¼ cups wheat-free, all-purpose flour

½ teaspoon plus ⅛ teaspoon xanthan gum

¾ cup turbinado sugar

2 tablespoons cocoa powder, unsweetened

1 teaspoon wheat-free baking powder

¼ teaspoon salt

6 beets, peeled and steamed

¼ cup 100% maple syrup

⅓ cup unsweetened applesauce

2 tablespoons lemon juice (juice from about 1 large lemon)

1½ teaspoons wheat-free vanilla extract

Cream Cheese Frosting (see recipe in this chapter)

1. Preheat the oven to 350°F. Line 12 cupcake tins with liners.

2. In a large bowl, whisk together the flour, xanthan gum, sugar, cocoa, baking powder, and salt so that all of the ingredients are evenly dispersed throughout the mixture. Set aside.

3. Pour the beets into your food processor or blender, slow adding small amounts of water if it becomes too thick. Process the beets for a solid 2–4 minutes, depending on how powerful your machine is, until completely smooth.

4. Add the maple syrup, applesauce, lemon juice, and vanilla, and pulse briefly to incorporate. If you are not using a high-efficiency blender, add 1 tablespoon of water at a time if mixture is too thick.

5. Pour the beet mixture into the bowl of dry ingredients, and mix just enough to combine.

6. Equally distribute the batter between your prepared tins, and bake for 18–22 minutes, until a toothpick inserted into the center comes out clean. Let cool completely before frosting.

Cream Cheese Frosting

This frosting can be a wonderful topping for any cake or cookie.
Unlike the store-bought varieties, this simple frosting only has four ingredients.

INGREDIENTS | MAKES FROSTING FOR 15–18 CUPCAKES

2 tablespoons unsalted butter, softened
3 ounces cream cheese, softened
½ teaspoon wheat-free vanilla extract
1 cup powdered sugar

1. In a large mixing bowl, mix the butter, cream cheese, and vanilla until smooth with a handheld blender.

2. Add the powdered sugar and beat until smooth.

3. Store any frosting in airtight container in the refrigerator for 3–5 days.

Pumpkin Pie with Pecan Crust

This pie is a perfect dessert any time of year, not just during the holidays.
You can use nonfat milk in this recipe to lighten it up, and it will still taste delicious.

INGREDIENTS | SERVES 8

1 (15-ounce can) puréed pumpkin
¾ cup milk
¾ cup 100% maple syrup
3 egg whites
2 teaspoons cinnamon
1 teaspoon pumpkin pie spice
1 Pecan Crust (see recipe in this chapter)

1. Preheat the oven to 350°F.

2. Mix all the ingredients except the crust together in a medium-sized mixing bowl until well combined.

3. Pour batter into prepared pecan crust. Bake about 55–60 minutes, or until a toothpick inserted into the center comes out clean.

Pecan Crust

Anyone eating this pie crust will not believe this is made with pecans.
So simple and tasty, and wheat-free.

INGREDIENTS | SERVES 8

¾ cup pecans
1 cup blanched almond flour
⅛ teaspoon salt
¼ teaspoon baking soda
½ teaspoon cinnamon
½ teaspoon pumpkin pie spice (cinnamon, ginger, allspice, and nutmeg)
1 teaspoon wheat-free vanilla extract
4 tablespoons coconut oil (or cold butter)
3 tablespoons 100% maple syrup
1 egg

1. Preheat oven to 350°F.

2. Place the pecans in a food processor and process until you have a coarse flour.

3. Add the almond flour, salt, baking soda, cinnamon, pumpkin pie spice, vanilla, coconut oil, maple syrup, and egg, and pulse until a ball of dough forms.

4. Using the palms of your hands, press the dough into the bottom and up the sides of a pie pan. Spread into a thin layer throughout the sides and bottom. Bake for 10 minutes.

Blueberry Frozen Yogurt

This wonderful, light dessert can be made with any berries you have on hand.
You can also use frozen berries and defrost them before you mix with the yogurt.

INGREDIENTS | SERVES 14

¾ cup milk
¼ cup turbinado sugar
4 cups vanilla Greek yogurt
2 cups strawberries, puréed

Simply Homemade

Store-bought frozen yogurt and ice creams maybe have over twenty ingredients in them! This recipe is a perfect example of how easy it is to make your own frozen yogurt at home with only four ingredients.

1. In a medium-sized bowl, mix the milk and sugar with a handheld mixer until the sugar is dissolved, about 1–2 minutes on low speed.

2. Stir in the yogurt and strawberry purée.

3. In an ice cream maker, freeze according to manufacturer's instructions. You can spoon the frozen yogurt into a tall, upright plastic container to place in the freezer for up to a week.

Mini Apple-Cranberry Crisps with Quinoa Crumble Topping

Your house will smell heavenly when this is cooking!
You can substitute or add different fruits if you'd like as well.

INGREDIENTS | MAKES 4 MINI APPLE-CRANBERRY CRISPS

Crisp

3 tart apples, cored and chopped into 1" pieces

2 tablespoons unsweetened dried cranberries

1 tablespoon 100% maple syrup

1 tablespoon lemon juice or juice of ½ fresh lemon

1 tablespoon cinnamon

1 tablespoon almond flour

1 tablespoon unsalted butter, melted

Topping

½ cup quinoa, rinsed and uncooked

½ cup wheat-free rolled oats

1 tablespoon chia seeds

1 teaspoon cinnamon

1 tablespoon 100% maple syrup

1 tablespoon unsalted butter, melted

1. Preheat oven to 350°F.

2. Place chopped apples, cranberries, maple syrup, lemon juice, cinnamon, almond flour, and butter in a medium-sized bowl. Mix thoroughly until well combined. Pour the apple mixture evenly into 4 mini greased ramekins.

3. In a medium-sized bowl, place quinoa, oats, chia seeds, cinnamon, maple syrup and butter. Stir until completely mixed. Sprinkle on top of the apple mixture in each ramekin.

4. Bake for 35 minutes or until topping is golden brown. Serve immediately with vanilla ice cream or whipped topping if desired.

Quinoa Pumpkin Chocolate Chip Squares

Quinoa adds a wonderful texture, protein, antioxidants, and fiber to these squares.
You won't feel guilty having your second!

INGREDIENTS | MAKES 20 SQUARES

2 cups wheat-free all-purpose flour
½ cup ground flax seed
1 teaspoon pumpkin pie spice
1½ teaspoons cinnamon
1 teaspoon baking soda
½ teaspoon salt
½ cup butter, at room temperature
2 tablespoons turbinado sugar
3 tablespoons 100% pure maple syrup
1 egg
1 cup cooked quinoa, cooled
1½ teaspoons wheat-free vanilla extract
1½ cups pumpkin purée
¾ cup dark chocolate chips

1. Preheat oven to 350°F. Spray a 9" × 9" or 9" × 13" baking dish with nonstick cooking spray.

2. Mix flour, flax, pumpkin pie spice, cinnamon, baking soda, and salt in a medium-sized bowl. Set the bowl aside.

3. In a large bowl, mix the butter, sugar, and syrup until thoroughly combined. Add egg, quinoa, and vanilla and mix again.

4. Slowly add in pumpkin and continue to mix well. Once completely mixed, slowly add flour mixture. Feel free to add small amounts of water in increments of 1 teaspoon if batter seems too thick.

5. Once the flour mixture is thoroughly mixed, add chocolate chips and mix well.

6. Place in oven and bake for 40 minutes or until you place a toothpick in the center and it comes out clean. Allow to cool for 15 minutes before cutting into squares.

Wheat-Free Resources on the Internet

The American Celiac Disease Alliance

This national organization represents the needs of all those who suffer from celiac disease as well as wheat allergies. This organization fights for proper standards on labeling of gluten-free foods and products.

www.americanceliac.org

Bob's Red Mill

Bob's Red Mill is a company that offers a wide selection of whole grain products, including many gluten- and wheat-free items. They are so careful about the safety of their products that they built a separate packaging division just for their gluten- and wheat-free foods.

www.bobsredmill.com

Celiac

This is a wonderful site to visit for everything from A–Z regarding wheat and gluten allergies. This website also includes research on celiac disease as well as offering information on support groups and organizations.

www.celiac.com

Food Allergy Gourmet

This website was designed by a mother with children of multiple food allergies. This site contains recipes as well as important tips on traveling and eating out at restaurants. Food Allergy Gourmet helps take the stress out of living a life with food allergies and also sells their own fresh, allergy-free baked goods.

www.foodallergygourmet.com

The Gluten-Free Mall

This store has every wheat- and gluten-free ingredient and dietary food product you could ask for. This store offers more than 1,000 gluten- and wheat-free items and is also part of Celiac.com's website.

www.celiac.com/glutenfreemall

Living Without

This website caters to the millions of people suffering every day from various food allergies and sensitivities. This is a fantastic resource for anyone newly diagnosed with any type of food allergy and it also has a large section of recipes to browse through.

www.livingwithout.com

The Mayo Clinic

This website is an excellent source for general background of illnesses and conditions, including an extensive area on food allergies.

www.mayoclinic.com

Wheat Allergy Problems

This website is current and extremely informative on all aspects of wheat and gluten allergies as well as celiac disease. This site explains the wide variety of symptoms for wheat allergy, intolerance, and sensitivity.

www.wheatallergyproblems.com

Wheat-Free

This website was created to help those with not only wheat but also gluten allergies. This site is a terrific place to go for all areas of living a wheat-free life.

www.wheat-free.org

Five Day Wheat-Free Meal Plan

	Day 1	Day 2	Day 3	Day 4	Day 5
Breakfast	1 cup Easy Breakfast Quinoa 1 tablespoon almond butter	1 serving Vegetable-Egg Scramble with Fontina Cheese 1 orange	1 Egg and Avocado Breakfast Burrito 1 banana	3 Coconut Flour Pancakes 1 cup mixed berries	3 Crustless Vegetable Quiche Cups ½ grapefruit
Lunch	1 serving Apple, Walnut, Cranberry, and Spinach Salad with Chia-Balsamic Vinaigrette 1 piece grilled chicken breast	1 Grilled Cheese 1 cup Fresh Tomato and Basil Soup	1 serving Quinoa, Kale, and Roasted Tomato Salad with Feta Cheese 12 almonds	1 serving Warm Chickpea Salad with Spinach	1 cup Black Bean–Quinoa Chili 1 Crispy Corn Fritter
Dinner	1 serving Sausage and Asparagus Risotto 1 serving Simple Zucchini-Parmesan Sticks	1 serving Parmesan–Chia Seed Crusted Chicken with 1 serving Warm Tomato Bean Salad	1 serving Healthy Mexican Casserole 1 serving Sweet Potato and Black Bean Hash	1 serving Slow Cooker Pulled Pork 1 serving Raw Broccoli Slaw with Fruit, Veggies, and Walnuts	1 serving Parmesan Crusted Tilapia 1 serving brown rice pasta with Roasted Garlic Sauce with Cheese
Optional Snack/ Dessert	1 Chocolate–Peanut Butter Smoothie	1 cup plain Greek yogurt ½ cup blackberries	1 cup Blueberry Frozen Yogurt	1 Peanut Butter Cookie	Frozen Chocolate-Covered Banana Bites

Standard U.S./Metric Measurement Conversions

VOLUME CONVERSIONS

U.S. Volume Measure	Metric Equivalent
⅛ teaspoon	0.5 milliliters
¼ teaspoon	1 milliliters
½ teaspoon	2 milliliters
1 teaspoon	5 milliliters
½ tablespoon	7 milliliters
1 tablespoon (3 teaspoons)	15 milliliters
2 tablespoons (1 fluid ounce)	30 milliliters
¼ cup (4 tablespoons)	60 milliliters
⅓ cup	90 milliliters
½ cup (4 fluid ounces)	125 milliliters
⅔ cup	160 milliliters
¾ cup (6 fluid ounces)	180 milliliters
1 cup (16 tablespoons)	250 milliliters
1 pint (2 cups)	500 milliliters
1 quart (4 cups)	1 liter (about)

WEIGHT CONVERSIONS

U.S. Weight Measure	Metric Equivalent
½ ounce	15 grams
1 ounce	30 grams
2 ounces	60 grams
3 ounces	85 grams
¼ pound (4 ounces)	115 grams
½ pound (8 ounces)	225 grams
¾ pound (12 ounces)	340 grams
1 pound (16 ounces)	454 grams

OVEN TEMPERATURE CONVERSIONS

Degrees Fahrenheit	Degrees Celsius
200 degrees F	95 degrees C
250 degrees F	120 degrees C
275 degrees F	135 degrees C
300 degrees F	150 degrees C
325 degrees F	160 degrees C
350 degrees F	180 degrees C
375 degrees F	190 degrees C
400 degrees F	205 degrees C
425 degrees F	220 degrees C
450 degrees F	230 degrees C

BAKING PAN SIZES

U.S.	Metric
8 × 1½ inch round baking pan	20 × 4 cm cake tin
9 × 1½ inch round baking pan	23 × 3.5 cm cake tin
1 × 7 × 1½ inch baking pan	28 × 18 × 4 cm baking tin
13 × 9 × 2 inch baking pan	30 × 20 × 5 cm baking tin
2 quart rectangular baking dish	30 × 20 × 3 cm baking tin
15 × 10 × 2 inch baking pan	30 × 25 × 2 cm baking tin (Swiss roll tin)
9 inch pie plate	22 × 4 or 23 × 4 cm pie plate
7 or 8 inch springform pan	18 or 20 cm springform or loose bottom cake tin
9 × 5 × 3 inch loaf pan	23 × 13 × 7 cm or 2 lb narrow loaf or paté tin
1½ quart casserole	1.5 liter casserole
2 quart casserole	2 liter casserole

Index